Black American Students
in an Affluent Suburb

A Study of Academic Disengagement

Sociocultural, Political, and Historical Studies in Education
Joel Spring, Editor

Spring • The Cultural Transformation of a Native American Family and Its Tribe 1763-1995
Peshkin • Places of Memory: Whiteman's Schools and Native American Communities
Nespor • Tangled Up in School: Politics, Space, Bodies, and Signs in the Educational Process
Weinberg • Asian-American Education: Historical Background and Current Realities
Books (Ed.) • Invisible Children In the Society and Its Schools
Shapiro/Purpel (Eds.) • Critical Social Issues in American Education: Transformation in a Postmodern World, Second Edition
Lipka/Mohattffhe Ciulistet Group • Transforming the Culture of Schools: Yu'pik Eskimo Examples
Benham/Heck • Culture and Educational Policy in Hawai'i: The Silencing of Native Voices
Spring • Education and the Rise of the Global Economy
Pugach • On the Border of Opportunity: Education, Community, and Language at the U.S.–Mexico Line
Hones/Cha • Educating New Americans: Immigrant Lives and Learning
Gabbard (Ed.) • Knowledge and Power in the Global Economy: Politics and the Rhetoric of School Reform
Glander • Origins of Mass Communications Research During the American Cold War: Educational Effects and Contemporary Implications
Nieto (Ed.) • Puerto Rican Students in U.S. Schools
Benham/Cooper (Eds.) • Indigenous Educational Models for Contemporary Practice: In Our Mother's Voice
Spring • The Universal Right to Education: Justification, Definition, and Guidelines
Reagan • Non-Western Educational Traditions: Alternative Approaches to Educational Thought and Practice, Second Edition
Peshkin • Permissible Advantage?: The Moral Consequences of Elite Schooling
DeCarvalho • Rethinking Family-School Relations: A Critique of Parental Involvement in Schooling
Borman/Stringfield/Slavin (Eds.) • Title I: Compensatory Education at the Crossroads
Roberts • Remaining and Becoming: Cultural Crosscurrents in an Hispano School
Meyer/Boyd (Eds.) • Education Between State, Markets, and Civil Society: Comparative Perspectives
Luke • Globalization and Women in Academics: North/West-South/East
Grant/Lei (Eds.) • Global Constructions of Multicuitural Education: Theories and Realities
Spring • Globalization and Educational Rights: An Intercivilizational Analysis
Spring • Political Agendas for Education: From the Religious Right to the Green Party, Second Edition
McCarty • A Place to Be Navajo: Rough Rock and the Struggle for Self-Determination in Indigenous Schooling
Hones (Ed.) • American Dreams, Global Visions: Dialogic Teacher Research With Refugee and Immigrant Families
Benham/Stein (Eds.) • The Renaissance of American Indian Higher Education: Capturing the Dream
Ogbu • Black American Students in an Affluent Suburb: A Study of Academic Disengagement

Black American Students in an Affluent Suburb

A Study of Academic Disengagement

John U. Ogbu
University of California, Berkeley

With the assistance of
Astrid Davis

LAWRENCE ERLBAUM ASSOCIATES, PUBLISHERS
2003   Mahwah, New Jersey   London

Lawrence Erlbaum Associates, Inc., Publishers
10 Industrial Avenue
Mahwah, NJ 07430

Cover design by Kathryn Houghtaling Lacey

Library of Congress Cataloging-in-Publication Data

Ogbu, John U.
Black American students in an affluent suburb : a study of academic
    disengagement / John U. Ogbu.
        p. cm. — (Sociocultural, political, and historical studies
        in education)

    Includes bibliographical references and index.
ISBN 0-8058-4515-1 (cloth : alk. paper)
ISBN 0-8058-4516-X (pbk. : alk. paper)
1. African Americans—Education—Social aspects. 2. Academic
    achievement—United States. 3. Educational equalization—
    United States. I. Title. II. Series.
LC2771 .043 2003
371.829'96'073—dc21   2002032692
                                                                    CIP

Books published by Lawrence Erlbaum Associates are printed on acid-free paper, and their bindings are chosen for strength and durability.

Printed in the United States of America
10 9 8 7 6 5 4 3

Contents

III   Community Forces

Preface

Our anthropological study of public school education of minorities began in 1968 in Stockton, California, with a focus on societal and school factors that contribute to many of these students' lower academic achievement. We subsequently examined these factors comparatively and found similar results in six societies: Britain, India, Israel, Japan, New Zealand, and the United States. However, when we began to compare the academic achievement of different minorities in the same societies and in the same schools, the differences among them could not be explained by societal and school factors alone. For example, in Britain, East Indian students did better than Afro-Caribbean students, even though both groups were discriminated against in society and school. In the United States, the differences in the academic achievement among Black American, Mexican American, Chinese American, Japanese American, and Vietnamese American students, as well as students from the Caribbean and Central and South America, cannot be attributed to discrimination in society and school alone; to mere differences in culture, language, and pedagogic style; or to differences in social class background.

Our comparative research led us in the early 1980s to examine differences in the community forces of the minorities and their possible contributions to the differences in academic achievement among the minorities themselves. *Community forces* include the ways minorities interpret and respond to schooling; these interpretations and responses extend to cultural and language differences. We treat this point more fully in chapter 3.

The comparative research suggests that there appears to be two sets of factors influencing the academic engagement and achievement of minority students: (a) Societal and school factors (the system), and (b) community factors. However, current research, discussions, policies, and practices regarding the academic achievement gap focus almost entirely on system factors. We argue that the minority community should be studied so other factors that may also be contributing to the problem can be discovered.

Since the late 1980s, we and some of our students have been studying the community forces in Oakland, San Francisco, and Union City, in California. The studies were conducted among Black Americans, Chinese Americans, and Mexican Americans. An opportunity to add Shaker Heights, Ohio, to the study communities came in 1997 with an invitation from some members of the Black community in that suburb.

There is no assumption that community forces are the only cause of, or play the most important role in, the academic gap. However, community forces can and should be studied in their own right just as societal and school factors are studied in their own right. Furthermore, examining the contribution of community forces to the academic gap does not mean exonerating the system and blaming minorities. We believe, however, that community forces and their role should be incorporated in the discussion of the academic achievement gap by researchers, theoreticians, policymakers, educators, and minorities themselves who genuinely want to improve the academic achievement of African American children and other minorities.

ORGANIZATION OF THE BOOK

This book is divided into four parts. Part I includes three chapters, two of which describe the problems to be explained. The problem of the academic achievement gap between Black and White students is described in chapter 1, and the academic disengagement of Black students is the subject of chapter 2. In chapter 3 we review some conventional explanations of the pattern of Black school performance and then offer an alternative perspective as well as a framework for the present study. We report our findings in parts II and III. In part 2, which comprises chapters 3–7, we present our findings on societal and school factors that contribute to the twin problems of academic disengagement and low school performance. These include race relations; Pygmalion or internalized White beliefs and expectations; leveling or tracking; and the roles of teachers, counselors, and discipline. We then take up community factors in part III. These chapters are about the educational impact of opportunity structure, collective identity, cultural and language or dialect frame of reference in schooling, peer pressures, and the role of the family. We summarize our findings on community forces in chapter 12 and offer our recommendations in chapter 13.

Acknowledgment and Dedication

We thank the Black community and the school authorities of Shaker Heights whose mutual support made this book possible. We are grateful to many more people in the community and in the school system than we can mention here. Parents. students, teachers, counselors, school administrators and others volunteered their time and shared their knowledge with us. Our special thanks go to Emmanuella Groves, Greg Groves, and Reuben Harris of the Caring Community who initiated our invitation to conduct the study. We were very impressed throughout the study by their kindness, their knowledge of their community and its educational problems, and their commitment to the improvement of Black students' school performance.

We also owe special thanks to Dr. Mark Freeman, the Schools superintendent and his school system for providing the financial support of the study. Although we alone are responsible for the interpretations of the school experience of Black students in Shaker Heights, these interpretations have been made possible by Dr. Bernice Stokes, Executive Director of Elementary Education and other schooled authorities who provided us with every available data we asked for.

We are grateful to Mr. Stuart Math, Dr. Mano Singham and our host and hostess for their contribution to the study. Mr. Math shared his movie on Shaker Heights which contributed to our knowledge of the history of race relations in this suburban community. Our writing benefitted from Dr. Singham's analysis of the contemporary Shaker Heights community and the academic performance gap between Black and White students. We thank our wonderful host and hostess for providing us with a quiet place to write our notes and reflect on our study.

Finally, but not least, we thank our editors at Lawrence Erlbaum Associates—Naomi Silverman, her assistant, Erica Kica, and others who helped in no small way to make this book possible. Many thanks to our superb and patient production editor, Marianna Vertullo.

We dedicate this book to the people of Shaker Heights and their school system for their concern about Black students' academic performance and how to improve it. To address this concern we have identified in the book several factors that can be used to develop policies and practices in the community and at school to reconnect Black students with learning and enhance their school performance.

Introduction

One evening in the spring of 1997, we received a telephone call from a group in the Black community in Shaker Heights, Ohio. It was about the low school performance of Black children in that suburb. The caller told us about a recent article in *The Shakerite*, the high school newspaper, on the school performance gap between Black and White students. Members of the Black community were angry both about the school performance gap and its exposure in the article. The caller invited us to suggest what should be done about the academic achievement gap.

We explained to our caller that we were primarily researchers and had no programs for increasing students' academic performance; however, we could offer some suggestions after studying the situation. Our subsequent visit to Shaker Heights in May 1997 was jointly sponsored by the community and the school district. After the visit, we proposed an ethnographic research endeavor that was accepted by the community and the school district, with the latter financing it.

The mutual agreement by the community and the school district was particularly important for the study. The school district was financially responsible for all phases of the study. The community gave us unlimited access to children, parents, other adults, and various community events and activities. During our initial visit, members of the community provided us with transportation and accompanied us to meetings with school personnel and student groups as well as with community groups. Some of the community groups included Whites and Blacks. We also made two public presentations. The first was to a mixed audience of school personnel, students, parents, and concerned citizens. Many felt that the lack of a solution to the academic gap threatened the racial harmony they had developed over the years. They listened attentively and wanted to know what to do about the problem. The second presentation was to an almost exclusively Black community audience in a church. They, too, listened attentively and raised questions about the causes of and solutions to the problem and what to do about it.

Shaker Heights is an upper middle-class suburb outside Cleveland, Ohio, with a population of about 30,000. Singham (1997, p. 2), described it as a carefully planned city, "with tree-lined streets winding past well-maintained homes with manicured lawns, lakes, parks, and red-brick schools nestled in campus-like grounds." Blacks and Jews were initially prohibited from living in Shaker Heights through real estate covenants. Then there was a roundabout turn during the civil rights period of the 1960s, when it became a model of a voluntarily self-integrated community, discouraged "White flight," and promoted diversity. At the time of our study, about one third of the community was African American. Some other minorities were present but not in a significant number.

According to the 1990 census, about 32.6% of the Black households in Shaker Heights and 58% of the White households, had an average annual family income of $50,000 to over $100,000 (Stupay, 1993, p. 8). The average household income ranged from below official poverty level (about 10%) to millionaires, with a median family income of $66,000. It was a highly educated community, with an estimated 61% of the residents over 25 years old holding at least a bachelor's degree, about three times the national average. Among the many Black and White residents were academics, professionals, and corporate executives. The self-image of Shaker Heights residents was that theirs was a middle- and upper middle-class community (Singham, 1997).

The school system was (and still is) one of the best in the nation. The community's pride in its excellence in education was reflected in its motto: A community is known by the schools it keeps. In addition to high academic standards, the school district had many excellent extracurricular programs. It was estimated that 85% of Shaker Heights high school graduates went to college, many to some of the best universities and colleges in the nation. More Shaker Heights graduates than those from comparable school districts were National Merit Scholarship finalists or semifinalists. For these reasons, relatively affluent people were attracted to live in Shaker Heights. They were willing to pay the very high school taxes that the community voluntarily assesses itself in order to maintain its high standard of education. It had the highest school tax rates in Ohio and at one point the highest in the nation (Singham, 1997).

However, there was a problem: A wide gap in academic achievement existed between White and Black students. The deep concern of many residents of Shaker Heights, Blacks and Whites, over the academic achievement gap, was succinctly expressed in a question that an African American woman asked us during our public presentation to a mixed audience:

> In this community we have large numbers of Black families which are stable and in which both parents are well-to-do, educated, professionals, upholding all the virtues that are assumed to be the prerequisites of educational success. And yet, the children of these families still seem to under-perform when compared with similar White families. What is going on? (Singham, 1997, p. 5)

We were touched by the question but at the time could not offer her a satisfactory answer. We designed our subsequent study to examine some of the reasons Black children whose "parents were well-to-do, educated and professional" were academically disengaged and not achieving. The significance of the study lies beyond Shaker Heights, because the racial gap in academic achievement exists nationwide. In 1999, Shaker Heights joined with 12 other affluent and high-quality school districts in a nationwide network to deal with the same problem (Belluck, 1999).

THE RESEARCH PROBLEM(S)

We set out to discover some of the reasons for the low school performance of Black students in the Shaker Heights schools. One possible reason that came to our attention during our first visit was the disengagement of Black students from academic work. Consequently, our second objective was to discover why Black students were disengaged from their academic work.

One assumption underlying the study is that two sets of factors affect minority students' school performance. One set consists of societal and school factors; by *society* we mean national and local mainstream White society. The societal and school factors are usually the focus of most research. In our research framework we designated them system factors. The second set of factors, which we call community forces, are the beliefs and behaviors within the minority community regarding education that minority students bring to school. These two sets of factors are not mutually exclusive. We examined both but focused more on community forces, for three reasons. One reason was that we were informed by some people in the community during our first visit that the U.S. Office of Civil Rights was investigating the school district for the low school performance of Black students. However, throughout our study we did not see anyone from the U.S. Office of Civil Rights conducting such a study. The only trace of U.S. Office of Civil Rights we found was a flyer announcing a meeting on March 15, 1997, at which someone from the U.S. Department of Education would speak. The flyer encouraged people to attend the meeting because the speaker wanted their input in discussing "the representation of minorities in higher level classes in the Shaker Heights District."

The second reason we did not focus on school factors is that an extensive study of these factors had just been completed by a committee of school personnel and community members. The committee, known as Project ACHIEVE, was established by the school board in January 1996 and submitted its report on March 5, 1997. The primary task of the committee was to determine the nature of and reasons for the widening academic achievement gap between Black and White students. The school district seemed quite sensitive to this problem, noting that it was not only a local but also a national phenomenon. Before the committee began its work, there were many discussions of the problem by teachers and other school personnel, parent–teacher organizations, and between school officials and community groups. The committee reviewed the literature on the problem and commissioned technical studies, including a comparative analysis of the performance of Shaker Heights students with other students in the state and the nation on proficiency and other standardized tests. It analyzed and compared the performance of Black and White students on several measures of academic success in the district from the 1980s to 1996. The report listed possible causes of the lower academic achievement of Black students. Among these causes were (a) societal *or* community-centered factors (e.g., lack of enriched preschool opportunities and experiences, isolation of education from other community activities, racism or vestiges of racism), (b) parent-centered factors (e.g., lack of involvement in education, low expectation of Black students, high expectations of the school system, (c) school-centered factors (e.g., low expectations of Black students, tracking, lack of communication with parents), and (d) student-centered factors (e.g., low ability, negative peer pressures, belief that academic success is "acting White"). The report included recommendations for dealing with each set of factors. It also described some remedial projects already in place.

We studied the report of Project ACHIEVE and the technical studies commissioned by the committee. We also studied other documents and previous studies of the students' academic performance. On the basis of our review of these materials and the data we collected during our first visit, we concluded that many societal and school factors contributing to the academic achievement gap were already known, and to some extent, were being used in policy decisions and change. We did not feel that we would be contributing anything substantially new by focusing on societal and school factors.

Neither the report of Project ACHIEVE nor the other documents we studied discussed the set of factors we call community forces, yet our impression during our first visit was that in Shaker Heights, as elsewhere, community forces might be contributing to the academic achievement gap. We concluded that community forces were not recognized as a possible source of the academic disengagement and low achievement. This, therefore, became our third reason for focusing on community forces. We believed that knowledge of the community forces and their inclusion in the discourse, policies, and practice regarding the academic achievement gap would contribute to the closing of the gap.

Fieldwork Methods

Because our theoretical framework suggested the examination of a host of interlocking factors, we used ethnography as the most appropriate method for the study. As ethnographers, we lived in Shaker Heights and interacted on a daily basis with African Americans in the community and at school. In this way we became more or less members of the Black and school communities. Our interaction enabled us to establish good rapport and to interact informally and formally with students, school personnel, and people in the Black community. Our goal in this daily interaction and rapport was twofold: (a) to understand the people's own ideas about schooling, and (b) to observe how students actually went about getting their education, how their parents went about implementing their educational expectations, and how the school personnel went about educating the children. In other words, the interaction and rapport with the people allowed us, as it were, both to "get inside the heads of the natives" and to evaluate their behaviors on the basis of their beliefs about schooling. We used four techniques to collect the data in this regard: (a) group and individual discussions, (b) individual interviews, (c) formal documents, and (d) participant observation.

The research lasted over 8 months, including 4 months of continuous fieldwork. The study was conducted in two phases. First, we visited the community in May and early June in 1997, meeting with groups of school personnel, students, and members of the Black community. With members of each group we discussed their understandings of the reasons for the racial gap in academic achievement. These discussions were tape recorded, and some were also videotaped. The discussions were transcribed when we returned to Berkeley. During this initial visit we also observed some classroom lessons. As already mentioned, the school district provided us with statistical and other studies of the academic gap as well as with evaluations of various remedial programs for students in need of additional help. To prepare for the second phase of the research we studied the documents and transcriptions of the discussions and the documents from the earlier phase.

The second phase lasted continuously from September to December of 1997. This was a period of intensive fieldwork during which we lived in Shaker Heights. Our research at this time fell into passive and active periods. The passive period began on our arrival in September. In this period we did not conduct any formal research but rather worked on the logistics of the study with school officials. We met with the authorities at the central administration building and the elementary, middle, and high schools. We were promised access to the schools and classes we wanted to study, permission to interview students, and other assistance. It was suggested that we should wear nametags, but we explained that this would make it difficult to blend with the school community. In a few schools we wore the nametags initially; later we were only required to sign in and out as visitors. We declined two other suggestions, namely, to submit a log of hours spent on the research and to provide a list of classes we visited. We explained that these would not be compatible with ethnographic research.

We spent the first few weeks familiarizing ourselves with the various schools and with the Shaker Heights community, especially the Black segment of the community. One major problem we did not satisfactorily resolve was finding an accommodation conveniently located for the study and acceptable to the Black community. Because housing was difficult to find, we accepted the offer of a room in the home of a White school board member. This soon made our status in the Black community somewhat problematic. Even though we spent almost all our time doing research at school and in the Black community, and used our residence primarily as a place to sleep, some Blacks still thought that living in the home of a White school board member would bias our research in favor of the school district. We were initially very concerned about this perception but eventually decided to keep our residence partly because we could not find other housing and partly because we did not think that living there would bias our research. Our residence continued to be a matter of discussion throughout the study, and we used every opportunity to reassure the community members that our residence did not and would not interfere with our study. When people asked for our research findings, as they often did, we told them that it was too early to come to conclusions, because ethnographic research took a long time. The concern over our residence in the home of a White family was a strong indicator of the mistrust the Black community had for the school system and the White people who controlled it.

Data Collection. During the active period of the study we occasionally visited and observed in (a) three elementary schools, with kindergarten through 4th grade students; (b) one upper elementary school, Woodbury, attended by all 5th and 6th graders; (c) the middle school, attended by 7th and 8th graders; and (d) the high school, which serves grades 9–12. We spent one full day a week at the elementary schools; on that day, we spent more time at Woodbury than at the other schools because leveling, or tracking, began there, and we wanted to study closely the process of how students became tracked before the middle school. We spent two days a week at the middle school and the remaining two days at the high school.

We conducted 110 classroom observations, usually from the start to the end of the lesson. We observed classes of different racial makeups, classes on the same subject taught at different levels, and classes on different subjects. We also observed the same teachers teaching the same courses at different levels as well as the same teachers teaching different courses and teachers of different races and genders.

At the elementary schools, we assisted teachers with small tasks when they requested help. Teachers at the middle and high schools encouraged us to participate in class discussions. This was very helpful in establishing rapport with students. We took notes on the attitudes and behaviors of both teachers and students in the classrooms we observed. We generally used lunchtime to write our field notes. Although we did not conduct formal interviews with teachers, we interviewed many of them informally on several occasions and situations. For example, we talked with many teachers either before or after their classroom lessons, during math labs, conferences, special projects, and other events; some teachers took us out for lunch or coffee. On these occasions we talked at length about Black education in Shaker Heights. We describe in appropriate chapters our observations of teachers' interaction with parents attending open house at the middle and high schools, during a conference organized for parents to learn how to help their children with mathematics, and at workshops on how parents should help their children prepare for the state proficiency tests. Some teachers invited us specifically to discuss the academic problems of Black students or their own special efforts to do something about the academic achievement gap. Our interaction with Black teachers was particularly important, because these teachers provided us with both general teachers' perspectives and Black teachers' perspectives.

We interacted and talked with school administrators, counselors, and staff in groups and as individuals. During our first visit we had at least a 1-hour group discussion with members of the following categories of school personnel: teachers, counselors, administrators, and staff. We talked with security guards in the hallways, with librarians and, of course, with students. We attended school board meetings and forums for candidates for the school board and city council elections.

In the Black community, we interacted with a wide range of people. We attended meetings organized by community groups around the issue of Black education. We participated in and observed tutoring and other educational programs sponsored by community groups. On these and other occasions we discussed with parents and other adults the education of their children, including the academic achievement gap and students' disengagement from schoolwork. We greatly appreciated the many occasions on which parents and other members of the Black community invited us to their homes for lunch or dinner or to other social events. These always gave us an opportunity to learn the views of parents and the community on the education of Black children in Shaker Heights.

Formal ethnographic interviews were conducted only with students who had their parents' consent. Elementary school students were interviewed in the classroom when the class was not in session. One student was interviewed at home. All middle school students but one were interviewed during tutoring sessions in the community; the one exception was interviewed at home. All but one middle school student interviewed were taking at least one honors class. Among high school students, two were interviewed at home, and the rest were interviewed in the library or the room reserved for our study. Most high school students came from classes we were observing; a few students were those we had come to know in other situations. Their interviews were conducted during lunch or free periods. We conducted a total of 28 student interviews. They were taped and later transcribed when we returned to Berkeley.

Data Analysis. During an ethnographic research project the ethnographer tries to develop a kind of "mental construct" of what is going on from what he or she has heard, observed, and read. He or she begins to notice meaningful groups of the data. Some of the groups of data fit the concepts in the ethnographer's conceptual framework; others emerge during the research. In general, the meaningful groups of data constitute the coding categories or topics for data analysis. We followed this procedure in our Shaker Heights study. The concepts from our conceptual framework (see chap. 3), together with others we found during the study, constituted the coding categories for our analysis and interpretation. We began our coding by reading several times our observational descriptions, group discussions, interviews, and other documents to find relevant passages. We coded a passage as belonging to a topic if the passage was an explicit or manifestly implicit statement about the topic. We then studied and summarized the passages under each topic and considered the relevance of the findings to the twin problems of academic disengagement and poor school performance. By summarizing and studying the interviews, group discussions, and documents we came to understand how the natives of Shaker Heights mentally and socially constructed their social reality in education, or their points of view. As we show in various chapters, the natives' point of view varied by race as well as by school status, such as being a student, school personnel, or parent. Finally, we studied the interrelationships among the categories to gain an overall sense of what was going on with respect to the students' academic disengagement and school performance.

Writing Style

We now say a word about the style of this book. In presenting our findings, we have chosen to let our informants—students, school personnel, parents, and other members of the community—address the issues as much as possible in their own words, for two reasons. One reason is that some of our findings run counter to current academic and popular discourse regarding Black or minority school performance. For example, we anticipate that some readers will not accept our findings reported in chapter 2, namely, that Black students in Shaker Heights do not work hard or to their full capacity. Their low-effort syndrome is a significant part of their academic disengagement. Current discourse, on the other hand, attributes their low school performance primarily to societal and school factors. The discourse tends to represent Black students as victims or marginalized people who, with some justification, fail by "resisting" the marginalization. In general, schools are held almost entirely responsible for the students' failure and for lack of parental involvement. There were people in Shaker Heights who shared this perspective. Our response to this conventional discourse is to give voice to our informants, whether they are students, school personnel, or parents; we let them represent themselves as active human agents. Our informants are articulate in describing or explaining their own roles in the issues of academic disengagement and performance.

Another reason for giving voice to our informants is one current criticism of ethnography within anthropology. It is evident from our research in Shaker Heights that ethnographic write-up is not merely the construction of the researcher based on selective interpretations. Some critics have charged that the conventional ethnographic writing process tends to exclude the views of the subjects. As a solution, they suggest that the researcher should "give voice" to the people being studied. However, there is a problem with this criticism and the recommended remedy. The natives' own account of their social reality is also a social construction rather than the reality that is out there. A case in point is Shaker Heights natives' self-portrayal, of which there are at least two versions. The version constructed by Whites, or the dominant group, is that this suburban community is a racially harmonious community. The other version, constructed by Blacks, is the opposite. Our own finding or construction, which we present in chapter 4, is that it is a mixture of both. Furthermore, the ethnographer and the people he or she studies may disagree about the interpretation of a particular event or phenomenon. We have found this to be the case not only in Shaker Heights but also in our previous studies in the United States. For example, we found that Blacks in Shaker Heights and other communities in the United States appear to hold a cultural model of teaching and learning which, when compared with the cultural model of some other minorities, is less conducive to school success. Yet they rejected the model when we described it to them. The cultural model is discussed in chapter 11. In the case of a disagreement, we prefer to report our own construction, because the construction of the natives is not more valid. It is important to remember that the ethnographer, as it were, gets inside the heads of the people by means of formal and informal interviews and discussions to discover their own constructions of their social reality. The ethnographer then combines the people's constructions with his or her observations and other relevant data to construct his or her understandings of the particular social reality, which is reported in the ethnographer's account.

I

Black Academic Achievement and Its Explanations

1

Black–White Academic Achievement Gap

HISTORICAL AND NATIONAL CONTEXTS

The gap between Blacks and Whites in academic achievement is historical and nationwide. The historical and national nature of the problem from the time of slavery to the 1970s has been described elsewhere (Ogbu, 1978). A part of this history can be seen in the school desegregation movement and compensatory education legislation. Thus, a few years after the U.S. Supreme Court decision in 1954 that school segregation by statute was unconstitutional, several southern school districts began to publish the gaps in test scores of Black and White students. They used the lower test scores of Blacks to justify their opposition to school desegregation. They argued that Black and White children should not be educated in the same school because the former were not as capable as the latter (Ogbu, 1978; "Under Survey," 1956). Compensatory education began in St. Louis, Missouri, as a remedial program to improve the school performance of urban Black students. By 1960 it had been adopted in New York City, and by 1965 it could be found in many urban school districts nationwide. It became a federally legislated intervention program in 1965 (Gordon & Wilkerson, 1966; Ogbu, 1978).

Differences between Black and White students are not limited to the gap in grade point average, they are found in course level enrollment, performance in specific courses, rates of participation in gifted programs and in special education placement (Artiles & Zamora-Duran, 1997; Gelb & Mizokawa, 1986; Harry & Anderson, 1994; Heller, Holtzman, & Messick, 1982; Patton, 1998; Russo & Talbert-Johnson, 1997). More Black than White students drop out without completing high school (P. R. Brown & Haycock,

3

1984; Fine, 1991; Oakland School District, 1999; Wehlage, 1989). Blacks are overrepresented among students held back for not performing at grade levels or for not meeting high school graduation requirements (Council of Great City Schools, 1999; Oakland Unified School District, 1999). They perform considerably lower than Whites on standardized tests, such as the state proficiency tests and the Stanford Achievement Test (College Board, 1993; L. S. Miller, 1995; Patterson Research Institute, 1997; Slade, 1982). Their lower academic performance can also be seen in qualifications for college admissions (College Board, 1999). The gap begins at the elementary school and widens as students pass through higher grades. By the time they are in the 12th grade, Black students are about 2 or more years behind their White peers in reading and mathematics (Berkeley Unified School District, 1985).

SHAKER HEIGHTS BLACKS COMPARED WITH NON-SHAKER BLACKS

Black students in some school districts do better than other Black students elsewhere in the country. For example, Black students in Shaker Heights perform considerably better than other Blacks in the rest of the state of Ohio and in the rest of the nation. The superior performance of Shaker Heights Blacks to other Blacks was noted in the report of Project ACHIEVE (1997). In her technical study for Project ACHIEVE, Whittington noted that (1996, pp. 3–4) in 1995–1996 school year, fourth-grade Blacks in Shaker Heights scored higher on a reading proficiency test than Blacks elsewhere in Ohio. In the eighth grade, Shaker Heights Blacks scored 37% in mathematics, 83% in reading, 77% in writing, and 48% in science, compared to 21% in mathematics, 64% in reading, 45% in writing and 23% in science. The mean SAT scores of Shaker Heights Blacks in 1996 was 485 Verbal and 471 Mathematics, compared with 464 Verbal and 441 mathematics for other Blacks in the state, and 434 and 422, respectively, for other Blacks in the nation as a whole. Finally, Shaker Heights Blacks earned more credits in foreign languages, mathematics, and science than other Blacks in the state and in the nation in the 1995–1996 school year.

SHAKER BLACKS COMPARED TO SHAKER WHITES

The school authorities in Shaker Heights were fully aware of the superior performance of Black students in the district compared to Blacks in other areas of the state and country. Their major concern, however, which was also the focus of our research, was that Black students in Shaker Heights were not performing academically like their White counterparts in Shaker Heights. This was evident in various measures analyzed by Whittington (1996) for Project ACHIEVE. The 1997 report of Project ACHIEVE summarized the gap as follows:

> An examination of the grades earned in the school district reveals that a significant achievement gap exists between African-American and White students. While African-American students in the Shaker school score higher than the state average for African-Americans on the Ohio Proficiency Tests at all levels, as a group they score significantly lower than the White students enrolled in the school district. A comparison of aggregate scores on the Stanford Achievement Test in Shaker Heights also demonstrates higher performance level on the part of White students over their African-American counterparts. As a group, White students in the school district maintain [a] higher grade point average than African-American students. While this disparity reflects a local, regional and national problem, changing this reality in the Shaker Heights City School district serves as [a] powerful motivating force to task group members involved in the effort of Project ACHIEVE. (1997, pp. 2)

Whittington (1996) concluded from her analysis of the 1995–1996 school year data that in every measure of academic performance there was a considerable gap. We summarize next the gaps between the two groups in specific measures of academic achievement in the district based on an interim report of Project ACHIEVE (1996) and studies conducted by Stupay (1993) and Whittington.

Proficiency Test Scores

On the proficiency test, differences were evident at almost all grade levels tested and were larger in some academic areas, such as math and science, than in others, such as writing and reading. In the fourth-grade proficiency test in 1995, White students scored 98% in mathematics, 99% in reading, 95% in writing, and 94% in science. In contrast, Black fourth graders scored 73%, 90%, 74%, and 51%, respectively. Among sixth graders, the scores for Whites were 86% in mathematics, 97% in reading, 93% in writing, and 79% in science; for Blacks the rates were 28%, 70%, 67%, and 21%, respectively. White eighth graders scored 92% in mathematics, 100% in reading, 93% in writing, and 91% in science; the comparable scores of Black eighth graders were 37%, 83%, 77%, and 48%, respectively.

SAT Scores

The mean SAT scores of Black students in 1996 were 485 Verbal and 471 Math, whereas those of Whites were 600 and 598, respectively (Whittington, 1996).

Course Level Enrollment

The two groups differed in level of their course enrollment. Stupay (1993:23) found in 1993–1994 that proportionately fewer Blacks than Whites took advanced mathematics and science courses. Furthermore, overall, the Blacks' share was 3.9% of the total 4.2% of the enrollment in general education and 43.1% of the 70.3% in the college prep. The proportion of Whites in these lower level courses were 0.2% and 25.3% respectively. In the higher level courses, Blacks were underrepresented with only 4.3% of them out of 17.3% of the enrollment in the Honors and 1.1% out of the 8.1% enrollment in the AP courses. In contrast, Whites made up the vast majority of those enrolled in the higher level courses, 12.3% of the Honors and 6.4% of the AP.

Grade-Point Average

The Project ACHIEVE committee found that Black students received 80% of … the Ds and Fs out of … the 50,000 high school semester grades issued by the departments of English, mathematics, science, and social studies over the 5-year period from 1989 to 1994. Furthermore, the proportion of the D and F grades received by Black students increased from 76% in 1989–1990 to 83% in 1993–1994. The unweighted grade-point average (GPA) of Black students during the same period was 1.6, compared to 2.87 for White students. In the graduating classes from 1992 to 1996 the average GPA of all Black graduates was 2.20 (1.99 for Black males and 2.42 for Black females). The overall GPA of White graduates was 3.34 (3.27 for White males and 3.42 for White females).

Judging from Stupay's (1993, p. 10) study of students' academic achievement at Shaker Heights from 1983 through 1992, the academic achievement gap was not a recent development.

High School Graduation Ranking

Racial differences in high school graduation ranking first came to our attention early in our fieldwork. One school official shared with us some graduation figures he was discussing with a teacher when we arrived at his office. We don't remember the year of the graduation. There were 400 students in the graduating class, almost evenly divided between Blacks and Whites. Seventy-eight percent, or 156 of the Whites graduated with honors; that is, their GPA was 3.0 or higher. In comparison, only 2.5%, or 5 of the Blacks graduated with honors.

In the graduating classes from 1992 through 1995 there were only 22 Blacks of 310 students ranked in the top 20%. Of the 22 Blacks, 4 were males, and 18 females. At the other end there were 295 Blacks out of 325 graduates who made up the bottom 20%; 195 of the Blacks were male, and 100 were female. Out of 787 students in the top half of the graduating classes there were only 145 Blacks, 41 of whom were male and 104 of whom were female. The bottom half had 809 students, 620 of them Black: 345 Black males and 275 Black females.

College Attendance

The proportion of high school graduates who went on to college was different for the two groups. Among Whites, 93% of the males and 87% of the females went to college. The corresponding figures for Blacks were 69% and 79%, respectively. Here, as in the high school graduation rankings, there were more Black females than Black males going on to college, a reverse of the situation among Whites.

In almost every school we visited there was some direct or indirect evidence of racial differences of the performance status. Indirect evidence was usually in course-or-class level representation. For example, during our early visit at Woodbury Upper Elementary School, one school official drew our attention to some learning disability and skills classes that had mostly Black students. In four basic skills classes of about 8 students each, we noticed only 1 White student. We did not know if this was typical or there was something special on the day of our visit. After a discussion with the school official, we came away with the impression that most students in the "academic enrichment" or "gifted" classes were White, whereas most students in "remedial" or "skills" classes were Black.

Racial differences in course-level enrollment were more easily observed at the middle and high schools. We saw instances where a teacher taught the same subject as an honors class with mostly White students and then as a college prep class with mostly Black students.

LOCAL KNOWLEDGE OF THE RACIAL GAP

Members of almost every segment of this suburban community knew and talked about the racial gap in school performance. It was a matter of great concern to school authorities, who had sponsored several studies of the problem and used some of the findings to develop remedial programs. The problem became more widely known and discussed in the community, especially among Blacks, following the publication of an article about it in the high school newspaper, *The Shakerite,* in the spring of 1997.

We encountered discussions of the racial differences in course-level enrollment and in school performance in the community, at school, and during various remedial programs. For example, during one meeting of the Minority Achievement Committee (MAC), one student commented on the small number of Black students in the honors and AP classes. He went on say that a Black student felt uncomfortable when he or she found that he or she was the only Black, or one of only a few Blacks, in such a class. At several other MAC meetings at the middle and high schools teachers and students discussed the relatively low academic achievement of Black males in particular. From various accounts of MAC history, we learned that the MAC program began because some teachers and other school officials were concerned about the low academic performance of Black males. The program was initiated in the early 1990s in an attempt to address the low academic achievement of Black males. The customary practice at that time was to post three academic rolls every 4 weeks: (a) an Honor Roll, with names of the highest achieving students, with GPAs of 3.5 and above; (b) a Merit Roll, for students with GPAs of 3.0 to 3.49; and (c) a Recognition Roll, for students with GPAs of 2.5 to 2.99. There were usually few, if any, Black students in the posted achievement categories. The MAC program was designed to encourage higher academic achievement among Black students. When the program started, the minimum GPA required for admission was 2.5. At the time of our research the qualifying GPA was 2.7. When the program was evaluated in 1996 it was found that it had indeed been effective in improving the academic achievement of Black males. The scholars not only achieved higher GPAs but also were less likely to drop out of school than their Black peers who were not in the program (Project ACHIEVE, 1997, p. 15).

Black students' low academic performance was also a topic of discussion at tutorial and other remedial programs for elementary and middle school students. These programs were designed to help students pass state proficiency tests. The discussion at a PROBE (Proficiency Review of Basic Essentials) session serves as an example. The PROBE program prepared middle school students who were taking the proficiency examination for the first time. Apparently, some high school students who were going to repeat the test participated in the review. Most of the middle school students in the PROBE program came from skills classes, because such students would have difficulty passing the proficiency test without this extra help. We were told that no middle school student in the skills class passed the proficiency test the year before, whereas no student in the honors classes failed. The failure rate in 1996 was highest among Black males.

Teachers and other school personnel often brought up the subject of the academic achievement gap. They also discussed racial differences in enrollment in honors and AP classes as well as the programs the school district had introduced to eliminate these problems. One school official lamented that the problem persisted in spite of the district's effort. One teacher reported that he wanted to increase Black enrollment in the Honors and AP classes by making Black parents more aware of the requirements for these classes. He reasoned that if the parents knew more about the requirements, they would more likely prepare their children to get into honors and AP classes. He did not explain why his plan was not implemented.

The Black community was aware of the academic achievement gap. Some members of the community had served on the Project ACHIEVE Committee in 1996. The mission of the committee was to find ways to improve the academic achievement of "all students," but it ended up focusing on "the disproportional low achievement of African-American students" (Project ACHIEVE, 1997, p. 2). We don't know how widely the report of Project ACHIEVE was read in the Black community, but we suspect that the report and the *Shakerite* article increased the community's awareness of the problem. After the report was released, some community groups emerged to deal with the problem; other groups already in existence began to focus on the racial gap.

One indication of the Black community's concern over the low school performance of its children was that it was members of this community who initiated our invitation to look into the problem. During our initial visit, community members provided us with transportation and accompanied us to our meetings with school personnel, student, and community groups. Another indication was that many parents and other members of the community attended the two public presentations we made during that visit. One of the presentations was given in a large church in the community. The packed audience was attentive and concerned.

The publication of the Shakerite article on the academic achievement gap not only made Black community members more aware of the problem but also angered them. At issue for them was not the accuracy of the reported facts but rather the public disclosure and discussion of the gap. This community sensitivity to the article can be seen in a dialogue between a community representative and a Black school counselor that we report in chapter 7. The Black school counselor and the community representative expressed the general sentiment and anger of the community over the academic performance of Black students as well as the community's disapproval of the publication of the article. The community believed that White people published the article to make Blacks in Shaker Heights look bad!

The White community also was concerned about the racial gap in academic achievement. This was evident in the attendance and discussion at our first public presentation. During the question-and-answer period that followed the presentation, most speakers ignored us and the substance of our presentation. Instead, they expressed their concerns and diverse views on the academic gap: its causes and possible remedies. Some blamed it on the use of biased standardized testing to track children early into ability groups. Others believed it was the result of low teacher expectations, peer pressures, or differences in learning styles. Some suggested closing the academic gap by eliminating tracking and standardized testing, removing from the school district teachers who had low expectations of Black students, and educating Black parents to monitor their children's TV watching and their peer group membership. A Black male graduate from the district said that Black students needed to feel that the school system recognized their cultural identity and cared for them. A White woman asked how such issues could be addressed. She was told to learn to "care." She interpreted this as a personal criticism, to which she responded that "it was precisely because she cared that she bothered to come to meetings like this to begin with." (Singham, 1997, p. 2). The audience applauded. Another White person, a father of a biracial student, entered the dispute, accusing the woman and other Whites of not wanting to give up the power they had historically used to control the Black education system and oppress Black people. He, too, received applause as he stormed out of the meeting.

There was no consensus among the students about the stage of the children's school career when the academic achievement gap began. Some students believed that it was not a significant problem until the upper elementary school. One student summed up this view by saying that the problem could not be traced to "the foundations laid in kindergarten ... [and that] it's something else that occurs later on in life, you know, like around fifth, sixth, seventh, eighth grade."

School counselors had no common opinion about the time in the students' school career when the problem began. Counselors' opinions seemed to depend on the age of the students under their charge. High school counselors said that it started mostly at middle school. One high school counselor who processed the admission of ninth graders said that eighth grade Black male students were "perfectly capable of doing very good school work, [but] were [already] grossly, seriously underachieving [emphasis added]." Black males entering ninth grade did not see themselves as learners. The ninth graders themselves knew this (see chap. 8, on internalization). The counselor was not sure when Black males began to feel this way or when they developed their self-image as nonlearners. She said that one of the biggest challenges was to find out just when the problem began and why. She suggested that middle school teachers should monitor the behavior and attitudes of Black male students. Middle school counselors believed that the problem began at the elementary school. One counselor who had worked with elementary and middle school students said that the problem began as early as the first grade or even at kindergarten. He declared emphatically: "It doesn't just start at middle school. You can see this building very early in kindergarten first. Some people could even probably take it to preschool now with so many preschools."

2

Academic Disengagement in Shaker Heights

STUDENTS' BELIEFS ABOUT WHAT IT TAKES TO MAKE GOOD GRADES

From elementary school through high school, Black students considered Shaker Heights schools to be exceptionally good. They believed that their school system had higher academic standards than any other school in the state. Because the students thought that the reputation of their school system was due to its high standard of academic achievement, we asked them what it took to make good grades in their school system.

Specifically, to learn what Black students believed it took to do well in Shaker Heights schools, we asked them the following hypothetical question: "What advice would you give to your relative (cousin) who is transferring to Shaker schools so that he or she would succeed at Shaker?" Some informants were themselves transfers and thus were often describing their own experience. The consensus was that it required more effort to succeed at Shaker than elsewhere. By effort they meant that a student must work hard, do classwork, do a lot of homework, and study a lot.

The majority of the students believed that the transition to the Shaker Heights school district was difficult because of heavy workloads, high standards, and high expectations of behavior and performance. Even elementary school students knew that Shaker's standard was high and that expectations were equally high. This awareness can be seen in the following excerpts from interviews with students at all school levels.

Elementary School

Anthrop: Now what kind of advice would you give to ... a relative who's coming from another state say, and they're coming to Shaker Heights, to Boulevard Elementary School. What type of advice would you give them?

Student: It's a very good school system. Um ... um, they help you learn. Like I know, um, some teachers give a lot of homework, like in Mrs. Rosack's (pseudonym) class, she give us a lot of homework in first grade. You have to be ready to listen, be ready to work. And that's it.

Middle School

Anthrop: If you had a relative who was coming to Shaker Heights from another state or somewhere else, and he didn't know anything about Shaker Heights, what would you tell him in order to do well here?

Student: Study a lot and do your homework.

Anthrop: OK. Do you think Shaker Heights is any different from other school districts?

Student: Mmm.

Anthrop: Or, would they need the same advice for other, like say, they were going into Cleveland schools? Would they need the same advice?

Student: No, 'cause Shaker is like, more higher level and stuff. And like the top–one of the top ten in Cuyahoga schools and stuff. So, I think you need to study hard, do your homework.

High School

The majority of the high school students believed that the transition to the Shaker Heights school was very difficult. Five students reflected on their own transition and how they suddenly found themselves doing more work than in their former schools.

---

[1]Anthrop stands for Anthropologist, the researcher interviewing students, school personnel, parents, or others making comments at a discussion meeting.

> *Anthrop:* If you had a relative that was coming from another state or something, to come to Shaker schools, what would you, what advice would you give them to do well here?

> *Student:* Well I just tell them they have ta (sic) apply themselves because like its, it's a hard switch from like [where I came from]. Well, when I came here, I came in the 10th grade and I came from Cleveland Public School, so I had to adjust [my] work habits and stuff like that.

> *Anthrop:* OK, and how was that adjustment, was that really hard, or manageable.

> *Student:* It was hard at the beginning because I came from doing like maybe three nights a week homework, to doing four or five nights a week homework. And that was in all my subjects.

Transfer students reported that workload in honors and advanced placement (AP) classes in their former schools was equivalent to the workload in college prep and skills classes at Shaker. They were not comparable to the workload in the honors and AP classes at Shaker. Consequently, those who enrolled in the honors and AP classes at Shaker because of their high grade-point average from their former schools usually had difficulty adjusting. They often found that they had to do almost twice as much homework as they did in their former schools. One such student described his experience this way.

> *Anthrop:* What about um, students who come in from other districts? Um, that's another reason that some people give for Blacks not doing well. They say that it is because they come into Shaker late, and that's why they're behind. Do you think that that's true?

> *Student:* Yeah. I think in Shaker, they push, they [push you] above [the way they push you in] Cleveland or whatever, and all the other school districts around here. It's hard to get up to this [shaker] level or whatever. I do think the college prep, these college prep classes are basically the same [in other school districts], 'cept for like computer labs. But the honors classes, they're the ones that they're basically talking about [as being more difficult things]. [Transfer students] can't get up there or whatever.

Some transfer students from school districts with similarly high standards and expectations as Shaker adjust more easily. The next transfer student had attended a Montessori preschool program and was a good student in a school system with high standards and expectations. When she arrived at Shaker she was placed in advanced classes and was doing quite well.

> *Student:* In the Montessori programs like, I guess we all were considered as, you know, high achievers. And we were all excelling, and, you know, I took the upper level classes as soon as they were available. Um, because I don't really remember but my (inaudible) always tells me stories about um, my transfer into the public schools. At Shaker they made me take some sort of test, and, um, they gave me like … I don't remember if it was like they gave me a seventh-grade test in the fourth grade and I passed it. Or if they gave me a test and I tested out as a seventh grader. But … um, it was something and I just had, you know, like great scores; the scores blew like the principal away and she put me in every honors class I could be in.

BLACK AND WHITE ACADEMIC EFFORT COMPARED

Both students and school personnel compared the academic efforts of Black and White students. Students did so directly; school personnel did it indirectly. However, both groups agreed that Black students did not work as hard as White students.

Students

Black students often voluntarily compared their own academic efforts with those of White students. They believed that they did not work as hard as White students. This comparison began at the elementary school level. One elementary student observed that Blacks did not study as much as the Whites and recommended that the former "should stop watching a lot of TV and read books more." Asked why they should follow his recommendation, he replied "Because I know a lot of White people who their mother tells them, they told me, they're not allowed to watch TV."

Middle and high school students were explicit and emphatic in their comparison. They believed that Black students preferred to take college prep and skills classes because those classes were easier and had a smaller workload; students did not have to work very hard. In contrast, White students preferred to take Honors and AP classes because they were more willing to work hard. One 11th-grade student described the course preferences of Black students and their reasons as follows:

Student: Um, well in the Shaker School system, uh, the preference [of Black students] seems to be the lower classes, like college prep classes, and not so much the honors and the advanced placement classes. Um, obviously the work is easier, and the standards of getting by are much lower. Um, and 'cause a lot—a lot of people that go to school, their goal is just to get by, and not to excel. And um, unfortunately a lot of um, uh Black students have that mentality … so they tend to take those lower classes.

Racial differences in students' academic efforts were discussed at length by a group of high school students. Here is a relevant segment of that discussion:

Anthrop: OK. Do White students work harder than Black students?

Male Student 1:   I would say—

Female Student 1:   A lot harder, yeah.

Anthrop: Yeah? (Several students responding and talking at once.) Wait … a minute. I hear some say, "yes." I hear some say, "no."

Male Student 1:   I wanted to ask a question. Are you talking individually or as a whole?

Anthrop: As a whole in the sense that—(students talking and laughing at once). Wait! (Continued student laughter.) Wait. (Student voices quiet.) Wait. That there are more White students in AP classes. Why are there more of them in AP classes or honor classes? Why? (Calling on a student:) Yes. (Two female students respond almost at the same time; student laughter.) Well, one after the other. The lady in the white shirt, whatever. Go ahead.

Female Student 1:   There are more White students in AP classes because they work hard.

Anthrop: Could you speak louder? Because they work hard?

Female Student 1:   Well how come Black students in College Prep classes don't like to work hard? (Students talking at once.)

Anthrop: I don't know; that's what I want to know. (Student laughter.) OK. The other person. Yes.

Female   Yeah. I just, I think that in general White people do work hard.
Student 2: The White people who are in AP and honors classes … do work
              harder than the Black people who are not doing very well [in
              the same classes], just because they're [i.e., White students are]
              more motivated or something. And they have better marks.

One student at a Minority Achievement Committee (MAC) meeting complained that Black students spend more time watching TV and playing video games, whereas White students spend more time working on computers. In general, the students believed that Black students did not work as hard as they should and could. This belief was expressed not only at group discussions during the first phase of the study but also at individual interviews conducted several months later.

School Personnel

Usually teachers and other school personnel did not openly say that Black students did not work hard—but they implied it in their actions. For example, some teachers did not give homework in their college prep and skills classes, which had mostly Black students. When asked, they would say that the reason they did not assign homework was that students would not do it. Teachers also expected and demanded less work from these students during lessons than they did from their honors and AP students. As we show in our case studies of lessons in chapter 7, teachers' perceptions and assumptions that students in skills and college prep classes were not hardworking influenced not only their homework policies but also their toleration of certain behaviors in class.

Although teachers and other school personnel did not openly say that Black students did not work as hard as White students, they discussed some factors that interfered with students' academic effort. Among these factors were students' engagement in part-time jobs to earn money to purchase material goods and the influence of peer groups. We discuss part-time employment in chapter 8 and peer pressures in chapter 10. We note here that teachers believed that White students were more engaged in schoolwork than were Black students.

LOW EFFORT SYNDROME:
A COMMON KNOWLEDGE

In spite of the fact that the students knew and asserted that one had to work hard to succeed in Shaker schools, Black students did not generally work hard. In fact, most appeared to be characterized by *low-effort syndrome*. By low-effort syndrome we mean that students were not highly engaged in their schoolwork and homework. The amount of time and effort they invested in academic pursuit was neither adequate nor impressive. From our observations in almost every schoolwork situation, our discussion with groups of students and school personnel, and our interviews, we can confidently say that Black students in Shaker Heights from elementary school through high school did not work as hard as they should and could to make better grades than their records show. The students themselves knew and admitted this.

Elementary School

From elementary through high school students there was a near consensus that, as a group, Blacks did not work hard in school. Students often reported that they themselves did not work hard. The way they often described themselves was that they did not work as hard as they should and could. They would also add that most other Black students they knew did not work hard. Among the few who believed that they worked hard was a fourth-grade student who was motivated by his desire to go to college. As he put it, he worked hard "because you have to try hard to do stuff in order to get in college and stuff." In contrast, other Black students "try just enough to get by." The sixth grader in the following exchange is an example of an elementary school student who could work harder and make better grades but "just tried to get by."

Anthrop: OK, and if you had to rate yourself as a student, do you think you work as hard as you can, you work just enough to get by, or you don't really work that hard to get good grades?

Student: I work, um, enough just to get by.

Anthrop: OK, how come you don't work as hard as you can?

Student: Cause I watch TV, and it drags me out, and I try, I mean last week I tried real hard to just stay on task, but it's, its extremely hard. I'm distracted really easily.

Middle School

A higher proportion of middle school students believed that Black students got poor grades because they did not work hard in class and did not do their schoolwork. In fact, most middle school students described their own academic effort as "just enough to get by" or said that they could work harder but did not. These included students in honors classes—that is, even honors students reported that they were working hard enough "to get by" and that with that level of effort they were doing well. Middle school students generally agreed that Black students avoided honors classes because those classes required a lot of work and effort.

High School

High school students had the most to say about low-effort syndrome, because they knew more about it than the younger students. Furthermore, several of them did not hesitate to report that they themselves did not work as hard as they could. In the words of one student:

> I mean, I'll do homework on occasion just to make sure my grades, just to make sure I maintain a 3.0, but I won't do anything overly. Like, like, say this math class, and everything worth 5 points. So if he [the teacher] gives us like 20 problems, I'll do it, but if he gives us like 40 or 50 problems and [it's] worth 5 points, I won't do it.

During a high school group discussion one male student said that Black students blamed teachers for their poor academic performance. He believed, however, that the reason for the poor grades was that the students did not work hard and did not usually do their assignments:

> OK, um, with me, I have talked to a lot of young Black males who are not … achieving. And what I've mostly heard is, most of them blame it on their teachers. [They claim that] their teacher doesn't like 'em, so they give 'em a bad grade …. But one of the things that I [think] is wrong … Is that they find an excuse why they're not achieving. They find excuses for not doing their homework or schoolwork, like, "Oh, yeah, well, um, I had to do this that night. I had to—" I mean, I could accept … some excuse [like] if you had family problems or something. But most of them just always find an excuse—. We tried to help these kids [through] this MAC program, and some of 'em, no matter what we said to 'em, just really don't find the need to achieve. I mean, they feel it's easier to [do other things], than work hard for your grades; rather than just to sit back, to come to school with … plans. We probably just see 'em in school, you know, most of 'em, I mean smoking things. You know what I'm sayin'? They find other things to do with their time. And some of 'em don't find homework as being of importance, which [on the contrary] is very important, I mean, to pass and to study.

Several students agreed with him that Black students got poor grades partly because they did not do their schoolwork or homework, not because teachers did not like them.

SCHOOL LEVEL AND ACADEMIC EFFORT

Academic efforts decreased markedly from elementary to high school. At least half of the Black students we encountered at the elementary school were enthusiastic about their schoolwork, and some indicated, directly or indirectly, that they wanted to make good grades. For example, the fourth grader we quoted earlier said he tried to do make good grades in order to go to college. As we moved to the upper elementary school, however, we observed more students who were less enthusiastic about their schoolwork.

For example, the sixth grader whom we also quoted earlier said that he worked hard enough "just to get by." At the middle school we interviewed and observed many more students who did not work hard or worked just enough to get by. These students did not think that they lacked the ability to get make better grades. They could do better if they worked harder, but they chose not to. Their description of their academic effort, including their study habits and those of other Black students in Shaker in general, matched our own observations. Academic effort was lowest at the high school. The majority of the high school students interviewed or observed admitted that they did not work hard. Yet, like elementary and some middle school students, they asserted verbally that making good grades to go to college was important. They would like to make good grades, and they could do so, but they admitted that they did not work hard and did not do their homework.

WIDESPREAD CONCERN AND DISCUSSION

We have seen that students individually reported that they and other students they knew did not work as hard as they should and could. We now turn to three situations in which their lack of effort was often discussed and concern expressed as to what to do about it. These were (a) classroom lesson periods, (b) MAC meetings, and (c) community tutorial sessions.

Classroom Discussions

On a number of occasions students' academic effort was discussed during lessons. The classes were made up of White and Black students, with racial variation depending on the type of class. Most of the discussions, how-ever, occurred in classes with a majority of Black students and therefore were situations where lack of effort affected teaching and learning more. On one such occasion a student pointed out that most of his classmates were content with being average. Another complained that people always talked to him about the value of doing well in school but that it didn't mean anything to him; whatever message they were trying to communicate to him did not get through. A third student said that teachers often talked to students about the importance of education and the need work hard to do well in class; however, most of the students didn't care. Toward the end of the discussion, someone said that his classmates would rather have "freedom" than "calculus." That is, calculus, or academic pursuit, was less important and less meaningful than other pursuits.

MAC Meetings

MAC meetings are occasions when factors affecting students' perfor-mance and what to do about them are discussed. At one meeting at the middle school some students explained why they did not pay attention in class or do math and other assignments. They did not understand why they had to learn math and some other subjects. Other students reported that they did not study or do their homework at home because they did not have enough space or because they spent too much time watching TV. Still others said that they habitually put off doing their homework because of distractions from friends and talking on the phone. Several students said they did not know how to study how to prepare for tests.

At a high school MAC meeting one student shared with the group how in the fifth grade he had changed the negative behaviors that prevented him from getting good grades. Before then he often got into fights. He made the decision to change when he received an F in a class and was al-most suspended for bad behavior. He knew he had behavior problems and that he got poor grades because he did not do his schoolwork and homework, so one day he decided to stop getting into fights, to behave well, and to get serious about school and work hard. Since then he has been a successful student.

At MAC meetings students are often reminded, or they reminded them-selves, of the need to prioritize, to set academics above sports, to budget their time, and give up some present desires for academic pursuit. A recur-rent theme was the need to develop good study habits and concentration skills. Students were advised on the importance of doing their homework, taking notes in class, and studying after school. Some students reported having difficulty focusing on tasks. As a result, they failed tests for which they knew the answers. Such was the case of one student who described her experience at a "sisters" MAC meeting. She understood the problems in the test but failed the test because she was talking while taking the test.

Tutoring Sessions

Lack of concentration or lack of focus on tasks was evident during tutoring sessions in the community. Students often did not concentrate on assignments or follow through to complete assignment. For example, on one occasion 12 students were each given a package of materials to read before attending the next session. When the students arrived on that day, only 3 had read the materials. Nine students had not only not read materials but also reported that they had lost them!

Students were good observers of their own academic attitudes and behaviors and of those of their peers. They did not hesitate to discuss typical attitudes and behaviors that affected their schoolwork in general and their test scores in particular. A high school student assisting at one tutoring session summed up the attitudes and behaviors that typified the approach of some students to their examinations, the consequence of which, predictably, was low performance:

> Well, it all depends on the person. If they wanna learn, if they're willing to learn and stuff like that, they'll do the homework and study for the test. But some of—some of us like to rush outside or stuff like that. They just rush into things and then when the test come *(sic)*, they, you know, put their faces on the table in their faces, they like, "I don't know this," 'cause they should have studied instead of outside. 'Cause people they do outside, go out to the malls and the movies and stuff, hang around they *(sic)* friends; but don't wanna do no work or anything.

Classroom Observations

We now turn to our observations of students' efforts in the classroom. What we observed in these classrooms was consistent with the attitudes and behaviors students described at interviews and group discussions. As we describe later, we often saw students arriving late to class, coming without the proper materials, talking among themselves during the lesson, not paying attention, and barely doing classwork. These attitudes and behaviors are described in more detail in the case studies we present in chapter 7. The cases cover different school levels and different types of classes: regular, re-medial, and academic enrichment classes at the elementary school; skills, college prep, and honors classes at the middle school; and general educa-tion, college prep, honors, and AP classes at the high school. In addition, there were special programs, such as tutoring centers for Grades K–12 to provide students with after-school academic support by the faculty, certi-fied teachers, and college students; programs to help low-and underachiev-ing students, starting from Grade 1; and programs in basic academic skills or general education classes for students in Grades 7–12.

HOW STUDENTS EXPLAINED THEIR DISENGAGEMENT

Several reasons were given by students, school personnel, and others for the low-effort syndrome of Black students in Shaker Heights. Some we discuss in subsequent chapters; here we focus on students' own views.

The Norm of Minimum Effort: They Don't Want to Do the Work

A kind of *norm of minimum effort* appeared to exist among Black students in Shaker Heights schools. The students themselves recognized this and used it to explain both their academic behaviors and their low academic performance. We can best explain what we mean by a norm of minimum effort with some of the self-descriptions of students. Consider the case of one student with whom we had established good rapport before our inter-view. We also talked at length after the interview. During the interview he said that he was considering attending college in Florida or California. He considered himself a good student, at least good enough to go to college. When we asked about his grade-point average (GPA), he said that it was "about 1.9 right now." He said he could work harder to get higher grades, but didn't. The reason he did not want to work harder was that he be-lieved he could be admitted to college to play football. Another example was a high school student whose homework attitude and practices we discussed earlier. He claimed or boasted that he would he would "do homework on occasion just to make sure ... I maintain a 3.0, but I won't do anything over that." Many self-claimed "smart students" stated that they could work harder and make better grades but that they didn't.

The norm of minimum effort existed at all school levels, especially among the males. At every school level some students reported that they did not work hard in school simply because they did not want to do so (the norm of minimum effort). This was the main reason given by middle and high school students for the reluctance of Black students to take honors and AP classes. Instead, they preferred to take college preparatory and general education classes, because these classes required less work. Two eighth graders described the preference for courses requiring minimum or less work:

> *Student 1:* I think they don't take it 'cause they don't want to do like the work, 'cause its more work than regular college prep classes ... and I think that's the only reason they don't take it.
>
> *Anthrop:* OK, um, do you think that the school does, you know, encourages Blacks to take those classes?
>
> *Student 1:* Yes.
>
> *Anthrop:* OK, and why don't Blacks take them?
>
> *Student 2:* Well usually, they start out in those classes, but they just don't do the work and then just slack off and they end up in the lower classes.

The belief that Blacks preferred basic skills and college prep classes because they didn't have to work hard in those classes was even stronger among high school students. Because this belief was widespread, it was not surprising to hear the following statement at an interview with an 11th-grade student:

> Um, well in the Shaker school system, uh, the preference seems to be the lower classes, like college prep classes, and not so much the honors and the advanced placement classes. Um, obviously the work is easier, and the standards of getting by are much lower. Um, and 'cause a lot of people that go to school, their goal is just to get by, and not to excel. And um, unfortunately a lot of um, uh, Black students have that mentality ... So they tend to take those lower classes.

"It's Not Cool" to Work Hard or Show You're Smart. Some students did not study or work as hard as they should have and could have because of peer pressures. Among their peers, "it was not cool to be successful." We asked students during a class discussion at the high school why Black students were not doing well academically. According to one female student, some Black students believed that it was cute to be dumb. When pressed for an explanation, she said that it was because they couldn't do well and that they didn't want anyone else to do well.

Boring and Uninteresting Courses.   Another reason was that the courses were boring or uninteresting. The following student contended that students who were really smart didn't put forth effort because the classes were boring and uninteresting.

Anthrop: Do you know any people who, like people who you know would say, "That person's really smart," and they don't really try in school?

Student 1:   Yeah, I know a lot of people that are like that. Like they score real well on like the SATs and stuff, they just don't do the work 'cause they don't [want to], they're bored with it, they're not pushing themselves enough.

Students wanted to be motivated.

Motivate Me If You Want Me to Learn.   Still another reason that Black students did not work as hard as they could was that the school did not motivate them. It is ironic that, when asked who was responsible for the kind of work students did, students said that it was their responsibility to work hard to make good grades—yet when they discussed their own effort they said that they could and would work harder if the school motivated them. One 12th grader who admitted he did not work very hard still put the blame on school:

> I mean like, I know myself, I can do the work if I applied myself. But its like school is ain't interested. I mean it's ain't interested because you know, its based on my future, what, [if] I can take that extra step and put more uh energy into my work, I'll probably have all As. But, I mean, [the school] just don't motivate … the things here don't motivate me.

Poor Study Habits

Students might not want to work hard. Many, however, who wanted to did not know how to study. Poor study habits were a recurring theme in our interviews and discussions with students as well as in our observations at school and community programs. Because Black students did not know how to study and how to do their schoolwork they often did not think through their assignments before starting to do them. They generally had difficulty completing their work successfully. They also had difficulty with tests because they did not study or did not know how to study for the tests.

Lack of good study habits was discussed several times during community tutoring sessions for middle school students. At these tutorials similar problems at the high school were also discussed. One specific problem was that students often rushed through their assignments or to answer teachers' questions without understanding them. The adults running these programs repeatedly advised the students about the need to learn to understand assignments and questions before commencing to do them. We observed examples of such behaviors in skills classes at the middle school. Students would rush to give the answer, right or wrong. Some teachers described this behavior as the "Black learning style." One elementary school teacher believed that such behavior distinguished the Black learning style from the White learning style. She illustrated the difference with an incident that we witnessed in her class. A White male had come up to the teacher for clarification on an assignment; he also wanted to know what he should do next. The teacher explained the assignment and told him to complete the first step before going on to the next one. This prompted the teacher to talk about cultural differences in learning style. She said that it was typical of her White students to make sure that they understood an assignment and were doing it correctly before moving on to the next assignment. In contrast, it was typical of her Black students "to jump right out there" and attempt to do the assignment or answer a question, "whether or not they understood it or know the right answer." She was not alone in her observation; we also heard other teachers reminding Black students to think through a question before answering it.

The problem of poor study habits was also discussed at several MAC meetings. On one occasion the group discussed the use of cards as a study aid. One student described his use of the cards and recommended the strategy to his peers. He told them that his study skills improved after he learned how to use study cards. He said he used to procrastinate a lot, but when he started using the study cards it helped him. Students' inability or unwillingness to follow through assignments and instructions was yet another a problem discussed at the meetings. We also observed this both in class assignments and in tutoring programs in the community. As we reported earlier, during one tutorial session only 3 of the 12 students had read their assignment. Most had lost the materials.

Inability to Focus on Tasks

Another problem was an inability to concentrate or focus on the task at hand. This was readily observable during lessons. Often students were doing other things during lesson: Some were inattentive, others did not sit still, some would be engaged in private conversations or reading magazines and materials unrelated to the lesson, some would be lying with their heads drooping on their desks during lessons. Lack of concentration and focus was also evident at the community tutoring session. At one tutorial session a student leader "burst" one table of girls who were not paying attention.

Students did not take notes and probably did not know how to take notes during lessons. In several college prep and skills classes, in particular, we found that students did not regularly take notes or take notes even when teachers advised them to do so. Some who took notes did not know how to use them to study for examination. The twin problem of note-taking and preparation for examination was discussed at one MAC meeting. Some students admitted during the discussion that they did not know how to prepare for tests; they put off studying for exams until it was too late. After describing their practices, students were taught how to prepare for tests in order to make better than a C grade. One students shared his strategy for preparing for tests. He said that "one could be smart about studying for an exam … Usually," he continued, "the teacher would tell you when a test is coming up, so you should be aware of that." What he apparently meant was that students should listen to the teacher's announcement of a forthcoming test and then study for it. A female student said she was "a very organized person" and that she sometimes took notes and studied them. But then she would not be able to find them later to study for her tests. She really didn't understand why this always happened to her. Apparently she was not as well organized as she thought she was. Another student said that sometimes he took notes as the teacher directed but that the notes didn't mean anything to him; that is, he did not understand his notes!

Blaming Teachers

It was not uncommon for students to blame teachers for their failure, a practice reported by the students themselves. One believed that there was something wrong with teachers: They would tell students to study one thing and then would turn around and test them on something else. On hearing this, another student mumbled "They tryin' to fail us 'cause we Black." There was also another complaint, namely, that teachers "go back

to stuff that you have already done, and throw that in on the test." Suggestions made by students to do better on tests include taking a practice test
or peeking at the tests. We then asked them how these strategies would
help them do well at the high school. There was no response.

Toward the end of the discussion, students were asked what they could
do to make sure that they were always prepared for tests. Once again, a student reminded the group that teachers usually notified students about im-
pending tests; teachers also encouraged students long before the exam time
to go and see them if they were having problems or had questions about the
upcoming tests. Students, however, preferred to wait until close to the examination date before trying to see their teachers. One student said that students believed that going to see the teacher just before the exam was
"thinking smart" because "the information that you get during the conferences is fresher when you are tested the next day." He reminded the others,
however, that it did not always work and that for some it was too late. Even
at the high school some students did not do their homework, did not know
how to take notes at all or did not take notes during lessons, did not plan
ahead or know how to study for their examinations, or know how to con-
sult their teachers or seek advice from their counselors.

Other Priorities That Derailed Academic Effort

Almost everyone talked about lack of prioritizing as a factor that affected
Black students' school performance. By this they usually meant that Black
students put other things, or preferred to do other things, before their
schoolwork. The competition between peer groups' activities, TV, and
phone on the one hand, and schoolwork on the other, was discussed by
students and school personnel on several occasions. A student once remarked that students sometimes forgot to do their homework or study because of friends, TV, and phone, thus putting these as priorities above
academics. Students understood that school was the first priority, but they
tended to switch them around. Why switch them? One student explained
the switch by saying that he worked hard enough at school and did not
think that he should be doing schoolwork at home.

One major issue in prioritizing was deciding between sports and academics. It was evident from student interviews that for some of them
playing sports was more important than doing academic work to get good
grades. We report in more detail in chapter 8 the case of a student, noted
earlier, who considered himself a student who was good enough to go to

college to play football even though he had a GPA of 1.9. His popularity at school came from playing sports, and he was sure that he would go to college. Therefore, he did not think he had to work hard in his academic courses because his future lay in sports rather than in academics. Teachers recognized the competition between sports and academics. As we show in chapter 6, some teachers tried, but apparently not successfully, to encourage the students to put academics ahead of sports.

In chapter 8 we show that even at the high school many students had not made the connection between schooling and their future positions in adult life. A teacher in one class tried to impress on the students the importance of considering how their education would help them in the future. Several of the students prefaced their responses about their future goals with "When I grow up." The teacher reminded them that they were already grown up. He told the students that in some other societies people of their age would be old enough to be married and have a family with children to support.

Part-time jobs posed another competition. Some students held part-time jobs to earn money to supplement family income; others, however, did so to purchase material things or pay off credit card debts. Whatever the reason, it appeared that students worked too many hours and that this interfered with their schoolwork. The extent of part-time employment and its consequences for school performance were described by two school officials at a meeting with us:

Male school official: Credit cards [have] become very popular with the local billionaires' company. Uh, and I think there's a concern that's been raised nationally about any student working beyond 20 hours a week. There is a direct relationship between the number of hours and a declining academic performance. And I think it's long past due studying uh the degree to which our students are involved in this work experience. And the degree to which parents support this uh 30, 35-hour work week that many students are in my experience this year—. I've taken informal surveys and found unbelievable percentages of students that are putting 20 hours plus uh into a work week, and uh, uh, that are not appearing for these after-school things, let alone many other activities, uh because we value work so much in this culture, so that's, that's—

Anthrop: But not only that, but you are working to get something now rather than putting it off.

Male school official: Absolutely. Tommy Hell—, and so forth. Etcetera. Etcetera. It's un—, unbelievable.

Anthrop: OK.

Female school And to add to that, most of my students who need to come in,
official: can't because they work. I mean, I mean that is the most frus-
                trating thing, if you have a kid who, they need to come in, and
                they can't because they work. And maybe it's because they get
                more *satisfaction* (emphasizes word) out of doing well at work,
                then doing not so great at school. It's not, I don't think it's, you
                know, a stupid choice to make if you do okay at work. People
                like you. Your friends are there. You work at (Hinans?). Every-
                body works at Hinans. You know, it's fun there for the most
                part, and you get satisfaction out of it, but then can't come in af-
                ter school.

The preference of Black male students for part-time employment to acquire material possessions rather than do their schoolwork to make good
grades was summarized by a frustrated male student who had worked
considerably with MAC scholars. He added, however, that the media
were partly to blame because of their failure to publicize the success of
Black professionals, Black people who had succeeded in life because of
their education:

> OK, um, with me, um I have talked to a lot of young Black males who are not
> um achieving. And what I've mostly heard is, most of them blame it on their
> teachers. They find an excuse why they're not achieving…. We tried to help
> these kids (through) this MAC program, and some of 'em, no matter what
> we said to 'em, just really don't find the need to achieve. I mean, they feel it's
> easier to come to school and just to sit back, rather than work hard for your
> grades and have plans; we just see 'em in school, you know, most of 'em, I
> mean smoking things. You know what I'm sayin'? They find other things to
> do with their time, and some of 'em don't find homework as being of impor-
> tance, which is very important. I mean, (if one wants) to study and pass….
> I've watched like lots of TV and I see like, most people you watch TV, you see
> like, maybe the, a White man that's in like the higher power, like even on
> these little make up TV shows. But you'll see like the Black man'll be like
> picking out of trash cans and things, and, and the Black man always got to
> get killed on the show.

Alternative Strategies

There was also a feeling that because of the failure of the media to present
to Black youth Black professionals who have succeeded because of education that young Blacks have come to view nonacademic routes as more
likely to lead to success in life. One of the students spoke about this:

I know of students who just do not see education as anything important, they look at, "I want to be this, so therefore I don't need to take this math class, and I don't need this science class, and I don't need to take social studies, I'm going to be a hairdresser." It's a personal thing. Education to them is not important. Education is not important because of what they desire to do and also because some people just, they have no, I don't want to say zeal, but they have no motivation for knowledge. Some people just don't care. As long as they can get by, then that's all that matters. As long as they can get by that's all that matters to them.

Residual Effects of Past Grading Practices

We conducted no systematic study of the grading practices of the teachers, but our discussions with various people, including students, indicated that in the past the school system passed students who did not perform at grade level, promoting them from one grade to the next. This was particularly the case with students below the ninth grade. Some informants said that this practice sent a wrong message to students, namely, that they would be passed to the next grade even if they did not work hard to earn passing grades. We learned that this was precisely the prevailing attitude among some Black students when the MAC program began. Many potential scholars had "lousy GPAs." When asked why their grades were poor, they would say that they did not take their schoolwork seriously because they knew that they were going to be passed into the ninth grade anyway.

We observed some college prep, skills, and general education classes in which there was minimal demand for students to perform. The requirements of teachers in one math lab with all Black students serves as a good example. However, from our discussion with these teachers we can emphatically say that their requirements and expectations were based on good intentions. At the same time, we found that there was almost no other requirement in this class except that students should to bring themselves and, if possible, bring a pencil to class. Some students did not even bring the pencil on the day we observed. When the class was in session one teacher went into the adjacent room to get a pencil for a student who did not bring one. He told the male student jokingly that if he didn't give the pencil back to him after class the student would have to wash and wax his car for the rest of the year. One of three male students in the row in front of us was particularly reluctant to pay attention to the teacher, who was trying to help him with the assignment. The teacher patiently waited until the student was willing to be involved in what the teacher was doing with the group. On the whole, students were allowed to do as they pleased.

As a result of experiencing little or no demand that they perform, students might not develop a good knowledge of the relationship between effort and grades. We came across several students in our classroom observations and in interviews who thought that they were good students but were, in fact, making "lousy grades." They also might feel that they were doing well or that they were "good students" when, in fact, they were not. This discrepancy could be seen among potential MAC scholars. Often potential scholars thought that they were doing better than they really were. One of the jobs of the mentors in the program was to help students learn to make those connections.

CONCLUSION

Data from various sources, including students themselves, led us to conclude that Black students in the Shaker Heights school system did not work as hard as they should and could. The reasons for this ranged from a norm of minimal effort, or working just hard enough to get by to grading practices that in essence endorsed the norm of minimum effort. The grading practices probably no longer exist; at the time of this study it was described to us as a thing of the past. What seems to emerge from the materials presented in this chapter is that Black students recognized the importance of working hard to make good grades, but they had not developed the habit of working hard to make good grades or making it a priority. We came across only a few students who were determined to work hard to make good grades in order to go to college. The reasons provided by the students and other informants for the effort disengagement require explanations. Thus, in chapters 8 through 11 we examine some factors behind the norm of minimum effort including why students considered their classes boring and wanted to be motivated by the school before they would work hard to make good grades. What were the reasons for their poor study habits? Why did they give in to other competing priorities and alternative strategies? Before we address these issues, we review some of the conventional explanations for the academic disengagement and present an alternative framework that guided our study in Shaker Heights.

3

Explaining the Academic Gap; Conventional and Alternative Explanations

Explanations of the school performance gap between White and Black students are not lacking. Hardly any of them, however can be applied satisfactorily to Shaker Heights. In this chapter we review some of them and point out their limitations.

INADEQUATE IQ

The idea that the lower school performance of Black students is due to inadequate IQ has persisted throughout the history of Black American education. Since the late 1960s, this idea has been reinforced by a number of publications (Herrnstein & Murray, 1994; Jensen, 1969). Herrnstein and Murray (1994), for instance, argued that Blacks do less well than Whites in school because of their lower IQ, which in turn, is attributed to inadequate genetic endowment. However, there is a problem with their argument when it is placed into cross-cultural perspective: Differences in group IQ are not necessarily the result of differences in genetic endowment. Consider the case of the Buraku minority in Japan, which has lower IQ test scores and lower school performance than the dominant, Ippan group in Japan, even though the two groups are of the same "race." On the other hand, as immigrants to the United States, the Buraku minority and the Ippan majority do equally well on standardized tests, and both make good grades in school (DeVos, 1973; Ito, 1967; Y. Nabeshima, personal communication, August 30, 1999; Ogbu, 2001; Ogbu & Stern, 2001; Shimahara, 1991).

Another version of the inadequate-IQ explanation asserts that Blacks' lower IQ is due to faulty family socialization, that poor Blacks do not develop high IQs because their mothers do not raise them with White middle-class mothers' childrearing practices. An underlying assumption is the *critical period hypothesis*, which asserts that without intervention during preschool or early years it is difficult for poor children to fully develop their "intelligence" (Kerber & Bommarito, 1965; T. R. Williams, 1972). This version of the inadequate-IQ explanation has had an enormous influence on the design of Head Start and other preschool programs since the1960s (Gallagher & Remy, 1987; H.L. Miller, 1967; Ogbu, 1978; White, 1973).

One problem is that this explanation is not a good theory of intellectual development. Intervention or preschool programs that are based on this reasoning have not raised the IQs of poor Black children, or of any other children, permanently, although the programs have served the children well in providing nutrition, health care, and other benefits (Darlington, 1986; Jensen, 1969; Ogbu, 1978). The few follow-up studies that have been conducted show that poor Black children whose IQs were raised through their participation in these programs were academically successful in middle and high schools. From our studies of Black students at the middle and high schools in several school districts with preschool programs, we do not believe that these programs are an inoculation against future school failure.

The inadequate-IQ explanation is also wanting from cross-cultural perspective. Immigrant minority children do better in school than Black and other nonimmigrant minority students even though they are not raised like White middle-class children and their IQs were not raised through early childhood intervention programs.

In the context of Shaker Heights Blacks the inadequate-IQ explanation is inapplicable. To begin with, their performance on IQ tests did not predict their academic achievement. Thus, although Black students in the school district scored lower than White students on the Otis–Lennon School Abilities Test, they performed considerably lower on the SAT than predicted by their performance on the IQ test. Neither did their performance on IQ tests predict their failure rate on the state proficiency examination or their share of the D and F grades in high school (*Project ACHIEVE*, 1996, p. 1).

SOCIAL CLASS STATUS

One persistent view is that Black students do not perform academically like White students because they come from a lower socio-economic background

(Bond, 1981; P. R. Brown & Haycock, 1984; L. S. Miller, 1995). The comparison is usually between poor Blacks and middle-class Whites. A favorite slant of this version begins with a comparison of Black Americans and European immigrants. The comparison goes like this: During Reconstruction, Blacks and Whites more or less had equal education. The school attendance and per capita expenditure for the education of the two races were about equal. Compared to White immigrants, Blacks had higher school enrollment, attendance, and educational achievement than the White immigrant groups. The relatively better position of Blacks continued until about the1930s (Lieberson, 1980). The two reasons given for why Blacks eventually fell behind the European immigrants are (a) the per capita expenditure for Black education fell about 30% below that for White education at the end of the Reconstruction, and (b) the White immigrants became members of the middle class by achieving higher socio-economic status—that is, they became assimilated into the mainstream. It is then concluded that Blacks are not performing like White students because either their schools have fewer resources or because they have not been assimilated into the mainstream to the same extent that other groups have been assimilated (Glazer, 1994). Other versions of the class-inequality explanation attribute the gap to unequal power relations between the classes (Anyon, 1981, 1997), class reproduction (McCleod, 1987), and class resistance (Weis, 1985).

None of the versions of the class-inequality can explain why Black students from similar social class backgrounds, residing in the same neighborhood, and attending the same school, don't do as well as White students. Within the Black population, of course, middle-class children do better, on the average, than lower class children, just as in the White population. However, when Blacks and Whites from similar socioeconomic backgrounds are compared, one sees that Black students at every class level perform less well in school than their White counterparts (Anton, 1980; College Board, 1999; Hu, 1997; Oliver, Rodriguez, & Mickelson, 1985; Slade, 1982; Stern, 1986). Class theorists often compare lower class Blacks with middle-class Whites. What the data show is that the lower academic performance exists among poor Blacks in the inner city (see Council of Great City Schools, 1999; Fordham, 1996; Payne, 1984; School District of Philadelphia, 1999); and among middle-class Blacks in the suburb (see Alexandria City Public Schools, 1993; Arlington County Public Schools, 1991; Council of Great City Schools, 1999; Fairfax County Public Schools, 1984; Montgomery County Public Schools, 1984, 1993; Prince George's County Public Schools, 1993; Stern, 1986).

The discrepancy between class status and academic performance of Black students is evident in Shaker Heights. As we noted in the preface, in this relatively affluent suburb White and Black social classes are not too dissimilar. Yet, as we saw earlier, Black students received 80% of the Ds and Fs in the 50,000 semester grades reported by various departments at the high school. The discrepancy between social class status and Black students' school performance was pointed out by a Shaker Heights resident who was neither Black American nor White American:

> "In the highest-achievement tracks [the advanced placement sections] you find only a handful of blacks [about 10%], while the lowest achievement tracks [called general education] have them almost exclusively [about 95%]." He went on to say that "When educational statistics are dis-aggregated by ethnicity, it is found that White … students on the average do better than black students elsewhere, just as white students do better than their counterparts in other school systems. He reported that in a survey conducted in February, 1997, the average Black SAT score was 813, while that of White students was 1118; Black students' average GPA was 2.20, compared to 3.34 for White students. (Singham, 1997)

RACIAL SEGREGATION

Black Americans have historically been discriminated against in education. Prior to 1954, Blacks attended segregated and inferior schools by law in the South or because of residential segregation in the North. Because school segregation by law was abolished, many Blacks have continued to attend segregated and substandard schools because of residential segregation (Anyon, 1997; Bullock, 1970; Mickelson, 2001; Ogbu, 1978). One consistent finding among researchers is that school segregation is a major cause of poor school performance among Black students (Mickelson, 1998). This explanation is inapplicable to Shaker Heights. Shaker Heights schools were voluntarily integrated when Blacks began to move into the city in the 1960s. According to Black and White informants, the community was determined to maintain its high-quality education for Whites and Blacks from the beginning. At the time of this study, the schools were not racially segregated in the traditional sense.

TEACHER EXPECTATIONS

Teacher expectations and their effects on Black students' academic performance have been discussed extensively (Irvine, 1991; Leacock, 1985;

Ogbu, 1974; Rist, 1970; Reed, 1988; Steele, 1992). Researchers have argued that Black students are taught by teachers who do not think that Black students are capable of performing like their White peers. Hence, teachers give them less challenging work, the result of which is lower performance. Some researchers note that teachers do not call on Black students as often as they call on White students to answer questions during lessons and, when they are called on, teachers give them more negative feedback to their answers to questions (Leacock, 1985). This sort of treatment contributes to the lower performance of Black students.

In Shaker Heights, parents and some school personnel were concerned about teacher expectations. Indeed, the topic was a major theme in a speech given in the school district by a major national figure during our research. The speaker told teachers to hold high expectations and high standards for Black students. There is no doubt that low teacher expectations can have adverse effects on students' school performance.

The problem with this explanation is that the situation involving low teacher expectations is more complicated than the proponents portray it. What is often overlooked is the role of students themselves in creating teacher expectations, low or high. As we discuss in chapter 7, in some classrooms we observed, low teacher expectations coexisted with students' unwillingness or refusal to do classwork or homework. It was difficult to determine which came first.

CULTURAL DIFFERENCES AND CONFLICTS

Since the late 1960s, it has been postulated that the low academic performance of Black students is caused by differences in and conflicts between Black culture and White American culture (Boykin, 1986; Gay, 1979; Hale-Benson, 1986; Hilliard, Payton-Stewart, & Williams, 1991; Irvine, 1991; Nobles & Mann, 1994; Pollard & Ajirotutu, 1997, 2000; St. Lawrence, 1977; M. D. Williams, 1990). With very few exceptions (St. Lawrence, 1977; M. D. Williams, 1990), the explanation based on cultural differences is not derived from empirical study of culture either in the Black community or at school or in the White community—at least, not in the anthropological sense.

Boykin (1986) presented the most elaborate description of the nature of the cultural differences and the learning problems they cause. According to him, Black students face a "triple quandary" in the realm of culture and schooling. The triple quandary is (a) that Black students simultaneously have to deal with three different cultural experiences, namely, European American culture and African American culture, which is rooted in African culture; (b) cultural hegemony that arises from their social, economic, and political oppression as minorities; and (c) self-contradictory socialization of Black children. We now examine briefly each of the three problems in comparative perspective.

Cultural Differences and Learning Conflicts

(1986) believes that Black students are compelled to master two incompatible cultures: (a) Black American culture, which is rooted in African cultures, and (b) European American culture. He suggested nine features of Black culture that distinguish it from White American culture; they include movement, time orientation, and verve. *Movement* is a part of Black psychological well-being; Black *time orientation* is more social, whereas White time orientation is more mechanical; and *verve* is the propensity of Blacks toward high-level stimulation. The problem that Black students face is that they are asked to master both of these two cultures that are sharply at odds with each other. To make matters worse, the public school does not allow them to learn and perform in Black culture.

We found some differences between Black culture and White culture but not necessarily as described by Boykin (1986). There were differences in dressing, hairstyles, jokes, sports, communication styles, styles of religious worship, attitudes toward schoolwork, parental involvement in school, study habits, time orientation, and peer group orientation. However, except for dialect differences and communication style, we did not hear from parents or other adults in the community, or from students at school, that Black children had difficulty learning the subjects in the curriculum because of cultural differences. In our observation of more than 100 classroom lessons from elementary through high school we did not record a single instance of cultural barriers preventing a student from learning the subject; that is, we observed no instance in which Black students said that they were unable to master a lesson because they were being taught European American culture and values and in European American pedagogy. It was during interviews that students reported that cultural differences in jokes sometimes resulted in White teachers disciplining Black students or Black teachers disciplining White students (see chap. 7, on discipline). On the whole, what we heard and observed was that some Black students did not want to or should not behave in certain ways that they considered to be White people's ways in and out of school.

We do not argue that cultural differences do not cause learning problems for Black students and other minorities. What we have found through comparative research is that the problems caused by cultural differences are temporary for some minorities; that is, some minorities eventually accommodate or adopt the "White ways" as presented to them at school and thereby become academically successful. Indeed, as we noted earlier, the minorities who are more successful in public school tend to be those whose cultures are more different from White mainstream American culture. They include immigrant minorities from Africa, Asia, and Central and South America (Caplan, Whitmore, & Choy, 1991; Gibson, 1988; Johnson, 1999; Suarez-Orozco, 1989). Furthermore, a study comparing African and Afro-Caribbean immigrant students with Black American students casts doubt on the hypothesis that the low school performance of Black American students is due to the fact that their culture is rooted in African culture, which is almost in dialectical opposition to White American culture: In her comparative study of African and Caribbean immigrant students with Black American students, C. Johnson (1999) found that the immigrants were more successful in the public schools. In our view, the relationship between African cultures and White American culture is similar to the relationship between the cultures of immigrants from Asia, and South and Central America and White American culture. They are *different* cultures, not *oppositional* cultures.

Cultural Racism and Hegemony

The second problem Boykin (1986) identified has to do with cultural racism and hegemony resulting from social, economic, and political oppression. Boykin argued that cultural racism and hegemony are manifested in the attitudes and actions of White school authorities (and their Black representatives) toward Black students. For example, public school authorities evaluate Black students by White cultural values and interpret Black values and behaviors as inferior to those of White people. The attitudes and behaviors of school personnel, therefore, show that the schools function as an institution in which Blacks are sorted and assigned to less desirable stations in society. This may happen even when there is no overt racism.

The suggestion that schooling involves cultural racism and hegemony needs to be examined in a comparative perspective. Public schools evaluate the values and behaviors of all minorities by White values and behaviors; however, not all minorities interpret or experience public school education as cultural racism and hegemony. Neither do cultural racism and hegemony adversely affect the school performance of all minorities even in the same school or classroom. Finally, not all values or behaviors of teachers and other school authorities are racist or hegemonic.

It appears that in current discourse on minority education there is some confusion or misunderstanding about the meaning of *culture* and the cultural role of schooling. We discuss this matter more fully later in this chapter. What needs to be pointed out here is that the knowledge, skills, values, and behavior taught and evaluated by the schools are supposed to be those that children need in order to participate as adults in the workforce and other positions. The mastery of curriculum materials (e.g., mathematics) and ways of speaking and writing (viz, standard English), ways or styles of learning (e.g., analytical thinking, problem solving), and other behaviors is the mastery of the knowledge, skills, values, and behaviors required to function competently in an adult role in contemporary economic and technological society (e.g., being an accountant, an engineer, a nurse, a taxicab driver; conforming to schedule, achievement orientation, independence, etc.). The curriculum and language of the public school are not intended or designed to replace the cultures and languages of ethnic minorities with those of mainstream White Americans.

These knowledge and skills are "White" only in the sense that schooling in the United States is based on White culture and language because White people are the dominant group in the United States that controls the economic and other positions in adult life. The same knowledge and skills taught in schools in China will be regarded as Chinese by any of China's 56 national minorities; in the same sense, in France they will be French, in Japan they will be Japanese, in Spain they will be Spanish, and in Russia they will be Russian. In each country, schooling will be based on the culture of the dominant group, and the language of instruction will be that of the dominant group or the culture and language chosen by the powers that be. For example, in former British colonies in Africa the leaders almost always chose to base their school curriculum on Western culture and to use English as the language of instruction.

We found in Shaker Heights teachers who taught the same subjects to Black and White students and evaluated them in the same way when they were in the same classes. Our impression was that the teachers were trying to foster knowledge, values, skills, and cultural practices they and society believed that the children, both White and Black, would need to function as adults in the economic and technological systems of U.S. society. This did not necessarily include the teaching of Black experience. We came across some instances in which Black students or Black adults wanted their experiences included in the curriculum. An example was a demand by high school students that the drama department put up a show about the Black experience. On another occasion, a representative from the community complained to a group of school officials that the school district was providing Black children with a "euro-centric education." He did not, however, explain what he meant by *euro-centric education.*

By and large, Black students and their parents did not complain of cultural racism and hegemonic education. On the contrary, some Black families moved to Shaker Heights specifically to give their children a "Shaker education." These families were willing to endure economic hardship or work more than one job to enable their children to attend Shaker Heights schools.

Socialized Ambivalence and Self-Contradiction

The third problem Boykin (1986) identified is that Black parents bring up their children to be ambivalent and more or less self-contradictory. On the one hand, Black parents teach their children to uphold mainstream American ideals. However, they also teach them to be cynical, skeptical, and on guard toward White people and White-controlled institutions, including the public schools, as well as toward Black authorities in the system whom they regard as White representatives. Because of this upbringing, Black children may come to school with values and beliefs different from those of school authorities. Furthermore, teachers who do not understand Black children's values and beliefs are also not aware that their own values and beliefs are different. As a result, the children face cultural conflicts in their relations with teachers.

We found some students in Shaker Heights who were ambivalent. They believed in the "American ideals," including success through education and hard work, but they did not work hard. They were also mistrustful, ambivalent, and skeptical, especially as they got older and moved up in their school career. We discuss in chapter 10 how the cultural problems in Shaker Heights were not merely caused by conflicts and hegemony, as Boykin (1986) suggested, but that they were due to incompatibility of beliefs held by the students.

LANGUAGE–DIALECT DIFFERENCES AND CONFLICTS

Inadequate Language

Several explanations based on language or dialect differences have been offered for the low school performance of Black children. The main explanation in the 1960s was the *language-deficit hypothesis*, which postulated that Black children experienced difficulties in learning to read because they did not have a fully developed language. That is, they were not proficient in standard English because their parents failed to teach them how to talk like White middle-class parents taught their own children to talk. This hypothesis also influenced the Head Start programs (Engelman, 1970).

Language Differences Per Se

Another explanation emerged after researchers discovered that Black Americans speak an English dialect that is "a complete language" but different from standard English (Labov, 1972; F. Williams, 1970). The new explanation, the different-language hypothesis, attributed Black children's reading difficulty to language conflicts. The conflicts were initially identified as structural interference from their dialect. It was thought that, in order to learn to read in standard English, Black children had to (a) learn to decode symbols making up standard English words, and then (b) translate the symbols into their own dialect before they could understand the meaning of what they read. White middle-class children, on the other hand, had only to learn to decode the symbols of other words of a language they already spoke—standard English. An additional problem for Black children was that teachers did not recognize the second task faced by Black children—translating the symbols into their own dialect—when they evaluated their language performance (Baratz, 1970). To eliminate the structural interference, Black dialect was used to teach reading, but this did not improve the children's reading success.

Sociolinguistic Interference and Miscommunication

The third explanation comes from the field of sociolinguistics. According to some sociolinguists, Black children's reading difficulty is not due to inadequate language development, or to language differences per se, although the latter are important. These sociolinguists said that the main problem lay beyond language or differences. It has to do with identity and cultural rules of using language. They explained that when the children learned their dialect in their speech community, they actually learned two things: (a) the structural rules of their dialect (i.e., grammar, phonology, and vocabulary), and (b) the cultural rules for using the dialect (e.g., how to talk appropriately in different situations). The difficulty the children experienced in learning to read standard English is partly due to miscommunication between the children and their teachers, who come from a different speech community with different rules for speaking English. To drive home this point, they said that Black children do not experience in their speech community the language problems attributed to them in school, a place where they have to communicate with school personnel from a different speech community. An effort has been made to improve reading proficiency from this perspective but it has met with little success (Gumperz & Cook-Gumperz, 1994; Ogbu 1994a, 1999).

Smitherman (1977) described other sociocultural differences between the use of standard English and that of Black dialect. She explained how differences in discourse rules may cause problems for Black students communicating with speakers of standard English. She believes that Blacks and Whites differ in call and response, signification, tonal semantics, and narrative sequencing. In the Black speech community, call and response can be readily observed during church services, but it also permeates other communication situations and events. This feature of Black speech can cause communication problems, because a Black speaker may be waiting for a response from a White listener who does not realize that a response is expected; the White person's behavior would be interpreted as inattention. On the other hand, a Black listener to a White person may respond verbally and therefore inappropriately when he or she is not expected to do so, causing the White speaker to feel that he or she is being interrupted. This difference in communicative style can cause problems between White teachers and Black students. Another difference in discourse mode that causes problems for Black students is narrative sequencing, or storytelling. Blacks use sequencing in nonacademic and academic settings. In academic settings they may use stories to illustrate an argument. Whites, on the other hand, consider storytelling in an academic setting or in writing as constituting verbosity and therefore inappropriate (see also Kochman, 1983).

Both dialect historians and sociolinguists have established that Black dialect is a complete and functional language but that there are important differences between it and standard English. The differences, no doubt, have some adverse effects on Black reading proficiency in standard English. However, from a comparative perspective, it should be noted that there are some other minority group students with different languages or dialects and with different rules of language use who achieve greater reading proficiency in standard English than Black American students do (Gibson, 1988; Oakland School District, 1996; Park & Chi, 1999). This suggests that there is something more researchers need to discover in order to understand why some minority groups achieve more proficiency in standard English in spite of speaking different mother tongues with different rules of language use, while other minorities, such as Black Americans, are less proficient.

Collective Identity, Speech Community, and Schooling

We show in chapter 9 that Blacks in Shaker Heights were bidialectical: They spoke Black English dialect as their mother tongue and standard, or "proper" English as well. Almost all the students we interviewed from elementary through high school answered our questions in Black English. Students also spoke Black English during group discussions and when talking with us informally. Adults in the community did the same. We can thus call Shaker Heights Black community a *bidialectical speech community.* This community had one set of rules for using Black dialect and another for using standard English.

Most of the explanations we have reviewed have contributed to an understanding of the low school performance of Black children. However, when placed in a comparative perspective (e.g., when Black students are compared to some other minority students, including immigrants from Africa), their shortcoming becomes apparent. The problem is that the explanations are limited in their focus. By this we mean that they (a) lack a historical perspective, (b) are noncomparative, (c) tend to analyze Black school performance out of context, and (d) ignore Black cultural models or Black people's own understandings of their social reality and the effects of such understandings on their interpretations of and responses to schooling.

AN ALTERNATIVE PERSPECTIVE: THE ROLE OF COMMUNITY FORCES

As a result of comparative research on minority education, we believe that to fully understand why members of a minority group do or do not do well in school, one has to study their own educational beliefs and behaviors and why they believe and behave as they do. To achieve this objective in our research in Shaker Heights, we adopted a cultural–ecological framework that allowed us to examine several interlocking factors that might affect Black students' school performance in the school district. The cultural–ecological theory of minority schooling takes into account the historical, economic, social, cultural, and language or dialect situations of minority groups in the larger society in which they exist. According to this theory, two sets of factors shape minority students' school adjustment and academic performance. One is the way society and its institutions treat or have treated the minorities. We call this part of the problem *the system*. The other set of factors arise from how the minorities themselves interpret and respond to their treatment; that is, their adaptations to the U.S. society and to their minority status, which depends on their unique history or how they became minorities in the United States. We call this second part of the problem *community forces*.

The system operates at two levels. The first level is the general treatment or mistreatment of minorities by society at large and in local communities. This treatment includes instrumental discrimination, or barriers in opportunity structures (e.g., economic, political, educational barriers, etc.), relational discrimination (e.g., social and residential segregation, violence and threats of violence, deceit, etc.), and symbolic discrimination (e.g., denigration of minority cultures, languages, and intellectual abilities). Ogbu (1994b, 1994c, Ogbu & Simons, 1998) has called these discriminations the collective problems faced by minorities. These collective problems affect minority education directly and indirectly. For example, discrimination in employment limits not only the economic benefits minorities could get for their education, but it also directly reduces the resources they have for acquiring education. Residential segregation often directly results in school segregation and inferior education.

This theory considers three types of treatment of minorities in education that influence their school performance. One is the educational policies and practices (e.g., school segregation, unequal school funding and staffing of minority schools). Another is how minority students are treated in the school and classroom (e.g., low teacher expectations, tracking, etc.). The third is how minorities are rewarded for their academic achievement, especially in the job market and in terms of wages (see Ogbu, 1974, 1977, 1978).

Discrimination in society at large and in education is an important cause of low school performance of minority students. However, discrimination alone is not the cause of the low school performance—otherwise, all minorities would be doing poorly in school, because all minorities experience discrimination in varying degrees, but some are doing well, and others are not. There are differences in the school performance of sub-group of minorities who belong to the same ethnic group or the same racial group. That is, minority groups with similar cultural or linguistic backgrounds do not necessarily perform alike. It is also apparent that cultural and language differences per se do not seem to account for differences in the school performance of minority groups, because minorities that are doing well academically are often those whose cultures and languages are more different from than similar to White American culture and language. Cultural–ecological theory posits that school performance differences among minorities are primarily due to differences in the community forces of the minorities. Community forces refers to the way members of a minority group perceive, interpret, and respond to education as a result of their unique history and adaptations to their minority status in the United States.

Prerequisites For Understanding the Role of Community Forces

There are some prerequisites for understanding community forces and their influence on the academic achievement of minority students. We discuss briefly only a few of them.

Formal Education in Contemporary Societies, Is a Formula For Preparing Children For Their Future Adult Cultural Tasks Or Roles. Contemporary societies use formal education to equip young people with the knowledge, skills, values, behaviors, and language required to perform in their future workplace as well as in the political and social domains. Examples of cultural tasks are the jobs of accountants, carpenters, computer software developers, doctors, engineers, lawyers, teachers, and truck drivers. In the United States, the public school and other educational institutions have been delegated to prepare children for these positions. As Wilson (1972) pointed out, the special problem faced by societies operating a modern economy is how to maintain enough increasing specialization with enough flexibility to adapt to changing technology and economy. Modern societies found the solution in formal education, such as that offered by public schools in the United States.

First, public schools provide all individuals with a general education at a high level of specialization, thereby ensuring an adequate supply of manpower. Also, public schools devote the first 12 years of schooling to intensive instruction in specialized areas. At the elementary school level, teachers provide intensive instruction in the subject matters of reading, writing, and arithmetic. Even though they teach other things, children's academic progress is measured by their performance in reading and arithmetic. High school teachers are specialists in instructing students in single subjects. Students are discouraged from committing themselves to a single area of study during their public school education, thereby ensuring flexibility. The 12 years of public school education, according to Wilson (1972), prepares U.S. youngsters for a wide variety of specializations. High school graduates can go on to specialize as a gas station service attendant or a grocery clerk in a few days or as an accountant, a doctor, an engineer, or a teacher in a few years. Furthermore, public school education imparts knowledge and skills, including learning skills, for learning new knowledge and skills that did not exist or were not anticipated during one's public school career. For example, a high school education provides the foundation for some people to become computer programmers and Internet communication experts.

A public school education not only imparts to the individual the specific skills and knowledge necessary to function in modern societies, but it also socializes the individual in values and behaviors necessary to adapt in the workplace. Some students have suggested that the school is in a better position to prepare young people for participation in the modern corporate economy than the family because of the close resemblance between the organizational features of the school and those of the corporate workplace. That is, the experience children gain from the structure of their family and how they are treated within the family does not prepare them well to adapt to the demands of the workplace in the modern corporate economy, whereas their experiences in school structure and treatment do (see Scrupski, 1975). LeCompte's (1978) ethnographic study of classroom socialization suggests just how public school experience prepares children for future participation in the corporate economy.

From this perspective, the public school is a delegate agency. All children—White, Black, and other minorities—go to school to acquire the knowledge, skills, values, behaviors, and language they will need as adults to qualify for and be rewarded in the workforce.

It is unfortunate that, in the discourse on minority education, there continues to be a narrow, if not misinterpretation, of the purpose and function of public school education as cultural transmission. By this is usually meant the transmission of the culture of mainstream White Americans and the displacement of minority cultures. Public schools are alleged to be ignoring the cultures and languages of minorities and attempting to replace them with those of mainstream White Americans. Some minorities perceive this as an unacceptable imposition of Eurocentric curricula and Eurocentric pedagogic tradition.

There are, however, other minorities who interpret public school education differently and pragmatically as a process of teaching and acquiring the knowledge, skills, values, behaviors, and language they need to qualify or obtain credentials for jobs and rewards in the adult opportunity structure. These minorities regard almost everything in the school curriculum and the language of instruction as learnable and do not question the pedagogic style of public schools. They are not worried that what they are asked to learn, or how to learn it, is Eurocentric. Among these minorities are immigrants from Africa and the Caribbean, Asia, the Middle East, and Central and South America.

Consider the case of an immigrant student from Trinidad whom we interviewed during our research in Oakland, California. Like other "foreign" or immigrant students, he did not expect the Oakland public schools to teach him the curriculum based on his native Trinidad culture, teach him in his language, or use his native teaching and learning style to educate him. During the interview he criticized his Black American classmates for insisting that the curriculum should be "relevant" for them to learn. He reported that in their world culture course, or geography, his classmates often were not interested in learning about places and geographical conditions in other parts of the world. "Back home" in Trinidad, he said, students taking a similar geography course acquired specific knowledge of countries and geographical conditions of other parts of the world. They studied the geography of England, America, and Russia. They studied wheat farming in Russia, the steppes in the Andes, mountains in England, and the prairies in the United States and Canada. He even boasted that he and fellow students "back home" probably knew more about wheat farming in Saskatchewan, Canada, than the people of Saskatchewan. He and other immigrant minorities we studied in Oakland adopted the same attitude toward their courses: To them, the public schools in Oakland were teaching subject matters or imparting knowledge, skills, and other attributes they needed to graduate, go to college, or obtain credentials for employment.

The education systems of former European colonies in Africa and the Caribbean play the same role as a delegate agency, like the public school system in the United States. These former colonies need accountants, computer programmers, doctors, engineers, lawyers, nurses, teachers, truck drivers, and other skilled workers to function in their modern economies. They know that they cannot produce accountants, computer software programs, doctors, engineers, lawyers, nurses, teachers, truck drivers, and other skilled workers for their modernizing economy, health and social needs with curriculum and pedagogy based on their indigenous cultures and languages. Therefore, they consciously design their education systems to teach the universal knowledge, skills, values, and behaviors that are compatible with roles in modern economic and political systems as they understand them. They adopt the language of their former colonizer, because it is a commercial language that gives them greater access to the global world of which they want to be a part; it also eliminates ethnic conflict over the legitimation of one language over many others for instruction. Consider the case of Nigeria, with more than 250 language groups! Whose language should be the language of instruction: Hausa, Igbo, Yoruba, or any of the other 247 languages? People of African descent in Africa and the Caribbean are not consumed by the thought that they are losing their cultural or language identity by adopting Western-type curricula and pedagogy for their manpower needs. Furthermore, they know that to base their formal education in their indigenous cultures and languages is to ensure that they would not become "modern" for centuries to come.

U.S. Society Is a Settler Society.   A *settler society* is a society in which the ruling majority consists of immigrants from other societies. Members of this immigrant majority have come to improve their economic, political, and social status. The dominant Whites in the United States are such immigrants (Stasiulis & Yuval-Davis, 1995) who have come to achieve "the American Dream." A settler society often has two types of minorities: In the United States, there are some non-White minorities who, like White immigrants, have also come to achieve the American Dream, but there are also other non-White minorities who did not come to achieve the American Dream but were made a part of the U.S. society against their will, through colonization, conquest, or slavery. Black Americans are such a minority group. As we explain in the next section, these two types of minorities have different perceptions of the United States, their place in society, and the role of the public school or American education system in getting ahead (Ogbu, 1978, 1994c; Ogbu & Simons, 1998).

There Are Different Types of Minority Status: Immigrants Versus Nonimmigrants.   In this section we outline briefly the differences between the two types of minorities: immigrants and nonimmigrants. The origins of non-White people in the United States or their initial terms of incorporation into minority status vary. Cultural–ecological theory considers and compares two ways of becoming minorities and their educational implications in the United States, namely, immigration and non-immigration. We use the term immigration both broadly and narrowly. In the broad sense, immigrant minorities are people who were not forced to become a part of the society by the U.S. government or by White Americans. Such minorities include immigrants, refugees, binationals, and migrant workers. However, for the purpose of this study we are restricting the concept of immigrant minorities to its narrow sense, namely, people who chose to emigrate to the United States permanently because they expected better opportunities (better jobs, more political or religious freedom, etc.) than they had in their homeland or place of origin. What is most distinctive of immigrant minorities is that they themselves chose to move permanently and become minorities in the United States in the hope of a better future (Palmer, 1990). These minorities do not interpret their presence in the United States as having been forced on them by the U.S. government or by White Americans. Indeed, they have immigrated to the United States for the same reasons that Whites Americans immigrated, namely, to pursue the "American Dream." To differentiate them from other foreign-born minorities, we designate them as voluntary minorities. Examples of voluntary minorities are immigrants from Africa, Central America, India, Japan, Korea, the Caribbean, Mexico, the Middle East, the Philippines, and South American countries.

Involuntary or nonimmigrant minorities, on the other hand, are people who are in the United States because they were initially colonized, conquered, or enslaved by White Americans. They have been made permanently a part of the United States against their will. The important thing about nonimmigrant minorities is that they did not choose, but were forced, to become a minority group in the United States society permanently. They did not become minorities because they expected to achieve self-betterment in terms of better jobs or more political or religious freedom—in short, in search of the American Dream. These minorities usually interpret their presence in the United States as forced on them by the U.S. government and/or by White Americans. Involuntary minorities include Native Americans, Alaskan Natives, Black Americans, original Mexican Americans in the Southwest, and Native Hawaiians.

Descendants or later generations of voluntary minorities are voluntary minorities like their foreign-born parents or grandparents. Thus, second-, third-, and fourth- generation American-born Chinese are voluntary minorities. It does not matter that it was their forebears rather than themselves who decided to emigrate to the United States. The community forces that developed among their forebears continue to influence their educational ideas, attitudes, and behaviors.

The exceptions are descendants of non-White immigrants who share an affinity with pre-established involuntary minorities—that is, they have the same ethnic, racial, or other relationship with other non-White minorities who were colonized, conquered, or enslaved. Such non-White Immigrants are often treated by White Americans as a part of the pre-established involuntary groups. They are segregated and forced to live in the same neighborhoods with the nonimmigrants; they intermarry with them, and their offspring attend the same schools as the nonimmigrants. In due course, the immigrants and their descendants identify with the nonimmigrants and assume the same sense of peoplehood or collective identity. This is what has been taking place among Black immigrants from the Caribbean and their descendants. Evidence for their assimilation into the involuntary Black American minority group can be seen in their involvement and leadership in the civil rights movements of Black Americans.

There are differences in the adaptations of immigrant and non-immigrant minorities because of their different modes of incorporation into society. For the purpose of our study, the most significant differences are in their frames of reference or reference groups, their cultural models or social construction of how U.S. society works, and their place in that working order. That is, voluntary and involuntary minorities differ as to what it means to be a minority in the United States. They also differ in their beliefs about and responses to economic, social, cultural and language barriers and in their sense of collective identity.

The way minorities interpret their history—whether they became minorities voluntarily or involuntarily, together with the impact of societal treatment or mistreatment—shapes the pattern of the collective solutions they forge for their collective problems in society at large and in education. Because of their different modes of incorporation, voluntary and involuntary minorities tend to interpret similar problems differently and forge different solutions to those problems. Thus, they differ in their interpretations of and solutions to instrumental barriers (e.g., employment difficulty, unequal wages); the latter usually include folk theories of how they can "make it" as minorities, their collective struggle, and alternative strategies for making it. Their solutions for social discrimination (social and residential segregation, threats of violence, etc.) include collective struggle (voluntary and involuntary minorities) and some degree of acquiescence (especially voluntary minorities). Both minorities distrust White Americans and their institutions, but involuntary minorities do so to a greater extent. Voluntary minorities develop a pragmatic trust in some societal institutions, such as like the schools, for instrumental reasons. Voluntary and involuntary minorities differ in their interpretations of and responses to cultural and language barriers. The collective identity (a sense of who they are) and the cultural and language frames of reference of the immigrants are perceived as merely different, and the immigrants' response to cultural and language barriers tends to be accommodation without assimilation (Fong, 2001; Gibson, 1988). The collective identity and the cultural and language frames of reference of the non-immigrants tend to be oppositional (Luster, 1992; Ogbu, 1992, 1999). These collective solutions constitute the minorities adaptations to U.S. society and to their minority status.

The adaptations, in turn, generate the community forces or beliefs and behaviors within the minority communities that influence minority school adjustment and performance. Five aspects of the community forces influence the academic achievement of minority students.

Frame of educational comparison.   Immigrant minorities compare educational opportunities and benefits in the United States with those back home. The frame of comparison of non-immigrants are the educational opportunities and benefits available to White Americans.

Beliefs about the instrumental value of school credentials.   Immigrant minorities believe more strongly that the way to get ahead or achieve upward mobility or the "American Dream" is to get a good education and good school credentials. To them, education is the key to success. They also believe that education can help them succeed more in the United States than back home. Immigrants' role models for making it in the mainstream corporate economy are White Americans or members of their own groups who have achieved professional success through education. Nonimmigrant minorities are not sure that education is the key to success. Many see little evidence among their own people for believing that success in adult life or upward social mobility is due to education. Their role models tend to be people who have made it through alternative strategies that require little formal schooling or school credentials. Leadership in civil rights movements or the collective struggle against "the system" is another source of role models.

Relationship with "the system" (school and school authorities). When one compares immigrant and nonimmigrant minorities in terms of their relationship with White Americans and the public schools, one finds significant differences. Such a comparison can be made with regard to three domains: (a) social distance or segregation, (b) conflict and mistrust, and (c) pragmatic trust. Because of their optimistic, pragmatic attitudes toward education and their relational interpretation of schooling, immigrant minorities are not deeply concerned about social or residential segregation. For nonimmigrants, segregation has acquired a secondary meaning of rejection and inferiority. The two minority types experience conflict with White Americans and mistrust them. But the twin problem is more serious for the nonimmigrants.

Of particular relevance to education is the difference in the minorities' interpretation of the relational part of schooling. The immigrants develop a pragmatic trust of the schools and school personnel. They believe that teachers are "useful experts" of the knowledge, skills, and language they need to succeed in the United States, that the schools will help them achieve the goal of their emigration to the United States. Nonimmigrant minorities interpret their relationship with schools and teachers within the context of the overall enduring conflict between them and White Americans. As a result, they are more concerned with how they are treated or represented in the curriculum and with whether schools and teachers "care for them" than with teachers' expertise in knowledge, skills, and language.

Expressive or symbolic beliefs about schooling: Issues of identity, culture, language and ability. Immigrants who perceive their cultures, languages, and identities as different are willing and able to adopt White or U.S. school ways and language. They emigrated to the United States expecting to learn a new language and new cultural behaviors so they could achieve the goals of their emigration. They do not feel that learning English and how to behave like Americans in some areas of life threatens their language or cultural identity. Neither do they think that being able to learn the language and behaviors required at school means that they must give up their own languages and cultures. To them, they are learning new ways to add to their own knowledge to achieve instrumental goals. Non-immigrants, who may perceive their cultures, languages, and identities as oppositional, are less willing and able to adopt White or the school ways and language. They are suspicious of the intentions of the school curriculum and language. Some fear adopting White or school ways because they think it would mean replacing their own cultural and language identity or that it requires them to give up their cultural and language identities in order to successfully learn the school ways.

Educational strategies: How the minorities go to school. The two types of minorities differ in the strategies they use to achieve their educational goals. The strategies of the immigrants are based on practical consideration and pragmatic trust in schools and teachers as experts who have something useful to offer even if they do not "care" for minorities or have their interest in mind. Another distinctive feature of their strategies is that they tend to match their educational aspirations and verbal commitment to education with behavior conducive to school success; students pay attention in class, follow rules, and do their schoolwork and homework. They work hard. Another feature of their strategies is that parents and community hold students responsible for school performance.

The strategies of non-immigrant minorities are overshadowed by their emphasis on social relations and caring rather than the practical considerations that schools and teachers are experts who have useful knowledge, skills, and language to offer. They are mistrustful of schools and teachers, and they feel alienated. Their high aspirations and strong verbal endorsement of education are not matched with behavior that is conducive to school success. Parents and community members tend to hold teachers and schools, rather than their children, responsible for school performance.

Community Forces

As they grow up, minority children learn about the community forces—the educational beliefs and behaviors—of their community that eventually affect their school adjustment and performance. The community forces also affect the educational strategies of their parents and communities in dealing with the educational system and in working with their children.

The community forces, together with societal and school factors determine more or less the school performance of minority children. However, according to cultural–ecological theory, it is the differences in the community forces that largely account for the school performance differences between immigrant and non-immigrant minorities.

The heuristic value of classifying minority groups as voluntary or involuntary is further enhanced by two other factors, which we already discussed. The first factor is that the U.S. public school and other educational institutions serve as a delegate agency to prepare children for future adult jobs that are vital to society and to certify positions in the corporate economy and other domains of society. From this perspective, the function of public schools is not to teach or destroy minority cultures and languages or replace minority identity with mainstream White American identity. From a comparative perspective, it appears that immigrant minorities more than the non-immigrants understand and evaluate the public schools as a delegate agency. The second factor is that some non-White minorities, but not others, have come, like White immigrants, to achieve the "American Dream." The difference in mode of incorporation affects the immigrants' perceptions of the role of the public school in minorities' ability to get ahead.

The cultural–ecological theory used for this study posits that the academic disengagement and performance of minority students are influenced by two sets of factors: (a) the system, and (b) community forces. The system includes societal or community educational policies, the treatment or mistreatment of minorities in school and classrooms, and how society or the community rewards minorities for their academic achievement. The factors that make up community forces are the frames of reference or comparison of the minorities; their instrumental educational beliefs and behaviors; their relationship with the educational system and the schools and their expressive beliefs and behaviors, including how they interpret and respond to cultural and language differences because of their collective identity; and their educational strategies.

In outlining our theory we have compared immigrant and non-immigrant minorities. In the Shaker Heights school district, however, the only significant minority group was the non-immigrant Black Americans. They constituted the study group. Furthermore, we did not study all the variables posited by the theory because of a lack of time and resources.

II

Societal
and School Factors

4

Race Relations

RACIAL HARMONY:
COMMUNITY SELF-REPRESENTATION

In a documentary film, "Shaker Heights—The Struggle for Integration" (Math, 1997), both Blacks and Whites described the history of race relations in Shaker Heights. Most of the documentary was made during our study. According to the documentary, when Blacks began moving into the city in the1960s, some White and a few Black residents organized what eventually became the Shaker Heights Community Association to halt "White flight."

The goals of the association were integrated housing, good race relations, and a good public school system with an outstanding academic performance and with good race relations. Since then, the people of Shaker Heights have created what they believe to be a diverse and desirable community. According to the characters in the film, "more than elsewhere in the nation, one could find in Shaker Heights integrated community-wide picnics, political rallies, Fourth of July celebrations and block parties and, within the school system, participants in *tai chi* on the high school lawn and more integrated classrooms. There were meetings of Black high school seniors in jackets and ties mentoring younger Black (males) at the high school, and Black and White sixth graders could be seen working (together) to build trust between children of different racial groups by falling into a circle of each other's arms." (Math 1997, p. 3). The people's effort to create and maintain a community with racial harmony was also noted by Singham (1997, p. 3) in his summary of the people's response to our first public presentation. According to him, "To attend a school orchestra or band function, with an overflow audience consisting of all ethnic groups watching and playing together in harmony is a model of what America as a whole might be if it could put its racial tensions behind it." He went on to say that the community was afraid that the academic achievement gap was a potential disruptive factor to the racial harmony.

We did not make a systematic study of these integrated situations and activities. However, we studied how Blacks in Shaker Heights, both students and adults, perceived race relations at school and in the community. We also examined how these perceptions, or their social constructions of the race relations, might influence the schooling of Black students.

COMMUNITY SELF-REPRESENTATION
AND THE CODE OF SILENCE

Frame of Reference

Blacks considered race relations in Shaker Heights to be far better than in nearby suburban communities and elsewhere in the nation. Several students compared race relations in Shaker Heights with those in Parma and other surrounding communities. They concluded that although Shaker was not perfect, it was, at least, a community where Blacks and Whites lived together and attended the same schools in peace. They were particularly pleased that White people in Shaker seem to have accepted the idea of racial diversity.

The Code of Silence

Although Blacks in Shaker Heights credited their city with better race relations than other cities, they were also critical of the patterns of race relations in their community. They described the public image or self-image of Shaker Heights as one of a well-integrated community with integrated schools. Whites, they said, thought of Shaker Heights as a community with a school system characterized by amicable race relations. Many Blacks rejected this self-representation. However, they believed that the self-image of harmonious race relations had persisted because there existed a sort of a code of silence: People were not expected to publicly discuss, and usually did not discuss racial problems in the community. A different image emerged when the code of silence was broken. Although support for the nondominant perspective on the race relations we describe later is based on data from Black informants, we also found support from some Whites and from our observations of White behaviors. As we show, the race relations problems are limited neither to Shaker Heights nor to the present.

National Comparison: Shaker High and Little Rock High

The code of silence broke down on several occasions during lessons. One such occasion was during a social science lesson. On that particular day, the teacher asked students to compare Little Rock High with Shaker High. He began the lesson by distributing copies of an article from *U.S. News and World Report* about Little Rock High School in Arkansas. He wondered how Little Rock compared to Shaker High. He challenged the students to compare racial integration in the two schools. On close reading, the article appeared to be comparing racial integration—or lack of it—in Little Rock High and Shaker High without mentioning Shaker Heights by name. The class proceeded to analyze the article. Both the teacher and the students pointed out similarities between the two schools: segregated cafeteria, honors and advanced placement courses had almost all White enrollment, Blacks and Whites seemed to use separate entrances to school, and so on.

There were racial differences even during the class discussion. More of the White students thought that Shaker High was more integrated than Little Rock High; more of the Black students believed the opposite was true. However, both White and Black students agreed that racial segregation in Shaker High was not limited to students' distribution in classes. It could also be observed in the hallways and cafeteria.

In general, White students were more reluctant than Black students to discuss race relations. We observed the greater reluctance of Whites in another class when we asked about differences in the way White and Black students behaved. A White student described Shaker as a castle containing things that were less than perfect. However, the residents of the "castle" did not like to discuss any matters that would suggest that there was something wrong in the castle. The young man was describing the *code of silence:* There were racial problems in Shaker, but these problems were not for public discussion. The majority view of White students was that Shaker Heights was a well-integrated community with an equally well-integrated school; therefore, there was no need to discuss race relations. A minority of the Whites disagreed, saying that their school was not well integrated. The dissenting students mentioned the "leveling system" (see chap. 8) as something that made Shaker High look like two different schools in one building.

School Curriculum and the Code of Silence

How the public schools, the Shaker community, and even society at large maintained the code of silence was revealed one day in an English literature class. The discussion started with a discussion of a poem by Claude McKay. The poem was about McKay's nostalgia for tropical fruits in his home country, Jamaica. There was a smiling photo of McKay in the anthology of his poems. The teacher next selected another poem by McKay from another anthology, *Black Voices*, (James, 2001). However, it was not about longing for tropical fruits; the mood was rather typical of McKay's style, sad and bitter about race relations in the United States. Someone said that Shaker High and similar schools across the nation did not usually include poems like Mackay's "America" in selected readings for students. When asked why the school would exclude such poems a Black male said that the authorities feared that reading and analyzing such works might change the way students' understood the social order.

Another student added that several themes in the poems in *Black Voices* were referring to bad things about the White man. The White man who established schools like Shaker preferred that students read poems portraying or suggesting that the writers were happy, including "a dude who missed fruit." Other reasons were mentioned for excluding Black literature in their curriculum. One was that Black authors were people at the bottom of society and were criticizing it and that White people didn't like that.

At this point a Black male said that Blacks themselves were not eager to read poems like the ones in *Black Voices*, because reading them could be upsetting. A White male added that White people were reluctant to read such poems because they were afraid of knowing the truth. Furthermore, race relations was a sensitive subject: White teachers at Shaker did not feel comfortable discussing the truth because it would make them angry and ashamed. Another White male said that it was easier to go with the flow. He added that students should read more poems like this to broaden their minds and knowledge. The discussion expanded to types of topics or ideas excluded in Shaker High curricula, especially in the history curriculum. A Black male believed that there was a conspiracy underlying school curricula: White people excluded certain materials from the school curricula to keep Blacks ignorant of their history and collective experience.

White students usually did not feel comfortable discussing race relations even when it was in the context of a situation outside Shaker Heights or about a historical event. We observed this uncomfortable feeling in a class discussion of Jim Crow, Plessy vs. Ferguson, and Brown vs. Board of Education. At the beginning of the lesson, the teacher asked the students if they had heard of Plessy. Most Blacks and only a few Whites raised their hands. The teacher later told us that a previous class discussion of race relations was very emotional and that some students were so upset that they told their parents about it.

In another class, White students objected to some comments made by the teacher about the desegregation of U.S. public schools. He was responding to a question about busing from a White student. The teacher explained that Shaker Heights integrated its schools through voluntary busing. In contrast, school integration in Cleveland was done by compulsory busing ordered by the court. Some White students opposed the use of busing to achieve school desegregation even if it was voluntary. These students a lived in desegregated neighborhoods, leading the teacher to later confide in us that some people in Shaker Heights were content living in desegregated neighborhoods, while leading segregated lives.

Race Relations Among Students

The comparison between Shaker High and Little Rock High revealed the discrepancy between's Shaker self-image and the reality. We now turn to a similar discrepancy between self-representation and reality: in patterns of social relations between Black and White students. We discuss students' own portrayals of their experiences, teachers' observations, and our own observations.

Students at the elementary school did not feel that race was a factor in their friendship formation or peer relations, but from middle school onward, race became increasingly important. At a discussion with Black middle school students, some complained that the school was "racist" because students segregated themselves by race. One speaker described the cafeteria as "a place where people segregated themselves by race, although they didn't have anything against one another." We heard that Black and White students would hang around mainly with people of their own race. On several occasions senior high school students reported that peer groups and peer activities were organized along racial lines.

Teachers, too, believed that students' peer groups were racially based. One White teacher reported that racial segregation could be seen in the hallways and cafeteria. He had observed such segregation on a daily basis. Although we found some integrated groups and activities, our own observations were similar to what this teacher described. Some Black students reported having White friends but, as we discuss in chapter 10, the students who hang around mostly with Whites were accused of "acting White."

BLACK PERSPECTIVES ON RACE RELATIONS
IN SHAKER HEIGHTS

Black Image in the White Mind

Shaker Blacks believed that they were disparaged by Whites and misrepresented in White people minds. They further believed that the misrepresentation aroused an unnecessary fear of Blacks by the Whites, and White fear strained race relations. The misrepresentation and its consequences were mentioned in several interviews we conducted with middle school and senior high students. They were also discussed in other situations. The following discussion is based mainly on an interview with students. We should note that the students were not unanimous in their views.

When asked what White people thought of Blacks in Shaker Heights, two middle school students said that some White people thought highly of Black people, whereas some did not. Another student took a neutral position, saying that most White students were comfortable with Blacks because they were used to being around Blacks (at school). However, the same student admitted that Blacks and Whites were somewhat segregated in her school. At the opposite end, three middle school students believed that White people in Shaker did not think highly of Blacks. The following excerpts show how two of the students assessed the White attitudes:

> Student 1:   Uhh, well I really can't say [what White people think of Black people] because I'm not White. So I really wouldn't know what they think of us. But ... they probably [think like this] about us, "Oh yeah, they're just gonna come in and cause chaos," because um, it's like most, like the perspective [i.e., image] they have of Black[s]. Most um, perspectives of Black people is that they come from the projects or anything like that. And they're gonna cause total destruction in a clean-cut environment and so ... That's probably the reaction. So White people, when they think this way about Black people, living in the same environ-

ment [neighborhood] that they [White people] live in … but
that's not the case most of the time.

Student 2:   White people think that Shaker is getting too crowded. Like,
it's like more Black people [are] comin' to Shaker now. 'Cause
they like, some heard like the school and stuff like that. So it's
like, it's like cause, I had heard, like my mom had told me like it
used to be a lot of Whites over here … like years ago. And now
Blacks are gradually comin' in and Whites are kind of like
movin' away. But it's some Whites that won't let go. So they
won't move, regardless of what you know …

High school students were more vocal about what White people
thought of Blacks in Shaker Heights. They distinguished between public
attitudes and pronouncements of White people about Blacks from private
beliefs and actions. The public statements of White people were often
based on the community ideal or self-image, which was quite different
from the actual image in the minds of individual Whites. The public statements that reflected the ideal self-image was that Black people in Shaker
Heights were like White people in Shaker Heights and that the two races
got along just fine. Black senior high school students and some White students questioned this image. They believed that that was not really the
way White people thought of Shaker Blacks. Whites did not really believe
that Black people in Shaker were like them; neither was it really true that
the two races got along well. Blacks added that although White people
publicly expressed a commitment to diversity and good schools, privately
they were not deeply committed to the twin goal of diversity and good
schools; they avoided dealing with race relations problems in the public
school. Here is how one student described this distinction between the image and actual practice:

Like on a surface kind of level it's supposed to be all peaceful, like you know,
"We have no problems and you know everything's fine; and you know,
Blacks and Whites are equal and whatever." But I think there is, there is a
part of the White community of Shaker who does look at Blacks as being you
know, inferior. And whether they, I mean obviously they don't like openly
act out on these personal beliefs [because] that's illegal. But you know it does
seem that there is that feeling. There's not really like we have a race riot going on here or anything [to show that we have race relations problems] but
like I think the community as a whole, it is segregated. And, like you know,
the White community, they don't really know that much about the Black
community. They don't care to, they don't want to deal with it.

The next student summed up Black students' perceptions of what Shaker Heights Whites thought of Shaker Heights Blacks and their mutual ignorance of each other.

Anthrop: What do you think that the White community here in Shaker thinks of the Black community?

Student: Um, I don't necessarily think that they want us here and they [don't] like us here [in high school]. I just don't think that they do; [but] I don't know. Sometimes I just feel like I don't belong. Like when I'm in my classes and stuff, ... I think that the kids are probably they indirectly expressing their parents' attitudes toward Black people. You know, a lot of times, what you hear [that] come out of peoples' mouths is regurgitated from exactly what their parents [believe] and what [White students] hear at home. And I just think that they have a warped view of Black people in general. I don't think they really understand. And I think Black people have a warped view of White people, too, ... [especially] if they haven't been with them. I think it's very important that if we're all supposed to be diverse or something, we need to, you know, [be open with each other]. We need to have forums talking about that. "What is it like to be a White person?" I don't know. I'm not White.

Black Image and White Fear

Shaker Whites were described as being afraid of Shaker Blacks because of their image of Blacks. Students recalled occasions when they observed White fear of the Black community. White fear of Blacks was not a recent development. White people had always been afraid of Black people, as one student noted:

I think that White people have always been frightened of Black people in Shaker Heights. Since the 60's when Blacks moved into the community, I think it's [White reaction?] always been based on panic and fear. People love the idea of having an integrated community, but still [maintain–retain] the basic stereotypes, "Our community gonna start to deteriorate and there's gonna be crime." And [White people think] that Black crime would be different from crime [committed by Whites] in all-White communities. [Their stereotyping leads them to say] "We know how to deal with that [White crime] 'cause we're White. But even if it is not a different crime from what we're used to, it is just [adding Black crime] on top of that .... It's like, "Goodness!" So yeah! I don't know. In addition, there's a fear of Black families, period. The fear of Black families is specially strong as you get down in the Ludlow and Moreland areas where it's primarily Black. I think there's just a panic surrounding Black families, period, especially [fear of Black youth].

We saw an example of the White fear of Blacks during a campaign for school board and city council elections. Some White candidates refused to participate in a forum organized in a church in a predominantly Black neighborhood. A day before the forum, two White candidates sent a letter to the organizers saying that they would not attend, because they believed that "the environment" would be hostile and uncivil toward them as White candidates. We attended the forum and saw no hostility or any uncivil behavior toward other White candidates who took part in the forum; in fact, we saw no difference in the treatment of Black and White candidates by the predominantly Black audience.

Racism

Racism was discussed by middle and high school students. When someone asked at the middle school how many people at the discussion meeting thought that racism "was a big deal," a student who talked "properly" replied that there was racism. Another said, "My teachers are." This student then began to mention names but was told not to do so. Others began to describe attitudes and behaviors they considered racist. Among them was self-segregation by race, which they attributed to White students' feeling that they were superior to Blacks. "Whites," one student said, "feel that they are superior to Blacks and do not want us to associate with them." He went on to say that White students' feeling of superiority was evident in their self-segregation in the hallways and cafeteria as well as in their dominance in honors and Advanced Placement classes.

Although most people believed that racism existed among students, not everyone had experienced it. Those who had not experienced it said they had made Whites fear them. According to them, racism was experienced by those who tolerated it. Whites did not behave in racist ways toward people they knew would not tolerate it. White people were, and had always been, "scared of [such] Black people."

Other students, and some adults, provided examples of racism either from their personal experience or from the experience of people they knew.

How Children Learn About Race Relations

Shaker children, White and Black, became aware of the pattern of race relations in their community early in life. White children, especially White males, began early in life to understand and assume that White people, especially White males, were superior to Blacks. This was illustrated by an incident in a kindergarten class. The kindergarten teacher began describing the incident, commenting that White children began as early as 5 years of age to think of themselves as members of the dominant group and as superior to Black people. Her point was that this particular incident illustrated how even a White boy of this age asserted the superior racial attitude of the Whites:

> I'm going to add an anecdote that happened in my own school. (Clears throat.) The gym teacher was having a class with kindergartners and the children were grouped into groups, you know, of mixed races and genders. And she called on one group, and she happened to name the little girl, one little Black girl who was in the group. She said, "Okay. Natasha's group or something." [I don't know what the child's name was.] "Uh, let's go do this." And then a little boy, a little White boy that was in the group, these are K's, he said, "Why is she calling this her group. I'm the White boy. This should be my group" So as early as 5 years old, people have ideas about who they are, and who other people are. And so it's not something that's so easy to pinpoint or fix, you know. It's a very deep thing.

Black children also began early in life to develop an awareness of the pattern of race relations, including their subordinate status. This happened both in the family and at school. In chapter 7 we give an example of its occurrence in the family. Here we describe an example of how it happened through school experience. This was the case of a Black teacher's son. Her son's experience was described at our meeting with a group of school personnel and is presented next in her own words:

> I teach here. And my kids were in the system, and I have one child in particular whose [experience is a good example of racism]. He's my youngest child, and he's very good in school. He's a good math student and ... works hard. He tries hard. He wants to do well. He dresses like, you know, the typical African American male. His hair is long. He has baggy clothes. OK. One day I dropped him off at the middle school last year after a dentist appointment. He made it to school. It was probably two o'clock in the afternoon. Somebody [at the school] said [to him], "Who are you? What are you doing here?" They made him prove [that] he belonged there. They made him follow them to his locker. He had to show them that he could open it. He had to, he was, he had to defend himself in his own school. And you have to constantly fight feelings of rejection, inadequacy, uh not being valued as a person or a student. Not being recognized as who he is by simply looking at him [was a terrible experience]. When you look at him, he's not valued. He looks like "one of those kids." And so, he has a constant struggle to keep his morale up, to

keep trying, to keep wanting to do this. And it's a *true* absolute frustration (emphasizes the word *true*).

Eliminating Racism

On several occasions, especially during class discussions and in interviews, suggestions were made about how to improve race relations not only in Shaker Heights but also in the nation as a whole. Some Black and White students were not happy about certain features of U.S. society in general. They appeared pessimistic about the possibility of making the United States a better society. Because we did not specifically question every student on how to improve race relations, not everyone we interviewed expressed an opinion on the matter.

At the elementary school only one student commented on changing race relations. He believed that the way to improve race relations in Shaker Heights was to eliminate prejudice and poverty. One middle school student thought that race relations in the United States, not just in Shaker Heights, could be improved by electing a Black president. Another stressed the importance of eliminating stereotypes. He felt that people should not be judged by the color of their skin.

As might be expected, high school students had the most to say about changing the race relations. They were, in fact, preoccupied with this issue even when they were not asked about it in interviews. Six of the ten students questioned specifically believed that it was important to change the race relations patterns in U.S. society as a whole and in Shaker Heights. Among those not asked about race relations some also said it was important to change it. High school students generally felt that society as a whole, and Shaker Heights in particular, should do away with stereotypes and should not judge people by the color of their skin. They also wanted people to abandon intellectual stereotyping. Finally, they wanted an end to discrimination in opportunity structure based on skin color and race. The last recommendation is summed up in the following students interview excerpt:

> I'd change the um, the whole structure of this society because I don't like the way it is right now. Like a lot of oppression like behind the doors ... I mean like [we should be] equal as in everybody, but its so much influence that has happened like over the years of like people growin', like stereotypes have been just like deep rooted into people's minds ... The way like how people are, like how some White people stereotype Black people as bein', you know, like no good.

RACE RELATIONS, COMMUNITY FORCES
AND EDUCATION

Distrust of White People and Their Schools

One strong impression gained during our initial visit to Shaker Heights was that many people in the Black community did not trust White people and their institutions. These impressions influenced our subsequent research plan to minimize the effects of the distrust on our findings.

School authorities apparently unaware of this distrust suggested that we introduce ourselves as researchers for the school district rather than as jointly sponsored by the Black community and the school district. As we noted in the Preface, the initial invitation actually came from people in the Black community. We did not go along with the district's suggestion because we felt that Black parents, particularly those whose children had problems, would refuse to participate or allow their children to participate in the research. Our initial impressions that people distrusted the school system were reinforced on many occasions throughout the study. For example, every now and then we heard of a "conspiracy" against Blacks or a "conspiracy" to deny Black children "equal education."

It was not only adults who distrusted White people and the school system; students did, too. We learned of the students' attitude from their responses to questions we explicitly asked about the extent to which their family and community trusted White people in Shaker Heights. Some students believed that Blacks did not and should not trust Whites.

> *Anthrop:*   So do Black people trust White people?
>
> *Student:*   No, I don't think so.
>
> *Anthrop:*   No? In uh, then do they trust them to educate their kids?
>
> *Student:*   I wouldn't think so.

Some people said that Blacks trusted Whites to some extent or with caution. The degree of trust depended on the extent of one's association with White people and on how comfortable the Black person was around Whites. But it was not safe to trust White people too much; those who trusted Whites too much did so at their own risk.

There was no indication from students or adults that Blacks had a pragmatic trust in the school system, teachers, and other school authorities— that is, they did not judge their teachers and schools primarily as useful because they were experts who offered valuable skills and information for their future in the job market and other domains of adult life. From this perspective, Shaker Blacks would strive to learn what the teachers were teaching, regardless of whether the teachers were particularly interested in them or cared for them as people both as Black people and as individuals. Pragmatic trust would make parents work more closely with teachers and other school officials because they would see the former as imparting useful skills and knowledge their children, things that they themselves could not provide. Children would observe their parents' attitudes and behaviors, internalize them, and approach their school learning as acquiring useful skills and information for their future. They would pay attention in class and do their schoolwork and homework. Rarely was schooling evaluated in terms of its instrumental or pragmatic function but more often was evaluated in the context of Black–White race relations.

In the absence of pragmatic trust, the attitudes and actions of teachers and other school officials were viewed with strong mistrust. Parents communicated to their children the belief that they had to be careful of teachers, whose ideas, words, and actions could not be trusted. Although only one student admitted outright that his father told him that White teachers were trying to fail him because of his race, discussions of the Shakerite article on the Black–White academic gap provided evidence that Black students and adults (including some school officials) were highly suspicious of the school authorities. Consider the Black community's interpretation of the article, given by a community representative and a Black counselor, which we present next. We learn from the dialogue that the article had served as a call for Black students to work hard or to improve their performance and thereby empower themselves. We also learn from the dialogue that the Black community suspected that Whites intentionally published the article to make Shaker Blacks "look bad."

Black School Counselor (BSC):   Most of the confusion now came about an article that came out condemning to our minority students. People should understand how we feel. Don't fight some institution and use Black children to do it. The person who did that [i.e., who wrote the article] needs to apologize to this [Black] community.

Anthrop (A):   I haven't read the article, so I don't know anything about it.

Community That's the article that brought up the achievement gap.
Representative
(CR):

A: Oh.

CR: The factual content was accurate, and it also served as a stimu-
              lus to create change with a lot of those Black students. A lot of
              them have now decided to do more to empower themselves.
              And they've created self-help groups. So, we can also look at it
              as a bell ringing, um, to start looking, "How can I empower
              change within myself," given we may have institutional rac-
              ism. We probably have that in any institution through out this
              country, but here's a point where self-empowerment and
              self-help have to begin, and the kids got that message.

BSC: Some of 'em.

CR: Many of them.

BSC: Some of them. I've called about this, this school—

CR: (simultaneously) Some of them—

BSC: I've had children tell me, "I want to go to another school."

CR: I know. I've heard that.

BSC: You don't know how, how the person's gonna react.

CR: I completely concur with you, but—.

BSC: I've heard defeat: "They tell me I'm no good, and I'm the (loser)
              in the battle." It doesn't affect me too well.

CR: But what we have to do is take that and do something positive
              out of it. And we have that facility, because no matter how you
              shake it, a 1.9 grade [point] average [GPA] for the last 5 years in
              high school! It's hard to put a positive spin on that. Uh, com-
              pared to White child, male, getting over 3.4 grade average. It's
              very hard to put a positive spin on that. It may be painful, and
              it's hurtful, but if you don't look at a situation and examine it
              holistically, you're probably not going to be able to find some
              resolution to it. It may be painful to know that 40% of our kids
              in the last 5 years have Ds and Fs. It is extremely painful. But
              the fact remains, that's what existed. What we have to do is not

to air it out on the headlines. What we have to do is bring in a
Doctor Ogbu so that Black, White, stakeholders, those in
power, those disenfranchised, have an understanding of what
are the underlying causes for this phenomenon, and then, and
only then can we start coming up with programs, implement
ideas to increase resolution and change systematically and not
put Band-Aids on this whole phenomenon that we've done for
the last 30 or 40 years.

Furthermore, this problem is not limited to Shaker Heights. As we noted
in chapter 3, Boykin (1986) pointed out that Black parents may socialize
their children to be mistrustful, ambivalent, and skeptical toward the public school and its personnel.

Race and the Interpretation of the Academic Gap

Because Blacks did not trust the school system, they did not accept the
schools' explanations of the academic achievement gap. Blacks believed
that the gap was due to racism. White people, including White school officials, in contrast, attributed the gap to social class differences. White
school authorities argued that Black students' low academic performance was caused by the low socioeconomic or poverty background of
students regardless of race. The overall lower performance of Black students was due to the fact that Black students as a group came from a
lower socioeconomic background than White students.

These differing racial perspectives on the academic achievement gap
can be seen in the following exchange between a member of the Black
community and a White school official:

White male In the district, the classes are split. You talk to a classroom
school official teacher, there's a group of kids who will do anything that's
(WMSO): asked, and there's another group of kids that will do almost
            nothing. And there isn't a lot of middle ground; so, they're
            kinda torn. [Teachers] can focus on the kids who won't work;
            and then, the kids who will work [will] sit there kind of bored.
            If [teachers] concentrate on the kids who will work, the kids
            who won't work just sit back and let things slide. It's kinda
            strange because when you talk about Shaker, we don't have a
            normal curve with the grades. We have a camel back, or, we
            have As and Bs, and we have Ds and Fs. We don't have a lot of
            kids in the C range.

Black Community Representative (BCR):	[In] your comments you both have given, are you referring to all kids, or to Black kids [when] you were speaking regarding the phenomenon?
WMSO:	No, I don't, I don't think it's Black or White. I think … in our district it's more economics. The … kids whose parents are professional, Black or White, tend to be pretty hard workers, 'cause … there's a push from home. And the—
BCR:	If that's true then, why do 80% of the Black kids over the last 5 years out of the high school, have the results that we're having? [i.e., discussing]
WMSO:	Well, our economics. We don't have, our population, if you eliminate race as … a factor, and you look at the students, and you just look at professional background uh, economic backgrounds, all the things that would give a student an advantage, uh, in the school district, like any school you walked into to, the kids who would have the greatest advantage, uh, if you looked at that, the kids who have the advantages do well. The kids who don't have the advantages in general don't. And there's kind of a middle ground. And then if you, if you go back and you just add race to it, you would find that a lot of the kids who have the advantages are White. A lot of the kids who have the disadvantaged background are Black.

And so you have a population that's really being pushed to go to Harvard and Yale; who, no holds barred, they're gonna get an education. And then you have another population economically and … the amount of parental help they can get, uh, they have a real disadvantage. It's real hard work to get caught up. So you, uh, [see], a big part of what you do in Shaker has as … much to do with economics as it has to do with race. |
BCM:	So you think it's an economic problem?
WMSO:	Well [what] I'm saying is that the kids who do well generally have a real economic advantage.
BCR:	But I guess my question,…. See I don't know all the economic statistics. I have some of them. But I just can't picture that with a 1.9 GPA of Black males in the last 5 years that there's a significant proportion of the Black population where there's lower income within Shaker [i.e., the proportion of Black males receiving a low

GPA is higher than the proportion of Black population with low income] I think ... it's very obvious ...

WMSO: There's only about 10% poverty rate in the district.

BCR: Well, I'm not talking about poverty. I'm talking about the—

WMSO: Then if you take $25,000 or less, I think that's only another 10%.

BCR: So that's 25% with less than $25,000. But then you have 80% who are not achieving. Eighty! Eighty!! You said 20% of your Black population—that has the 25?

WMSO: Pretty sad numbers [rest of comment unintelligible].

BCR: OK, and then you take the White population, and how many of them ... have parents who are both professionals, who have a good income, um?

WMSO: It's a higher percentage than Blacks. I don't have a number. I guess what I'm saying is that those kids have a tremendous advantage; and it's very hard for ... other kids who are in the middle ground to catch up.

At this point we joined in the exchange, pointing out that we had seen some data from other school districts indicating that there were differences in the academic achievement of Black and White students from similar family and socioeconomic statuses. Among Blacks, as among Whites, students from families of higher socioeconomic status and professional families did better in school than students of the same race from families of lower socioeconomic backgrounds and nonprofessional families. This suggested that differences in socioeconomic status were associated with differences in academic achievement within the same race. On the other hand, the academic achievement of Black students from families of higher socioeconomic backgrounds and professional families was lower than that of White students from similar family backgrounds; furthermore, the academic achievement of Blacks from families of lower socioeconomic backgrounds and nonprofessional family backgrounds was also lower than that of White students from a similar family background. These differences could not be attributed to social class differences. The data from Shaker Heights clearly showed that Black students from families of higher socioeconomic backgrounds did not do as well as Whites from similar higher socioeconomic backgrounds.

Neither did Blacks from lower socioeconomic backgrounds do as well as White students from similar socioeconomic backgrounds. The lack of similar school performance by Black and White students from similar socioeconomic backgrounds meant that something else, probably race, was implicated in the academic achievement gap.

The community representative and the school official resumed their debate:

BCR: That's really what we're talking about. In Shaker, 30% of the Black population had an income of $50,000–$100,000 or more [according to the 1990 census]. But far less than 31 percent of Black kids are not making two points [2.0 GPA] or more. So, that means that the advantages of high-income families are not reflected in the academic performance of Black students at high school. If Black children from high-income families do not do as well as White children from high-income families, what are other reasons for their lower performance? Does race have anything to do with it?

WMSO: Oh, I think [that] economics aggravate it, not that they cause it.

White Female   Yeah. I think there are there are some, ... I think there's lots of
School   variables that have to do with kids' performance, and race, of
Official: course [is one of them]. Everything that affects a child has something to do with his or her performance, ultimately. Uh, race, class, where they see themselves in society, whether they come from a single parent home, or, but you know, with two parents; ... there are lots of different things that affect [an] individual's performance. There are so many variables that we see.

Like their parents, many Black students believed that the academic achievement gap was due to racism. Some believed that the school courses were set up so that most White students would take honors and advanced placement classes while the majority of Black students would go to remedial, skills, and college prep classes.

5

Pygmalion in History, Society, and School

In this chapter we examine the beliefs of White Americans about Blacks' intellectual ability and how the internalization of the White beliefs by Blacks affected the academic attitudes and behaviors of Black students in Shaker Heights. *Internalization* is defined by Webster's Ninth New Collegiate Dictionary (1990, p. 632) as "the incorporation of values or patterns of culture within the self as conscious or unconscious guiding principles through learning or socialization." We found the nearest meaning to this definition in Shaker Heights during a lesson in which Sambo mentality was discussed. *Sambo mentality* was defined as a state of mind in which people unconsciously replay in modern society or in Shaker Heights the role (or mentality) of slaves. Several students at the class discussion gave examples of this mentality from their observations at school and in the community. The existence of the internalized beliefs and their effects on students' work became obvious when students responded to some research questions. Here is one such question we asked students at a discussion meeting with a group of high school students: "How many of you deeply think in the back of your mind, maybe White students are really smarter than Black students?" Several students raised their hands in affirmative.

PYGMALION IN HISTORY

History has taught us and [society has] persuaded us to think that Blacks are inferior to Whites and [that] Whites have more potential than Blacks. And since the birth of the United States society has always thought this way. And I compare the struggle in slavery, you know … all those things that have been wrong in history, to what happens in classroom today. In slavery those

[Black people] who thought differently than what society taught [them to believe] which was [that] Blacks are inferior to Whites, fought that struggle. And those who fought that struggle, most of those who fought that struggle succeeded. Sometimes in the classroom, [Black] kids seem to think, to have this mentality, this unconscious way of thinking that Blacks are inferior to Whites. And I think that [that] takes a toll on some Black students. [White teachers, counselors, etc.] might not be racist. They might not have anything [against Black students], any negative views of Blacks that [whether] they're White [or] Black [teachers and counselors]. They just survive in it. [They unconsciously act like society believes Blacks will act because they are inferior].

—A Black male student at Shaker High

Three important points are made by the student in this interview excerpt. One is that Black people as a category or collectively had known since slavery that (White) people believed them to be intellectually inferior to the Whites; the second is that Black people had come to believe that they were indeed not as intelligent as White people (i.e., they eventually internalized the White beliefs) and the third point is that even today one can observe the consequences of the internalized White beliefs in the classroom attitudes and behaviors of Black students.

Our observations at school and in the community during the study support the student's analysis. Some conversations with parents and other adults in the community, discussions with school personnel and students, student interviews, and in-classroom observations suggest that the White belief that Blacks were intellectually inferior to them had become an ingrained part of the thinking of some Shaker Heights Blacks.

ORIGINS OF THE INTERNALIZATION
OF WHITE BELIEFS

Students traced to slavery the origins of the internalization of the White beliefs that Blacks are intellectually inferior. White slave owners and White people in general believed that Black slaves were inferior to White people. They treated the slaves as if they were indeed less intelligent. After slavery was abolished, White people continued to treat Black people as inferior. High school students in particular elaborated on the long history of the intellectual denigration. It was evident during class lesson on Jim Crow, Plessy vs. Ferguson, and Brown vs. Board of Education that Black students knew far more of the White mistreatment of Blacks than did their White peers. When the teacher asked how many had heard of Plessy, it was mostly Black students who raised their hands. It was also evident during the same lesson that Black students felt the impact of the past mistreatment. We learned, for example, that one Black student was absent because she had gone to show a film somewhere about the Tuskegee experiment.

The Tuskegee experiment is a good indicator of society's belief that Black Americans are not as intelligent as White Americans. The experiment, which lasted from 1932 to 1971, was sponsored by the federal government. Initially, the purpose was to study the effects and treatment of syphilis, but the experiment eventually concentrated only on its effects, ignoring treatment. Black men from rural Macon County, Alabama, were chosen for the experiment because, according to one official, it was believed that Blacks there had lower intelligence than Whites. It is estimated that between 28 and 100 of the men died from the disease because they were not treated. The experiment was discontinued in 1972 when it was leaked to the Associated Press and President Clinton offered an apology to the participants in 1997 (Lehrer, 1997).

PYGMALION IN SOCIETY

Internalization of the White belief that Black Americans are not as intelligent as the Whites persists in Shaker Heights, as it does elsewhere in the nation. Although very little research has examined the subject, we have encountered it and some of its educational consequences in a number of ethnographic studies. What is particularly important is that a large segment of the Black community is aware that White Americans do not think that they, Blacks, are as "smart" as Whites. For example, in research conducted in Oakland, California, 82% of the 1,300 students surveyed reported that people in their families and community believed that White people considered Blacks less intelligent than the Whites (Ogbu, 1998). The internalization is, of course, strongest among the oldest generations. In a comparative study conducted in the early1990s, Stanback (1992) found that the internalization was probably strongest among Blacks born before 1930, followed by those born between 1930 and 1960. It was weakest among those born or who grew up during the "Black consciousness" period, or Black Power Movement (Stanback, 1992). We suspect that similar age differences would be found in Shaker Heights. However, we have made no separation by age in presenting the following explanations for the persistence of the internalization of these beliefs in Shaker Heights and the nation. It is important to bear in mind that most of our data for this chapter came from students rather than from the oldest generations.

Exclusion From Assimilation

We asked why White beliefs and Black internalization of these beliefs persist in the Black community and among Black students. One common explanation was that the beliefs were based on race and differences in skin color. White people would continue to believe that Black people were inferior as long as Black people remained a separate category based on skin color. Under this circumstance, some Blacks would continue to internalize the White beliefs. Blacks contrasted their situation with those of some White immigrant groups, particularly the Irish. In the past, other Whites believed that Irish people were intellectually inferior. However, the Irish escaped internalizing the belief that they were inferior because they were light skinned, intermarried with the other Whites, and eventually assimilated into mainstream White society. In contrast, because of their skin color, Blacks have not been able to escape the internalization through intermarriage and assimilation. One student who provided this analysis elaborated on it:

> [the Irish] got a little bit of intermarriage goin' on, and everybody looks the same now, you know. And so, I think that Black people are just supposed to [be different] and everybody is just like, whether you're mixed or you're um, [dark] Hispanic, they're all Black. Anybody with a darker skin is Black. And like I just find it kind of weird and I think a lot of these people view themselves in the same way. They can't do anything. And after so many times of hearing that, you know, you know, it starts to become you. You know. Like I guess its like—what's the saying? It's a saying like that, my mother says sometimes. Like, "Once you hear it so many times, then, it becomes what you are" [i.e., you internalize it].

Collective Mistreatment

There were collective experiences that reinforced and perpetuated the internalization of the White beliefs. Although Shaker Heights children themselves did not go through the experiences of their ancestors, they were nevertheless affected by memories of past mistreatment, including slavery. They did not have to have been slaves to internalize the beliefs about the mentality of the slaves; memories of the collective experience of the past influenced their thinking. Black students but not White students recognized this. Thus, one day when a teacher asked how a Native American student who read a book about all the horrible things done to his people would feel, a White student replied that the Native American student would not react like a victim of oppression, because those things did not happen to him personally. A Black male student countered by saying that the mistreatment of Black people in the past, such as Jim Crow segregation, indirectly affected Blacks of later generations such as himself.

Current Debate About Black Intelligence

Current discussions of Black intellectual and academic performances and their intellectual representations in the media maintain or reinforce the internalization of the White beliefs. Examples of this discourse include the following. In 1969, Jensen published his widely publicized article claiming that the gaps between Whites and Blacks in academic and professional achievements were due to differences in intelligence. A 1978 Newsweek poll found that 25% of Americans believed that Blacks are not as intelligent as Whites ("How Whites think," 1979; see also A. Campbell, 1971). The debate generated by the publication of The Bell Curve by Herrnstein and Murray (1994) was not lost on Blacks in Shaker Heights. Murray and Herrnstein argued that Black Americans are not as intelligent as White Americans. Several students talked about contemporary White debate over Black intellectual ability. One Black male described the impact of the contemporary White view of Blacks' intellectual ability on Black people's self-perception as follows:

Male Student:	Um, I believe that, uh, the image that [the White] society, you know, [through] TV, magazines, books and everything we look at and read every day, the image that [society] gives to Black people is that we're inferior. And unless you learn [otherwise], or something has happened to you in life to [counteract] that image, and [destroy] that way of thinking in your mind, you [are likely] to act [as if you are indeed inferior] ... in your everyday life. In everything you do, you do it as if Blacks are inferior to Whites. I don't know if that came out clearly [i.e., if you understand what I am saying]. (Muffled voices as audience members react.)
Anthrop:	So the public image or stereotype is internalized by Blacks.
Male Student (agreeing):	And we have this ... indirect way of thinking. Like it's ... an unconscious way of thinking. And unless we learn ... we learn [otherwise], then that's the way we go through life.

Another student reported in an interview that Black students were influenced by society's stereotype. "The real problem" was that the stereotype was unfair and generalized:

Anthrop: Well, what about the exception to the stereotype? The guy who's just trying to get a cab downtown.

Student: That's where it's so unfair and that's why things really suck. Because for the person who really is doing things right, and is trying, so to speak, and he doesn't have things going for him because of his skin color. That's the problem. If the society is looking down upon Black people, then that's a problem because that becomes what the person believes. But I do believe that [Black people] have those difficulties and it's, you might even need to have twice as many qualifications [to be accepted as equal by Whites].

Treatment of Blacks in the Workplace

The treatment of Blacks in the workplace also reinforced the internalization. This happened even to Black professionals or minority professionals when they were placed in new positions without mentors or clear specification of what they were supposed to do. The employees would be thinking that they were being scrutinized by White people who expected them to fail. In this situation the Black employees would develop self-doubts about their ability to perform well. One professional described the case of a young Black salesclerk in a department store. The salesclerk gave our informant an incorrect amount of change. The informant interpreted this to mean that the salesclerk had been placed there without proper training "just because the employers wanted to meet quotas." She said that without proper training the salesclerk was making many mistakes and would be eventually fired for incompetence. As we will see in chapter 8 Black students seemed to feel the same way. They said that White employers did not think that Black employees were as good as White employees. Therefore Black employees must "prove themselves."

Cultural Transmission

Black children in Shaker Heights, as elsewhere in the nation, became aware early in life that White people did not believe that Black people were as intelligent as themselves. Children in Shaker Heights began to internalize the White beliefs as a part of the beliefs and experiences of their parents and other significant people around them. There were adults in the Shaker Black community who lived with a sense of intellectual inferiority. They inherited these beliefs from their own parents or acquired them during their school career when they were classified and labeled as "mentally retarded" or disabled learners and placed in special education programs. The internalization might also have come from experience at work and other encounters with White people. The personal experience of the following student is an example of how adults in the family fostered the internalization of the White beliefs.

> You know … I guess the way to explain [the internalization] is like this. I've always been taught [that] it goes back to slavery. You know, when you think about how the different things that were put into a slave's head. That they [Black people] could not achieve well; that they weren't meant to achieve anything in life. And those kinds of ideas have [continued to influence Blacks] throughout the generations. Like my grandmother, she always says to me like, "You know, those niggers don't do nothin'. They'll never get anythin' done. You better do right [so that] you … might be able to get out [i.e., become somebody]. But like the rest of them [Blacks] are just like crabs in the barrel." And when you keep hearing this every time it affects you.

We found in a research project conducted in San Francisco that the internalization may begin quite early for some children. One incident at a preschool–afterschool class during a Black History Month program in February 1996 illustrates just how early children begin to internalize the belief that Blacks are not as intelligent as White people. Three Black Americans from San Francisco Health Department went to make a presentation on health to the 4- to 10-year-olds. One of the three public health officials was a doctor who talked about what she and other doctors did. When asked what they wanted to be when they grew up, many children replied doctors, architects, dentists, lawyers, and so on. Asked what they would do to achieve their goals they answered almost in unison, "get a good education." Finally, when questioned about what might make it difficult to attain their career goals, a 7-year-old boy said that Black people could not be doctors because they were not good (i.e., not intelligent) enough. Several other children agreed.

In a subsequent discussion among the Health Department workers and the daycare staff, these adults repeatedly said that in their communities children began as early as 3 or 4 years of age to understand that White people discriminate against Black people and do not believe that Blacks are as smart as White people. To further illustrate the seriousness of the internalization problem, the doctor described a visit to her health center by a 3½-year old boy. The social worker who brought the boy had told him that it would be a good experience for him to see a Black doctor. The boy replied that there were no Black doctors. When the social worker introduced him to the doctor, the boy repeatedly asked her if she was a real doctor. The basis of the child's skepticism became obvious when he said that "All doctors are supposed to be White."

PYGMALION IN THE SCHOOL AND CLASSROOM

School Experience and Internalization of White Beliefs

Some school practices reinforced the internalization of White beliefs that Blacks are not as intelligent as White people. These practices included teacher expectations, leveling, and disproportionate representation of Blacks in special education. We have found in our research in Oakland, San Francisco, and Stockton, California, evidence of the contribution of these school factors to the belief by Black people, including students, that they are not as intelligent as White people.

There was both explicit and implicit evidence of the internalization during formal and informal interviews we conducted with Black school personnel, students, parents, and others. One school counselor in Stockton, for example, reported that Whites' intellectual denigration of Blacks was prevalent in his school district, just as it was in the college he had attended in Arizona.

It was a status symbol among Stockton teachers to teach in a school with mostly White and therefore more intelligent students. Parents who had been placed in classes for the mentally retarded during their public school career reported living with a sense of intellectual inferiority.

As we have already noted, Black children become aware quite early in life and begin to internalize the belief of White Americans that Black Americans are intellectually inferior to Whites. In a study of more than 1,300 Black public school students in Oakland, California, 21%reported that school authorities do not believe that they are as smart as White students, compared to 5% of the Chinese students (Ogbu, 1998). Further evidence that Black students are sensitive to the issue of intelligence can be seen in their response to another question in the Oakland study. Black students "wished" they could prove to White Americans that they were wrong in thinking that Black people are not as intelligent as White people. Thus when asked why minorities went to school, Blacks asserted nearly three times as often (18%) as the Chinese (7%) and twice as often as Mexican Americans (9%) that they went to school to show Whites that they are smart (Ogbu & Simons, 1994).

Shaker Heights informants also reported that some teachers, both Black and White, assumed that Black students could not perform like White students (see also Project ACHIEVE, 1997). Those who performed well were perceived as "exceptional." Black students were aware of the assumptions and to some degree internalized them, and this contributed to their low performance.

Leveling, or tracking, reinforced the internalization. The following male student, speaking at a high school discussion, argued that leveling and racial distribution in classes symbolized the intellectual inferiority of Black students.

> I think, uh, [that] in Shaker the way the classes are set up, the majority of White people go to the honors and [advanced placement] courses. The majority of Black people go to the [college prep] courses. And I think that, that's a bad setup, because … you don't want to go into a class where you're one of four or five people of your race. I think that's a very intimidating situation. It is especially hard for a Black person to enter and perform well in … an honors class or an [advanced placement] class where there's gonna be four or five other uh people of their race, if not less. Or you know, so.

The way some White classmates treated Black students also reinforced the internalization. Black students reported that some White students did not want to work with them. We observed one instance of this in the hallway. In this case, White students ignored a repeated request of a Black classmate for information about their homework.

Belief That Doing Well in School Is a White Prerogative

For some people, the internalization of the beliefs that Blacks are not as intelligent as Whites translated into another belief, namely, that White students, not Blacks, were the ones who did well academically. Therefore, Black students who tried to do well were really trying to be like White students; they were "acting White." This was one of the themes emphasized the discussion, with high school students. In the following excerpt from that discussion White students were seen as the ones who could perform well academically:

Anthrop: OK. Is it true that Black students who are doing well are accused of acting like White people?—

Female   OK. I think part of our problem is we're proud individuals. We
student: truly are. We think one of the reasons to try to go and get that
              good education is to get that college degree. And one of our en-
              tire goal[s] in life is that this is what we want. But as we're sit-
              ting here, we know, we're slacking, because we've been acting
              like we're not going to get that [college education]. "Duh duh
              duh duh." Instead of being smarter than that and trying to
              reach and follow behind that [White] person who is doing well,
              we sit ... back and say, "Man," whatever, "duh, duh, duh, [the
              White students are] better. Duh duh duh." It's more because ...
              we feel inferior. Once we feel inferior inside, OK, forget it: [we
              say to ourselves] "I'm not even gonna try." Once we have that
              inferior feeling, it's like something turns us off. We're just
              turned [off] and stop trying.

Self-Doubt

Internalization of the belief that Blacks are not as intelligent as Whites gave
rise to self-doubt and resignation in regard to intellectual performance.
Self-doubt and resignation were described by both students and school
staff. We observed both during classroom lessons and in other performance
settings. Self-doubt sometimes began early in one's school career; in some
cases it began later, but it generally became pronounced about high school
time. We got some idea about the development of the self-doubt from the
following accounts by two school counselors at a meeting between school
counselors and the anthropologist (the researcher). In their experiences
from elementary through high school they believed that Black students,
particularly Black males, began before the middle school to give up thinking of themselves as capable of good academic achievement.

Female   Well, I want to take [the discussion of apparent lack of attempts
Counselor: to achieve] one step back which may explain part of what um,
              Linda's going through. Um, Linda talked about a manifesta-
              tion of what I'm going to say. First of all, we're talking it from
              the point of view of high school [i.e., as it happens in high
              school]. So it's difficult to know what the experience [situation]
              was prior to this. But, um, [I do because] I work with entering
              ninth graders who are under [ordinary circumstance] ... are
              perfectly capable of doing very good school work. [Yet] they
              are grossly, *seriously* (emphasizes the word) underachieving.
              And I see them as a group of ... mostly young Black male[s]
              who do not see themselves as learners. They do not see them-
              selves as participating in the educational process. I'm not sure
              what the reason is. I'm just making a statement of observations.

It's very disturbing. When you discuss it with them, ... it is so clear that they see that in themselves. That is, they [themselves] are very perceptive. They're very self-aware. They see themselves in the light that I'm describing, um. They aren't sure why this is the case, but they don't enter feeling that there is the expectation that they're going to achieve. Perhaps it is because they have a history of underachievement; so, why should it change when they enter in ninth grade. They haven't seen themselves as learners throughout ... the years they have been in school; And [a] part of our job is to try to change this kind of attitude, to change their attitudes about themselves, their level of self-confidence, um, their image of themselves as students. And once that happens, and it does happen because we've all observed it where kids have come in seeing themselves in that way and done dramatic turnarounds. Um, there is a whole other aura about the young Black males, about the way they feel about themselves, and about the way they participate in the educational process. There is also an aura about how they see themselves as belonging in this educational setting. When that dramatic change takes place in a group of those students. So, I'm not sure where that [resignation] begins, and I'm not sure how it grows. But I believe that one of our biggest challenges is to figure out a way, find a key, to unlock that.

Anthrop: Maybe people [counselors] at the middle school can help us, because ... That students at the elementary school are eager to learn. You are talking about high school. So would somebody give us some insights as to what goes on in the middle school [i.e., seventh and eighth grades].

Male
Counselor: Well, before you talk about the middle school, I just want to make a comment. I think what you said about us starting at the middle school [assumes that the children] are doing fine in elementary school. Um, having experienced a range of those grades in my own career, I know what you say, [because] it's often [reported] that way. It's often talked about that way. [But] my own experience, though, tells me that these things start as early as first grade, uh kindergarten. [The suggestion that it does not exist in the elementary school] is somehow either an erroneous assumption or a misconception.... Differences in the way students respond to school [by race] starts much earlier. And some of [the differences] you can see very early. Uh, I think that we have to just add that piece, and I make that comment. That it doesn't just start at middle school. You can see this building very early in kindergarten first. Some people could even probably take it to preschool now with so many more pre-schools.

Students agreed that self-doubt prevented some of them from seriously engaging in academic pursuit. In the words of one student:

> And I mean there are [students] who just don't … I feel that they just don't want to push themselves and I don't know why. And also I think there's people who just think they can't do it. Or they've been subconsciously somewhere, they been made to just believe that they can't do it. And then they're not expected to do it. Their parents don't set expectations, the school might not set expectations. It becomes like the norm for them to lack confidence that they can succeed. You know, the feeling to not do anything in school and be lazy and whatever. And like they feel like [this is the way] people are thinking of them, or expecting them to [behave]. And even if they're not [behaving this way] knowingly, they're doing that like subconsciously I think.

The same student went on to point out that the self-doubt was caused not only by the beliefs of the school personnel about Black students' intellectual ability and low expectations but also from internalization of White beliefs and memory of past White treatment of Black people. Consequently, there were students who had given up trying because they "lived in the past." He continued:

Student: Because most of them [those who don't work hard to make good grades to go to college], like wherever, they live in the past. They mostly talk ebonics, and they don't really go to school. And [they] don't go to college. They just stuck under the past. They're like adults, they don't have to do anything else. They don't have to work.

It was partly because of self-doubt that some students avoided honors and advanced placement [AP] classes. Doing well in these classes required a lot of effort, and some students doubted their ability to make those efforts. Students 1 and 2, quoted next, addressed the problem of effort and avoidance of honors and AP classes because of self-doubt during a discussion group, and the third student did so during an interview: All three students did not feel that they could succeed in these classes.

Anthrop: OK, now how about the honors and advanced placement classes? Um, when you're in your honors classes, um, are there lots of other Black students in your classes?

Student 1:   No. It's like two other Black people in my honors math class.

Anthrop: OK. Um, how about in general, in the lower classes, are there more Blacks in the lower classes?

Student 1: Yeah. 'Cause they don't try hard enough.

Anthrop: Why don't they try to take the advanced classes?

Student 2: They probably think they're not good enough for 'em ... they're probably not prepared to take them.

Student 3: I think a lot of Black people think that they can't do it. They say "AP, that's too hard for me." Ahh!, like they're dumb or something. And you're not dumb. It just takes more work, and you have to be willing to work. I mean, I don't know. I think it would be interesting to see like, what everybody turns up to be. And what they become as adults. And its like, "well, see I told you." You know.

Their White classmates also reported that Black students avoided or dropped out of honors and AP classes because they were unwilling or unable to keep up with the required workload. The following White student commented on this:

Anthrop: What do you think in general about the fact that there are not very many Black people in your [AP] class?

Student: Well, I don't really have a problem with it because those are the classes that I need to be in because I'm learning on that level, so it doesn't really bother me.

Anthrop: OK. And why don't Blacks take 'em?

Student: Well, usually they start out in those classes but they just don't do the work, and then just slack off and they end up in the lower classes.

The problem of academic self-doubt exists among Black students in every community we have studied, including Oakland (Ogbu, 1998), San Francisco (Luster, 1992), and Stockton, California (Ogbu, 1974). During a discussion about a math course with a Black school administrator in Stockton, the Black students told her, "You know, we're not as smart as they [i.e., White students] are. They don't have any muscles, we have muscles (for sports and athletics") (Ogbu, 2001; see also Grier & Cobbs, 1968; Howard & Hammond, 1985).

Redirection of Intellectual Ability to Nonacademic Pursuit

Some students suffering from self-doubt in the academic domain direct their "smartness" into nonacademic endeavors. In a discussion with the anthropologists, several students said that a part of the problem was not only that self-doubt made students avoid honors and AP classes but also that Black students directed their "smartness" to nonacademic pursuits.

6

Leveling

Most research on *leveling*, or *tracking*, has been concerned with its contribution to the reproduction of social inequality or social stratification in society. Prior to the mid-1960s, high school students formally enrolled in separate academic tracks, namely, Honors, Remedial, Essential, and Basic (Lucas, 1999). Some school systems dismantled the tracking system in the 1960s or 1970s, sometimes as a result of protest by Blacks and other minorities, as was the case in Stockton, California (Ogbu, 1974). The academic tracks were replaced by course tracks in which a student enrolled at a given level of a course in the same subject, as in the case of Shaker Heights. This has resulted in a new form of tracking. Researchers are still trying to determine the relationship between the new form of in-school stratification or tracking and stratification in society at large (Braddock, 1990; Lucas, 1999; Oakes, 1985).

Our concern in this chapter is different in two ways. First, we want to describe how and why Black students got into, or failed to get into, various course levels and then performed, or failed to perform, well. Second, we are primarily interested in the contribution of leveling or tracking to the academic achievement gap between Black and White students. To achieve these objectives, we analyze data from our ethnographic observations, formal and informal interviews with students, counselors, teachers, and other school personnel, rather than analyze statistics. Although we did not conduct formal interviews with counselors and teachers on leveling, we had at least one group session with each of them. In addition, we had informal discussions with individual counselors and teachers, as indicated in the Preface.

WHAT IS LEVELING?

What is leveling? No matter how leveling was officially defined, to most of our informants it meant "tracking." Elsewhere and throughout the nation, leveling is also known as tracking. Shaker Heights students first encountered leveling at Woodbury, the upper elementary school for fifth and sixth graders. According to school authorities, leveling was the selection of students at Woodbury to participate in either of two academic resource programs (ARPs). One was the academic enrichment program for students "who had the potential" for academic achievement. The authorities believed that those students needed advanced classes in math and other subjects. The second ARP was the Title 1 program, for skills improvement. This was designed for students in Grades 5 and 6 who were experiencing difficulty in specific subjects, such as mathematics.

During our research, the two criteria used to select students to participate in the enrichment and skills programs were test scores and teacher recommendations. Students were formally tested for placement in the programs. A student's performance in the state proficiency examination was also a good indicator of the program to which he or she would be assigned. Thus, in the year that preceded our study, no one in the enrichment program failed the proficiency examination. Teachers' recommendations were based on their observations of students' class performance and needs. Students recommended for the enrichment program were generally those who performed well in class and had impressed the teacher as having "potential." A student could also get into the program at his or her parent's request.

Changes After Our Research

Some changes occurred in the leveling process after our fieldwork was completed. A *Guide for Parents* issued for the 1998–1999 school year stated that the advanced level-classes (i.e., enrichment program classes) were "designed to be the most academically challenging." Students selected for the advanced program in language arts and mathematics should possess specified attributes necessary to succeed in those advanced classes. To continue in these classes a student must maintain at least a B grade. Although the Guide emphasized academic criteria, it also informed parents that the advanced classes were open and that they could place their children at any level (i.e., advanced or basic skills classes) they considered appropriate (Shaker Heights School District, 1998).

According to the Guide, the following criteria would be used for assigning students to skills classes: (a) failure in the fourth-grade Ohio Proficiency Test in Math or Reading, and (b) receiving the lowest test scores in class in reading or math. A letter of explanation was to be sent to the parent who was asked for permission to place his or her child in the program. There should not be more than 11 students per a teacher in a skills class. The students were tested before they entered the program and at the end of their participation these tests were designed to probe their ability to do well in the state proficiency tests. Children were to be transferred to regular classes when their test scores showed that they were ready for regular fifth-and sixth-grade reading or math. Later we describe the enrichment and skills classes as we observed them during the fieldwork, not as they operated after the changes.

LEVELING, RACE, AND CLASS COMPOSITION

Upper Elementary School

There were three levels of classes or academic streams at Woodbury Upper Elementary School. In a given subject, particularly mathematics and reading, students participated in skills, regular, and enrichment classes. Theoretically the three groups of students were studying the same subject matter for their grade level and had the same homeroom teacher. However, they studied the same subject at different levels. During a math period, for example, math enrichment students went to that program, in another room; math skills students also left to attend their program, in another room; and the remaining students in the homeroom received regular math instruction.

We did not obtain statistics on the racial makeup of the three groups in various subjects, but our impression was that there were no significant racial differences in class makeup before the upper elementary school. On entering Woodbury, the upper elementary school, there was a dramatic change in which the students were classified as skills, enrichment, or regular students. The difference in racial composition of these classes was apparent during our first visit to the school. While going to the principal's office, we saw some learning disability and skills classes that had mostly Black students. We indicate in Table 6.1 the proportion of Black students in the different classes we observed at the upper elementary school.

TABLE 6.1
Leveling, Race, and Class at the Elementary School

Teacher	Class Level	Total No. Students	No. Black Students
A	Learning disabled	4	4
B	Skills	22	17
C	Regular	19	9
D	Academic Enrichment	16	2

Middle School and High School

Students at the middle school (Grades 7 and 8) and high school (Grades 9–12 enroll in honors, college prep, and skills classes on the basis of the recommendation of their Woodbury teachers and their test scores. The proportions of Black students in these classes at the middle school and high school are shown in Tables 6.2 and 6.3. Theoretically, a parents could request that his or her child enroll in an honors/advanced, college prep, or skills class, but the usual procedure at the middle school and high school for assigning students to particular course levels was similar to the procedure at the upper elementary school, namely, use of test scores and teacher

TABLE 6.2
Leveling, Race, and Class at the Middle School

	Skill/CP		AP/Honors	
Teacher	Total No. Students	No. Black Students	Total No. Students	No. Black Students
E	21	13	18	2
F			23	3
G	Skill: 11	9		
H	CP: 20	9		
I	CP1: 21	16	AP: 27	6
	CP2: 22	17		
	CP3: 20	15		
J	CP: 23	11	Honors: 27	4
K	CP: 20	10		
	Skill: 12	11		

Note: CP = college prep; AP = advanced placement.

TABLE 6.3
Leveling, Race, and Class at the High School

Teacher	Class Level	Total No. Students	Total No. Blacks
A	10th-grade CP	22	19
B	10th-grade Honors	19	5
C	10th-grade Honors	25	1
D	CP	17	11
D	AP	28	2
E	CP	15	8
F	CP	15	10
G	Algebra lab	17	16

Note: CP = college prep; AP = advanced placement.

recommendations. There were similar uneven racial distributions in the course levels at the middle school and high school.

RACE AND INTERPRETATIONS OF LEVELING

Black Students

At the upper elementary, middle, and high school levels students attributed the uneven racial distribution of students in classes to leveling. Middle and high school students were almost unanimous in asserting that their present course enrollments had already been determined by the leveling at Woodbury. Assigning students to either enrichment programs or skills-improvement programs did not provide all students an equal opportunity to grow and excel. Every middle school student we interviewed said that there were few Blacks in the honors and advanced classes and that most Black students at the middle school were in College Prep and skills classes. Middle school students believed that there was some causal relationship between participation in the academic enrichment programs at Woodbury and enrollment in honors and advanced classes at the middle school.

Most high school students also believed that their course enrollment had been determined by their course enrollments at the upper elementary and middle schools. Those who participated in the academic enrichment program at Woodbury and enrolled in honors and advanced classes at the middle school were prepared for the honors and advanced placement (AP) classes at the high school. However, for students who started with skills classes at the middle school and then took skills and college prep classes at the middle school, it was very difficult, if not impossible, to take the honors and AP classes and do well at the high school.

At a meeting with the anthropologist, high school students discussed at length the effects of the leveling at Woodbury on the racial makeup of classes at the middle school and high school. Students blamed leveling for the uneven racial distribution and the academic achievement gap between Blacks and Whites. One female student summed up the views and general feeling of the students as follows:

> Um, [I'm] going along with what [Lorraine] said. Like somebody said earlier, [we] don't understand [why] all the sudden like, within [lower] elementary school everybody is too pretty much around the same [i.e., Blacks and Whites are about equally represented in the same class]. Then all the sudden their appearance in the classes at Woodbury is totally different. I think a lot of that happens between Woodbury and middle school because [it is at Woodbury] that the differential classes start. At that point they'll begin to have the enrich classes, advanced classes, and regular classes. *And* (with emphasis) I know like my mom had to talk to the administration about putting me in the enrich classes because it was just like, you know, I know that many of those people who are in those classes [when they were] in the seventh and eighth grade [honors/advanced classes] got the background, had the experience, and had the knowledge [at Woodbury] to see and to get into those classes. Once they got to high school the transitions were much easier to maintain and to stay in those honors and AP classes. So it's a lot more difficult [than] being in regular classes. [But if you were not in such enriched classes] at the elementary school and at the middle school, and then all the sudden [to] move into an honors or an AP class in high school that you're not used to [is difficult]. You're not used to having a heavier workload. You're not having, like more reading or more note-taking being required. So I think that's where the gap starts. Until then, the test scores were high enough to be in here. Everything was, you know, I'm doing well in math or whatever, but for whatever reasons they didn't want to put me in those classes.

The Black Community

Parents and other members of the Black community were critical of leveling. They blamed leveling for the "racial segregation" of most classrooms in Shaker Heights. They were particularly angry that only a small number of Black students were in the enrichment, honors and AP while most of their children were in college prep and skills classes. The most elaborate analysis and criticisms of the leveling policy and practice were made by one speaker during a community meeting. She espoused what sounded like *social reproduction* theory (McCleod, 1987).

According to this individual, middle class Blacks and Whites were not putting pressures on the school system to eliminate leveling, because the system was serving them well. The schools were designed to continually reproduce the existing social structure, which favored Whites and tolerated Blacks. It ensured that the two races would be educated separately or would not receive equal education. The Shaker Heights public school system was like an apartheid; she did not mind if Whites and Blacks went to separate schools—what bothered her was the negative intellectual evaluation of Black children in the school system. Community members also criticized leveling and the racial segregation of classes it caused because the segregation prevented Blacks and Whites from getting to know each other to achieve better race relations.

LEVELING AND PATTERNS OF INSTRUCTION

A recurring theme was that teachers taught better in enrichment, honors, and AP classes than they did in skills, regular or general education and college prep classes. This implied that White students, who dominated the high-level classes, were being taught better. Conversely, Black students, most of whom were in skills, regular, and college prep classes, received inferior instruction. We first present the views of students and teachers on the effect of leveling on instruction; then we describe our observations of the classroom instruction. We are not including parents' views on classroom instruction, because they were not usually specific in their criticisms. Our impression was that parents were not familiar with the classroom instruction.

Black Students' Perspectives

Current upper elementary school students did not discuss the difference in instruction between enrichment and other classes. They were probably not aware that there were differences. It was middle and high school students who, after reflecting on their experiences at Woodbury and how well the instruction at Woodbury prepared or did not prepare them for their present classes, discussed the instructional differences at Woodbury. They reported that students in the enrichment classes were taught better or were "made to learn more." One student briefly alluded to the better instruction of enrichment students as she reflected on own her experience at Woodbury:

Anthrop: What did you do that was different [in the academic enrichment program], i.e., different than the regular ...?

Student: We did stuff to really make us think. Like in Mrs. Parker's class, she did really make us think. But we liked it. She did make us do math and anything .... You really have to think when you go to ARP ... and sometimes you have to—when you go to ARP. Sometimes you have to struggle, and Mrs. Parker, she'll give you homework or something.

Most appreciations of and complaints about differences in curriculum materials, teaching styles, and quality of instruction at Woodbury came from senior high school students. Those who had been in the enrichment, honors and AP classes praised the curriculum materials and teaching styles. Conversely, those who had taken mostly skills, regular, and college prep classes were very critical of the materials and teaching approaches. The following three interview excerpts are representative of the high school students' appraisal of the instructions in the more academic and less academic classes.

Anthrop: OK, now some people have told me though, [that] it's very difficult to make a transition from college prep classes to advanced placement classes, not just because of the pace of work, but because the starting point is different. Like for instance, um, you can't just jump right into an AP class. Is that true or not true, or ...?

Student 1:   Um, I think um, another difference is [that] the teachers tend to take, I don't know, a different angle. Um, like he may be [teaching] the same thing in different classes, but, you [i.e., one class] might be reading a different book, looking at it more in depth, looking at more of the complexity of it. And I think that's a major difference. Like in [college prep], there's a lot of general, you know, perspectives of different things. And you know, honors and AP get deeper into the complexity of things. And that's the hard change [to move from college prep to AP] because you're not expecting um, you know, all this deep thought, and deepness in consideration ...

Student 2:   I think there's a lot, like in the college prep classes, there are a lot, there's a lot more busy work than in the honors classes. In honors classes, there's more reading and stuff and they get down to the point. And [in] college prep, they like say, just like little work sheets and stuff that are irrelevant. [What you do in college prep classes is] not really gonna help you out. And like projects, like in honors classes, they give you lots more reading; and [in] college prep, they give you these little projects and its not really relevant to anything. It's just like busy work basically.

Student 3:   My mom pushed and pushed and finally when in my freshman year, I was in honors English. And I mean I loved it, it was a completely different look on life. It was great and I got to talk and your teacher wouldn't stand and lecture you. But most Black kids aren't in AP classes.

As we show later, students' descriptions of the differential instructions were similar to some of our classroom observations.

Teachers' Perspectives

We asked teachers if there was a difference in the way they taught their college prep or skills classes and the way they taught their honors or AP classes. Most initially denied that there was a difference whatsoever. Some admitted that there might be a difference. But some differences were readily apparent to an observer. A case in which both the teacher and the observer were aware of the difference involved a teacher who taught the same English course as an honors class and as a college prep class; the two classes used the same textbook. When we asked the teacher if the honors and college prep classes read the same book and at the same pace, he emphatically answered "No." The honors class read at an accelerated pace. The teacher expected the honors students to engage in a more thorough discussion of a variety of subjects, including relationships between characters in the book. The college prep class read the book at a slower pace. From our observation there usually was only a little discussion of the book. Instead, the teacher would ask the students to answer questions such as "What kind of suit was [a character in the book] wearing?" In this college prep class and similar ones, instruction appeared to be more geared toward memorization of facts rather than comprehension and analysis.

The difference in teaching styles in the two levels of classes was most apparent in mathematics. One teacher described this difference one day to a group of parents whose children were in an algebra lab. He told them that in higher level mathematic classes—enrichment, honors, and AP math classes—the emphasis was on developing students' thinking and problem-solving skills. In the lower level math classes (skills and college prep classes) teachers emphasized remediation. As a result, students who went through the math enrichment program automatically received 2 years of algebra in high school, where the emphasis was on thinking and problem-solving skills. In contrast, other students, especially "those most at risk," went back to arithmetic when they entered high school and ended up with only 1 year of algebra. Furthermore, although the at-risk students might go through special algebra and geometry labs in high school, where attempts were made to teach them thinking and problem-solving skills, they rarely became adept at these skills. This was because when they returned to their regular math classes there was no continuity because instruction reverted to an emphasis on remediation. The teacher assured the parents that there were good intentions behind remediation but felt that "calculators did all these things for them," so there was no real need for the teacher to repeat it. Thus, teachers should stress teaching the children thinking and problem-solving skills. We return to this conference in chapter 11.

As we noted earlier, some teachers were looking for ways to increase Black enrollment in honors and AP classes so that they would experience the teaching styles that would adequately prepare them for math courses in college. One teacher tried to organize a program for Black parents to help them learn what to do to get their children into enrichment, honors, and AP classes. This teacher said that he would eliminate the leveling system and open honors and AP classes to all students. Another teacher, who taught several honors classes in one subject, reported having only seven "students of color," including one Native American, out of 65. He, too, said he would change the situation by encouraging students to adopt a more instrumental and pragmatic attitude. Students should not worry that they were the only one or one of few Blacks in an honors or AP class. He believed that successful Black students in these classes had usually developed self-confidence.

One teacher suspected that there might be a link between the teaching approach in college prep and skills classes, where Black students were in the majority, and low teacher expectations. As a result of low teacher expectations, Black students in the college prep pre-math classes did not learn enough to be able to do math in college. The amount of math work to which they were exposed was dismal. In this teacher's view, math was a subject that required practice and constant attention. This was not the case in college prep and skills math classes, where there was little or no homework and thus not much reinforcement to classroom learning. He wondered if the reason students in those classes did not do their homework was that teachers did not have high expectations about their ability and willingness to do the homework.

Classroom Observation

We observed instructional approaches at different class or course levels. We focused our observations on two things: (a) how teachers taught, and (b) the extent to which students were engaged with the lessons. We made about 110 classroom observations. In the following sections, our description of our observations shows both the instructional patterns for students at different class levels and students' attitudes and effort in selected classes.

Woodbury Upper Elementary School

On one occasion at Woodbury, one skills class appeared to contain more students than the regular classes. We were told that when a skills class was large it usually had more than one teacher, or there would be teacher's aides assisting the regular teacher. We also observed some skills classes that had as few as 4 students. This was the case of the class we describe. It was reported that students in skills classes were often absent. Some did not participate regularly because participation was voluntary. The irregular attendance was evident in the 1996–1997 school record, according to which some students missed 99 of the 180 days in the school year. To encourage more frequent attendance, teachers were asked not to excuse students from the class unless it was absolutely necessary. Teachers were also told not to schedule special events such as book fairs during skills class periods.

Case 1: Remedial Class. There were only 4 students in this class at Woodbury the day we made our observations. They were all girls. The teacher commented on the number of students who were absent. One girl reminded her that one absent student had told them on Friday that he would not come to school today because it is Columbus Day. The teacher remembered that she had discussed this with the student's mother.

The teacher reminded students that this was math and told them to finish the quiz from last week. She told one student who had already finished the quiz to begin working on the computer. We watched the youngster maneuver a program very easily. She then began playing a math game. The teacher later came to demand her attention, telling her that she had received a 70% on the quiz. The teacher showed the student the mistakes on her quiz. She went over the problems with the student, helping her to understand that had she not made these careless errors she would have gotten a much higher grade. The teacher also assured the student that 70% was not too bad but that she could have done better. The teacher told the student to correct her errors before resuming her computer game. The student did as she was told. The teacher approached the next student and inquired whether she had finished and checked all of her work. When the teacher verified that she had, the student was told she could work on the computer while the teacher corrected her paper. This student also scored 70% on the quiz. The teacher had a discussion with this student that was similar to the one she had with the first student. The teacher went over the work of the third student, to whom she first gave a 70% on the quiz, and on second thought, raised her grade to 80%. She praised the student but at the same time pointed out what she could have done to get a 90%. After the three students finished correcting their quizzes, they went to play Atlas on the computers. Each student was told to return her test the next day with her parent's signature. The fourth girl didn't finish her test as far as we could tell.

Case 2: An Enrichment Class. The instructional approach was different in the academic enrichment math class. During the lesson, students answered and discussed the teacher's questions. The students themselves asked the teacher several questions. Toward the end of the math period the teacher asked the class to help her choose a question she would ask the incoming fifth graders in order to select students for the same math enrichment program. At first she asked if she should use the same question she had used when she selected the current students. The students were enthusiastic and very involved in the discussion that followed. They suggested some alternative questions. It was significant that the students not only suggested questions the teacher could substitute for her own but also gave reasons for their suggestions. Some students explained that a particular question was more difficult and would really require a fifth-grade student to be "clever" to solve the math problem. The approach in this class was one that encouraged students to think of themselves as more capable than other students. This was evident in the statement made earlier by a high school student who had participated in the academic enrichment at Woodbury.

We do not think that the self-confidence of the academic enrichment students was solely due to the program. However, participation in it provided them very early with the opportunity to develop a good academic self-image. This contributed to their future self-confidence and academic success. In contrast, the instruction in the skills program did not provide students with the opportunity to develop a high academic self-image. Some students who attended the enriched classes often bragged about their grades and their knowledge. The opposite also seemed to be the case: Students who had not participated in the academic enrichment program tended to develop a low academic self-image This eventually may contribute to their school failure. One student who had been in the basic skills program at Woodbury said that she felt stupid being in the program.

Middle School

We observed some skills, college prep, and honors classes that were taught by the same teachers as well as at the same course levels. We describe our observations of math, English, and geography classes.

Case 3: Math Skills Class.   The same teacher who taught this class also taught the college prep math class described below. His skills class had nine Black students and two White students. The teacher once commented that many students in the skills class did not belong there, that they were capable of taking the next math level, namely, college prep math, but ended up in the skills class because of behavior problems.

This class was often disrupted by students, although they seemed interested in and somewhat involved with the lesson. The teacher told us that he tried to incorporate a lot of reading into this particular class, because most of the students' problem was that they did not read or did not read well. (Students' behavior is described in more detail in chap. 7.) The teacher did not punish students for their disruptive behavior. He said that punishing them by sending them to the office, did not help his teaching. If students missed time in class because he sent them to the office he himself would be contributing to keeping the student further behind in his or her classwork. This teacher does not assign homework in the skills class, because the chances of getting the work back were close to none. At one point some students who were very engaged with the materials asked if they could take the work home. The teacher said they could, provided they promised to return it with the homework the next day.

Case 4: College Prep Math Class.   This teacher's college prep class had 9 Blacks and 11 Whites. One day during our observation we noticed that he had transferred one of the students from his skills class to his college prep class. He was also considering moving a second student from the skills to the college prep class. While discussing the transfer later, he told us that a student transferring from the skills class to college prep class would have difficulty adjusting to the pace of work. He felt confident that the student he was moving from skills to college prep would be able to adjust because he would work with the student during his or her adjustment period.

Case 5: College Prep and AP English.   We observed the college prep and AP English classes, taught by this same teacher, several times. In the college prep class there were 16 Blacks and 5 Whites. The AP class had 6 Black and 21 White students. The teacher repeatedly told us that there was not much difference in the way he taught the two classes. In neither class did he tolerate disruptive behavior, tardiness, and lack of preparedness, yet during our observation he spent more time correcting these behaviors in the college prep class. He said that some students in the AP class did not belong there because they were not working at that level. He seemed very disappointed on one occasion and lectured the AP students about the level of expectations in the AP courses.

There were certainly differences in the way he taught the two classes. Although students in both classes read the same books, the AP students usually read at a faster pace. The students read aloud and enthusiastically. They discussed the reading critically. Students discussed the relationships between characters in the book and made inferences. In contrast, in the college prep class the teacher often read aloud for the students. There was hardly any critical analysis of the assigned reading; the emphasis seemed to be on building vocabulary and paying attention to details of the story.

Case 6: Skills Geography Class.   This classroom was bright and well decorated with pictures from around the world. When the lesson was about to start, the students asked "Are we taking notes today?" The teacher said "Just a little." They countered, "That's what you said last time, and we ended up taking two pages of notes." She laughed. The students began to grade their own homework. An African American student raised his hand and asked if he could answer some questions as they went over them. The teacher responded "Yes; I'll call on people." When a student got the answer wrong, she would say, "That's OK." She gave students credit for answers that were close to the right ones. Only a few students constantly raised their hands when she asked questions, but she wanted all students to raise their hands. At one point a student asked if there would be a test on the lesson and if they could use their notes. The teacher told the class that they would not need their notes for the test.

She continued to remind students to raise their hands when they knew the answer to a question. Whenever she asked a question she would wait until all hands were up before taking an answer. She permitted students to help one another. For example, at one point a student went over to another student who didn't know the answer to a question and helped him. There was no digression from the lesson or disruption such as we had observed in other skills classes.

Case 7: College Prep Geography. This class was taught by the same teacher. We asked her during a break if students in the skills class studied only Ohio geography, because that was what we had read in the syllabus. She replied that the contents of the lessons for the two classes were the same, that the only difference was that she gave more explicit instructions to the skills class about where to keep things. She said that college prep students got extra credit for being organized. She encouraged them to participate and raise their hands but did not wait until all hands were up to answer question, as she did in the skills class. She made an effort to call on a variety of students. Apart from giving college prep students extra points for being organized, this teacher used other incentives to elicit appropriate responses from students. For example, when she asked them to clear their desks to play bingo, she walked around the classroom handing out red coupons to students who responded quickly.

High School

At the high school we observed only one teacher who taught both college prep and AP classes. In other cases the different levels of classes were taught by different teachers.

Case 8: High School Algebra Lab. Sixteen of the 17 students in this class were Black. We sat at the desk as one of the teachers began to hand out the students' folders. We requested to see one folder with some writing on the back. It read, "Bud smokes. Weed smokers." The teacher laughed a little and commented, "I know. I would never have wanted my teachers to see something like that." The teachers began to reflect on their own classroom experiences as a students. One had graduated from Shaker Heights. At that time, there was more leveling, with the higher level classes being more academically difficult. Some former outstanding Shaker students found it interesting to be teaching students at the other end of leveling. Students at the opposite ends of leveling were different not only in ability but also in behavior. Commenting on the students' behavior, one of the teachers said, "You wouldn't believe the things that they talk about in our presence." Some of the girls in the class were told last week save their conversation for somewhere else. One in particular was asked whether she was embarrassed that everybody could hear what she was talking about. The student replied that she didn't care.

During our observation, three students wanted to borrow pencils. Another student waited for a teacher's help and made no effort to figure out how to do the classwork. The teacher then tried to assist him in getting started. Three other students were sharpening their pencils. As the teachers made their rounds, we recorded their comments to students. It was apparent from these comments that the teachers praised students for what they were able to do well and encouraged others to do better. One teacher, for instance, advised a student not to second-guess himself. The student had already solved a problem similar to the one the class was doing today. The teacher expected him to know how to do it. Another student sitting nearby began to laugh, shaking his head.

The second teacher told a student, "part of it is right" and then proceeded to help her correct her errors. The first teacher said, "like the way you wrote your answer out in work form." She then said to another student "very good," and then added, "You know you want to smile." The teacher told another student whose answer was wrong to read the problem again. The student complained that it took too long a time to read. This prompted the teacher to say "You flatter me." The reluctance or inability of students to read through the assignments seemed to be a recurring problem in this class.

One teacher also let the students know when they were being disruptive. She told one student to be quiet and another to stay focused. Another teacher gave us one female student's paper to look at. He said that the student had really "made it over the hump" in respect to both math and behavior. We asked the teacher if he had attended the conference at which a well-known national figure spoke of the importance of high expectations. The teacher replied that he had not attended and that although he understood the argument he felt that it was also important to show students some degree of success.

Case 9: College Prep Geometry. We got to this class a few minutes before it began and found the teacher sitting alone. We asked if we could observe his class, and he said he had no objection. The teacher told us that the class was for 10th graders, but we saw many older students who were apparently repeating the class. The teacher stood at the door, greeting each student by name. After the bell rang, one White male student entered. The teacher said to him, "You need to walk a little faster." Then a Black female student entered, and the teacher didn't say anything; he just changed the role sheet. Nineteen of the 22 students were Black. A student we had seen in a 10th-grade honors algebra class raised her hand and said, "Mr., Mr. ..." The teacher responded, "Just a minute. My name is Mr.—by the way, D."

The teacher tried to get everyone's attention but had some difficulty doing so. He caught off guard a male student talking to a girl, and said to him "Right, K? I told you I was going to keep picking on you when you talk." He asked the students to raise their hands when they wanted to answer a question. He demanded attention from one of two Black female students talking. The teacher said, "Shh!" and then continued the lesson, but the girls continued talking. He reminded one White student to keep following the lesson. The White student raised his hand for the next question. The teacher had a little exchange with one Black female student. He told her not to do her assignment if she did not understand the problem. But the student replied that she knew how to do it. The teacher reminded another student to stay awake. A few students finished their assignment in the time allowed during the class period. Two Black male students were visibly not doing any work when the teacher asked if they had finished. They said they had, but when he demanded to see it they didn't produce it. Still, they made no attempt to start working. Several students got up to leave the class before the bell rang. In spite of their disruptive behavior and slackness in their work, it appeared that students in this class felt pretty comfortable with their teacher. They were disruptive but not disrespectful.

Case 10: 10th-Grade Honors Math. It was recommended that we observe this class because it was taught by an excellent math teacher. The teacher had the reputation of being in control of his class and making sure that students knew that there was a definite line between teacher and students. He also made students do their work.

We waited outside as students filed in. All of them were on time. There were 2 Asians and possibly 1 American Indian student. There was only 1

Black male in the class of 25. There was a lot of low-level talking through-out the class; at times there was a lot of daydreaming, too. One student was facing away from the teacher for much of the period talking to an-other student diagonally behind him. A girl in front blurted out "Does anyone have a pen?" followed moments later by "What's the date?" She kept talking at a lower voice occasionally during the class period. A White male asked if he could turn in his previous day's homework. The teacher told him to turn it in the next day because he would need to study it for the next day's test. He gave back to the class the homework he had collected earlier, telling them to study it for the upcoming test.

When the teacher began the lesson for the day, the room quieted a bit, but there were still sporadic conversations. At the end of the lesson, the student who wanted to turn his previous day's homework asked again, "What should I do about my homework?" This was after the teacher had told him to take it home to study for their next examination. The teacher repeated his earlier response.

As the next class filed in we waited outside the class, waiting to thank the teacher for allowing us to observe. There was a White female among the in-coming students who kept staring at us. She didn't realize that we were watching her. She looked at our nametags, with a funny look on her face. This was quite unlike the reaction we had gotten from most of the students at Shaker. Shaker students had generally been very nice, even before they knew who we were or what we were doing in their school. They usually said "Hello!," and sometimes they would ask what we were doing, but they generally made us feel welcome. This was not the case with this particular student. She seemed to have some difficulty with our presence.

We noticed that in a class just across from this one every student was Black. The school personnel employee accompanying us explained that that was a math lab run by three teachers. It was for students who required more individualized attention than they could get in a regular algebra class. It was hoped that completing the math lab program would prepare them for college prep math. The school official recommended that we ob-serve that class, too. This was probably a polite way of telling us that there were hardly any Blacks in the AP math classes we had just observed.

Case 11: 12th Grade AP and College Prep English. This teacher taught both college prep and AP English classes. Before the class began, the teacher said that the difference between the two classes was simply that the

AP students read at a faster pace. A college prep student who overheard the statement disputed it.

In our observation we found that there was a marked difference in the amount of material covered in the two classes and in the way the materials were treated. Almost daily the AP students actively discussed their reading assignments. The students were usually enthusiastic and almost everyone was involved.

There also were daily discussions in the college prep class; however, the discussions were often not about the reading assignments. Instead, the students discussed issues relevant to their personal or racial group experiences. For example, the class discussed rap music, government conspiracy, and tracking in Shaker Heights schools. The ideas leading to these discussions may have come from the reading assignments, but the readings themselves were not discussed, partly because most students had not done the reading.

Although the teaching style in both classes appeared to be similar, the teacher demanded different amounts of work outside the classroom. The difference in the outside work affected the work done in the classroom.

Case 12: College Prep Social Studies.   On several occasions we observed a college prep class on Oppression or on Human Relations. These are two separate classes, but treat them as if they were the same, because the teacher chose to teach them as a college prep class. The classes were racially mixed; they also included students from different grades and ability levels. The teacher's policy was to offer the classes at one level to ensure that all students would be able to take it. We could not determine whether these courses were popular because of the subject matter or because of the teacher. The classes were usually overcrowded, with some students sitting on the desks and floor. Most students were very interested and actively engaged in the class discussions. Students were occasionally late, but the teacher did not apparently consider that disruptive.

Conclusions: Middle School and High School Observations

The case studies suggested that there were some differences in teachers' instructional approaches at different class levels. In the honors and AP classes teachers focused more on the subject matter and demanded more work and intellectual involvement from students.

In some college prep classes the lesson did not always focus on the topic of the day. Students were not actively intellectually involved, and there was less demand for their participation in class or that they do their homework. Of course, there were differences among the teachers in the approaches they used at a given course or class level.

Students in the honors and AP classes were more interested, able, and willing to engage in their lessons. This affected teachers' teaching style. They assigned homework more regularly to these students, and expected that the students complete the homework and discuss it in class. This was not the case with skills and college prep classes. Students were less willing and perhaps less able to do their homework and, hence, were generally given less homework. Their class discussions were not always or even usually on the topics of the class lessons, because they had not done the readings.

Both teachers and students were aware of the differences in expectations between honors and AP classes, on the one hand, and skills and college prep classes, on the other hand, in terms of classwork, homework, and behavior. Teachers and students sometimes compared the differing expectations. The exception was in the college prep Human Relations and Oppression classes. In these, students paid attention and were regularly engaged in discussions with one another and with the teacher, much like we observed students do in AP classes.

LEVELING AND ACADEMIC DISENGAGEMENT

At the early elementary school, participation along racial lines did not emerge as a factor in the academic disengagement of students. It was probably for this reason that the elementary school children we interviewed did not talk of racial disparity in class composition. This changed when we entered Woodbury, the upper elementary school. Here students began to talk about the racial disparity. Middle school and high school students were, of course, much more aware of the differences in racial representation in the skills, college prep, honors, and AP classes. These students attributed the under-representation of Blacks in the honors and AP classes to leveling as well as to counselors, teachers, school administrators, parents, and peers. We elaborate the roles of these agents and other factors in subsequent chapters.

SUMMARY AND CONCLUSION

The Shaker Heights school district had no overarching leveling or tracking program; that is, students were not assigned to general education, vocational education, or college preparatory education "tracks" that stayed with them more or less throughout their school career. Instead, they were assigned to different levels of the same course and in different subjects in a given school session. Nevertheless, this more or less resulted in de facto tracking along racial lines, because most Black students were enrolled in lower level classes, and most Whites were enrolled in higher level classes.

The tracking, or leveling, began at the upper elementary school, where the curriculum differentiated into three categories: (a) skills or remedial, (b) regular and (c) academic enrichment classes. Pronounced racial differences in enrollment between the remedial programs (mostly Black) and the academic enrichment programs (mostly Whites) began here. Middle schools and high schools had four curriculum levels: (a) skills or general education, (b) college prep, (c) honors, and (d) AP classes. Most students in the skills and college prep classes in each subject were Black, whereas most students in the honors and AP classes were White.

The potential for differential racial distributions of students at different curriculum levels starting at the Woodbury upper elementary school seemed to exist as early as the first grade. A clue to this can be found in a report of a first-grade teacher who had taught in the school district for 17 years; the report appears chapter 11. She had made several unsuccessful attempts to get Black parents to participate in a program for first-grade students with learning difficulties, most of whom were Black. Children who received help during this early period in their school career might avoid being assigned to remedial programs or learning disability curricula at the upper elementary school. One may assume that the failure of Black parents to get the help described by this first-grade teacher for their children during the early years contributed to the disproportionate assignment of Black students to the remedial programs and their underrepresentation in the academic enrichment programs at Woodbury Upper Elementary School. This was likely to happen whether student assignments were based on teacher recommendations, test scores, or both.

During interviews and group discussions, students pointed out that their academic tracks were often determined by the program to which they had been assigned at the upper elementary school. When they arrived at the middle school, counselors assigned them to various course levels in each subject on the basis of their performance at Woodbury and teachers' recommendations. In subsequent years and at the high school, students were assigned to their course levels based on their record of performance and teachers' recommendations. Students often said that their previous performance did not necessarily reflect their ability; however, counselors worked with the record before them: grades, test scores, and recommendations. In our discussions with counselors they seemed over-burdened with scheduling students for classes or school transfers and with students' behavior problems with teachers. They had little time for explaining to students the importance of enrolling in honors or AP classes. Blacks interpreted this to mean that counselors did not "care" and did not encourage them to enroll in the higher level classes. Some students be-lieved that they were actually discouraged from enrolling in the higher level classes until their parents intervened.

Black parents contributed to the uneven racial distribution at the mid-dle and high schools in part because they did not seem to understand the leveling system. They did not know enough about how honors and AP classes differed from skills and college prep classes. Perhaps it was for this reason that they did not emphasize to their children how important it was for them to take the honors and AP classes, did not prepare them to take those classes successfully, and did not intervene to enroll their children who had the potential in the honors and AP classes.

Finally, self-elimination played a role in Black underrepresentation in the honors and AP classes. Self-elimination took three forms. One was avoidance of the honors and AP classes because most of the other students in the classes were White. Another was lack of effort; that is, the students did not work hard enough to make good grades to qualify for those courses. The third mechanism was the personal decision not to enroll in an honors or AP class by a student who was qualified to be in the class by vir-tue of his or her academic records. In this case, after consulting with the counselor the student might decide not to enroll in spite of the counselor's recommendation because he or she did not think that he or she could han-dle the work. The counselor was not always the gatekeeper.

Students, teachers, and some other school personnel were aware that leveling affected instruction. In the next chapter we describe our observa-tions of differences in the instructional patterns at different course levels from upper elementary school through high school. Students who partici-pated in the academic enrichment program at Woodbury Upper Elemen-tary School believed that they were taught better and learned more than those who were assigned to remedial programs. Students in the honors and AP classes at the middle and high schools praised the curriculum materials and teaching styles, whereas those in skills, regular, and college prep classes criticized the curriculum materials and teaching styles. We found in our classroom observations that the latter paid less attention during lessons, were less willing to do classwork and less likely to return their homework, and were generally more disruptive than the former. Teachers acknowledged that they taught the same subject differently at different levels, even when using the same curriculum materials. For example, one teacher who taught the same literature with the same textbooks in an AP class and a college prep class usually assigned more reading materials to the AP class. The students in this class read and discussed, the assignments critically and enthusiastically. In contrast, students in the college prep class usually did not read the assigned passages; the teacher read them for the class. The students discussed not the reading assignment but rather their personal or group experiences. The ideas for the discussion of the personal or group experiences might, however, come from the reading.

7

Counselors, Teachers, and Discipline

We noted in the Preface that we did not conduct formal interviews with individual counselors and teachers. However, we interacted with them on a variety of occasions. The first of these was a "dialogue" meeting with counselors and teachers for about an hour during our first visit. We later had dialogue meetings with some individuals. Most of our interaction with these school personnel, however, occurred during the phase of our intensive fieldwork. In the case of teachers, we almost always talked with them before or after the 110 lessons we observed, at lunch, or when we dropped by for a friendly chat. We also shared many occasions in the community with Black teachers and other school personnel from the Black community. However, the primary purpose of this chapter is to describe Black students' (and the community's) perceptions of, and responses to, the role of counselors and teachers in the academic achievement gap.

COUNSELORS

Is the Counselor a Gatekeeper?

At the middle schools and high schools, school counselors assigned students to general, college preparatory, honors, and advanced placement (AP) classes. The assignment was based on teacher recommendation, students' classwork grades, standardized tests scores and, in some cases, at the parent's or student's request. However, counselors were generally regarded as responsible for class assignments. Thus, in response to the question of why there were so few Blacks in honors and AP classes the most common answer was that counselors did not "push" or "encourage" Black students as much as they pushed or encouraged White students to take those classes. Black students and their parents more or less perceived the school counselors as gatekeepers who were reluctant to let Blacks into the honors and AP classes. Their gatekeeping function and reluctance made it necessary for some Black parents to intervene to enroll their children in those classes.

It was widely believed that the reason the counselors were reluctant to let Black students take honors and AP classes was that they did not think that Blacks were capable of doing the work at that level. Here is how one student described the way counselors discouraged Black students from taking the more academically rigorous courses:

Student: I think most Black people aren't encouraged as much as ... White people are. Like the counselors, they encourage White people to take the hard classes and stuff, and the Black people like they discourage it a little bit more.

Anthrop: How do they discourage [Black students]? I've heard that before ...

Student: They say, "Um, I don't know if it'll—you might be able to do it [because] it's really hard, and I don't know if you'll be able to do it." They'll [i.e., counselor] say, "Well, it's a lot of reading or whatever," and that's basically what they say.

Anthrop: OK, has that happened to you?

Student: No, but they've never encouraged me to take any [honors and AP] classes. But like I know like my friends, they say that their counselors said, "Well, you know it's not an easy class; it's kind [of] hard" or whatever. But [as for me] I know I could do the work; it's just [I did not try] ... I regret it when I look back, since I'm a senior now.

Some students at a meeting of the Student Group on Race Relations reported their personal experiences of the counselors' gatekeeping role. One student said that a Black student might not be allowed to take an honors class even though he or she always scored very high on the tests. She added that she knew counselors who steered Blacks away from AP classes. She then went on to describe the experience of a friend who "scored off the chart" on the tests but her counselor told her she was "not mature enough" to take the upper level classes. The informant believed that her friend was mature enough to take the classes. Another student agreed, saying that she, too, had experienced that.

There was some disagreement along racial lines over the use of test scores to determine eligibility for honors and AP courses or for college admission. White students generally favored using test scores, whereas Black students opposed reliance on test scores or grade-point average (GPA) because that would limit "diversity." Blacks also complained that they and their parents were not fully informed by counselors that class assignment would be based largely on test scores. In any case, they considered test scores an insufficient basis for class assignment. We should point out that this information was made available to parents as a matter of the school district's policy.

At one point during our discussion with high school students someone brought up the issue of affirmative action in college admission. White students were overwhelmingly opposed to affirmative action. They said that it was unfair to admit a Black applicant with lower SAT scores while denying an admission to a White applicant with higher SAT scores. Countering this, Blacks said that there were many other factors that might have affected the test scores of the Black applicant. However, they did not specify the "other factors." They said that on paper a person with higher test scores might look better, but they repeatedly said that college admission should not depend primarily on test scores because that would limit "diversity." If students were admitted primarily because of their test scores, then people would be educated in an environment without diversity, and without diversity they would not be prepared adequately for the real world. It seemed from their argument that Black students were more concerned with the social benefits of schooling than with its instrumental or pragmatic values.

Parents' intervention was sometimes considered necessary to overcome counselors' reluctance to let Black students take honors and AP classes. Both students and parents discussed this strategy, often from their personal experiences. We first report the experiences of two students who got into the "hard classes" only because their parents intervened. The excerpts are from one of our discussions with the high school group that included both White and Black students.

Student 1:   Yeah! 'Cause counselors are basically the people that put you in the classes. And I had to, my mom talked to my teacher about getting me into [these] classes, and then she had to talk to my counselor about putting me into those classes, whatever. And I know other people have had a similar experience where they know their son or daughter needs to be in that class and they had to go and talk to the administration about putting them in the class and that was it.

Student 2:   Now, they're many—I'm not saying that um, [all counselors], you know, um [are] racist or whatever … But, um, it's like that. I know [because] my mom moved here to Shaker because she knew I had a lot of potential. And she came up with me to the school and talked to my guidance counselor. My mom sat down and found a Black guidance counselor for me who would talk with Mr. Cusick. He, the White guidance counselor was to be my guidance counselor. 'Cause like I say, [the Black counselor], understood. Later on my Mom really liked [the White guidance counselor's] attitude and things. But I think one reason [was] that the guidance counselor … can [be swayed or persuaded] … Anyone can be persuaded. OK? But it is, if you want something bad enough, you know, you'll fight the principal. You'll fight with the governor and the President of the United States until you get what you want. But it is a misnomer that um guidance counselors are not letting people get into these classes, because you can get into whatever class you want as long as you have the prerequisites you know, of course. But nobody's gonna stop you. They can try to [manipulate?] your opinion. (In feigned voice), "Well, well, I think, I think [whichever you think] (student laughter). (In firm voice:) "It's what I want." You see what I'm saying? And I'm, I'm gonna fight for a long time, but I didn't [want to], [kinda?] what you said. I agree (several unintelligible words).

Some parents described their own experiences in breaking through the counselor barriers to enroll their children in the honors or AP classes. One parent who was herself a teacher in the district reported her experience. Her daughter had called her from school one day to tell her that her middle school counselor would not let her enroll in an AP English class in her first year of high school because it was "too late." The counselor told her that her records had already been transferred to the high school. The mother said she was furious and immediately contacted someone at the high school. She demanded that her daughter be allowed to enroll in AP English. The daughter was eventually allowed to take the class and did well. Since then she continued to take and perform well in AP English classes throughout her high school years.

There was some consensus at the high school discussion meeting that parents could get their children into honors and AP classes by intervening against counselors' reluctance or challenging their decisions. However, many parents did not intervene because they did not know how or were not aware of what was going on. One male student described the efficacy of parent intervention quite well when he said "Um, here's a known fact that, um, none of these counselors or anybody in the school can stop anyone from getting into Honors and Advanced Placement classes. What is involved is being informed." A female student echoed, "Yeah."

Self-Elimination

Whether a student enrolled or did not enroll in an honors or AP class was sometimes a joint decision of the student and the counselor. For instance, a student and his or her counselor would discuss the student's record of performance in class and on standardized tests. If the record was weak, the counselor might suggest to the student that he or she not take the honors or AP class. The student, looking at his or her records and reflecting on his or her ability to keep up with the classwork, would accept the counselor's recommendation. In other words, it was not always an arbitrary decision of the counselor that kept the student out of an honors or AP class. One student described his experience of such a joint decision as follows:

> *Anthrop:* Do you take honors classes, too?
>
> *Student:* No. I'll be taken' some next year because my counselor, um, I wasn't doin' that well last year ... I was gettin' Cs and stuff ... So she wasn't sure if I wanted, if I, uh, [would be] able to keep up with the honor level. So she said she goin' see how this year goes and then you know, if I do well, I'll be able ta be moved up.

There were also students who took the initiative to request not to enroll in honors and AP classes that had been recommended for them by their counselors. They asked to be excused from these classes because they did not think they could handle the work. These were often transfer students who had been in honors and AP classes in their previous schools but, on arrival, they found that the standard of work and expectations at Shaker Heights were higher. They refused to enroll in honors and AP classes in spite of their counselors' recommendations, because they were afraid that they might not do well in these classes. One student who transferred to Shaker Heights disclosed to us his reluctance to enroll in high level classes because the standard and expectations were higher than he was accustomed to in his former school.

Anthrop:	You did not want to take the honor classes?
Student:	Yeah. 'Cause I mean that's extra stress. 'Cause I know that stresses me out now.
Anthrop:	So when you decided that you couldn't handle the AP classes, who did you go to and how did he or she deal with it. Was it a counselor?
Student:	Yeah, it was my counselor.
Anthrop:	And how did the counselor deal with it?
Student:	I just said that I couldn't function in all of the AP classes that I had because, first of all, I was adjusting to a new school. And then I was put into an environment where not only did I not know people, [but also] they were being kind of like really cold to me.
Anthrop:	Ok, and um, were you encouraged to drop them or stick it out a little longer?
Student:	In the one that I stayed in I was, in English. But there were actually more Black kids trying to take [that] AP English.
Anthrop:	Now, how did you get placed in the AP classes in the first place when you came in from another district?
Student:	Well, I've always been an honor student.
Anthrop:	Ok, so they basically looked at your records from the other school.
Student:	Right. And they said, "You can handle this." But Shaker is so much stronger than most of the Catholic schools in the area that I had to get adjusted to the workload.

Other students believed that some nontransfer Black students failed to prepare themselves for honors and AP classes because they had wrong priorities, because their parents did not recognize the importance of these classes, or because their parents did not prepare them for the classes. Some clues to this self-selection out of honors and AP classes can be seen in the following statement, made by a male student during the high school discussion meeting. First, the students themselves did not have a strong academic orientation but were easily distracted. Then, their parents, in spite of the sacrifice they made to live in Shaker Heights so that their children would get a Shaker Heights education, failed to provide them with effective guidance.

> In the sixth grade the students, um, elementary school, a lot of [Black students], would say something like this, "If the students learn, they're going to learn." But at the same time, when we're that young, a lot of us aren't worried about studying. We are mostly interested in looking at cars, looking at um, girls or guys, looking at a lot of clothes and things like that. When we start getting older [and into higher grades], and the whole thing [nonacademic matters] starts getting more attractive. And our attention is, you know, um diverting away from the books and things like that. So then, it's like this. Everyone is gonna be looking at those things, except those who have parents at home who understand, telling you, "Look ... Before you can even get those [material] things in the proper way, you're gonna have to stay in school, do your books and things like that." But some people's parents, they're not gonna be coming for whatever reason [admonishing their children because of the nature of their] jobs or something like that. There's a trade-off. You see what I'm saying? Are you [i.e., parents] gonna um, you know, work real hard to get 'em up here [to afford to live in Shaker so that your children can go to Shaker schools], and let them in a certain way, not talk to them [but not have time to guide them], or [provide them] the essential um things that they're gonna need to know to make it through this school system? Or are you gonna just get 'em there, and let them go [off?] on their own. You see what I'm saying?

Counselors' Perspectives

The counselors themselves were aware that some Black students and their parents were not satisfied with the counseling services at Shaker. They admitted that counseling services were not adequate because the department was understaffed, and as a result counselors were overworked. This was the explanation offered during the following heated exchange with a Black community member.

Female   There are three counselors, and um, with a, an enrollment of—.
Counselor 1   What do we have? About 850 students?
(FC1):

Male   Right.
Counselor
(MC):

Black   Yeah.
Community
Member (BCM):

FCI: So the students are divided among the three of us.

MC: Three of you, that'll pull you away [from?] also.

FC1:   And we have both grades [seventh and eighth].

MC: We have about 275.

FCI: We have seventh and eighth graders.

BCM: What do you think your contact time is?

MC: It really varies.

FC1:   Yeah.

MC: It, you really can't do an average because there are some kids you see all the time—

FC1:   —and some you don't.

MC: And some you almost never see.

Female   Yeah.
Counselor 2:

BCM: How many kids do you think you effectively see just during the course of a year?

MC: Uh, as far as dealing with individual situations, probably, specific situations with students and with their parents, uh, I would say at least half of them, like on a, where you really have to do something that, to deal with either a teacher or a class or whatever. And then the others, it's more incidental, uh.

FC1:   We have more time with uh eighth graders, uh, because we, we're scheduling them for the high school at the end of the year, too, and we meet with all of them individually—, on an individual basis, every single one.

As one can see in this exchange, there was no real discussion of the major complaints of students and their parents, namely, that students were not "pushed" into, and that they were not allowed to take honors and AP classes. The information provided by the counselors was mostly about scheduling students for school transition and handling behavior problems, especially relationship, with teachers. The counselors did not explain how they handled a student who wished to enroll in or to be excused from honors and AP classes. This omission was particularly important, because we had heard from many students about those who were discouraged from enrolling in the honors and AP classes by counselors who told them that the classes were hard. On the basis of his research elsewhere, the anthropologist suggested that students needed challenging classes and that counselors should convince the students that taking challenging courses was good for them (Ogbu, 1974).

Two other issues came up during the meeting with school counselors. One was that Black male students were "drifting" into nonacademic activities such as sports, believing that they were going to "make it" in this field. Black males believed that they were going to become stars and be rich; what they did not know, however, was that only a very few people who went into sports eventually made it into professional sports. Even those who made it into professional sports were still in a very risky occupation. For example, professional athletes do did not know whether they are going to be injured. It appeared that counseling at Shaker did into include working with students "drifting into sports" to educate them about the realities of putting sports before academics. The anthropologist shared with the counselors some findings from his previous research (Ogbu, 1974, 1998). In one study, he had found that many Black students invested a great deal of effort in sports. As a result, they had little time to study or do their homework. He also found that the coach was primarily interested in having his team win and was not particularly concerned about the players' academics. In Shaker, it was some Black teachers, not the counselors, who were advising students about the risk of abandoning academics for sports.

The other issue was the discrepancy between aspiration and academic achievement among Black students. Shaker Black students had very high academic aspirations but, as was evident in their record of performance, it was not clear that they knew how to realize that aspiration. Most of them wanted to go to college; some wanted to become lawyers, others wanted to become doctors, and so on. But did they know what required to go to college to become a lawyer or a doctor? For example, if a student wanted to become a lawyer when he or she grew up, what kind of education would he or she need to achieve this goal, and what would he or she need to get that education? In this regard, we usually asked students two questions: (a) "How do you get the college degree you desire?," and (b) "What steps would you take to qualify to become a lawyer, a doctor, etc.?" It was obvious from discussions with students and from our classroom and other observations that many Black students did not understand the connection between their present schooling, higher education, and future adult careers or professions. When questioned directly, students were usually vague in answering these questions.

We did not interview Shaker parents systematically about the process of getting their children successfully through Shaker Heights schools into college and then into professions. We have data from our research elsewhere (e.g., Stockton, Oakland, etc.) that are instructive (1974, 1998). Like their children, some parents in those studies were also vague about how to get their children successfully through public school, into college, and eventually into desired adult jobs. Some parents would say that they wanted their children to "go all the way." This answer suggested that they didn't really know. Parents who do not know what is required to succeed in public school, go to college, or qualify for a job or profession cannot advise their children effectively about these matters. We examine the role of parents more fully in chapter 11.

The lack of awareness of the connection between their present schooling and their future was an important issue for school counseling professionals, especially in the case of poor minority children. School counselors or others in the school system can provide the missing knowledge. It was our impression from the research done in Shaker Heights and elsewhere that some of these students are "fooling around" and not working hard because they do not really have an idea of how their present schooling fits into their future education and subsequently into their aspirations in the job market.

TEACHERS

Shaker teachers were perceived as producers of academic success and academic failure. To Blacks they mostly produced failure. We discuss this perception among Blacks with respect to encouragement, expectations, instructions, and equity and fairness.

Inadequate "Push"

Black and White Students reported that an unstated assumption in the Shaker school system was that every Shaker High graduate would go to college. During a class discussion, students said that to Shaker school authorities, maintaining this Shaker image was more important than the students themselves. Good grades were the most important thing because "you can't go to college without them." For this reason, the school "pushes"

students to do well. The types of college that Shaker graduates were expected to attend determined the push they got, according to White students. One White male put it this way: "The school pushes you depending
on which [college] you are interested in." But from the point of view of Black
students, the push also depended on the student's race. One of them said
that "[school personnel] push low-performing White students and pay attention to them, whereas they don't push the same with Blacks."

Blacks also translated this lack of adequate push to mean that "teachers
don't care." In one high school discussion group a Black male reported that
Black students who had aspired to go to college were not encouraged and
therefore did not strive to achieve their goals. A female student concurred:

> I think your teachers have a big part in how well you're doing because if you
> have a teacher, and you're stuck with someone in fourth grade [the grade be-
> fore leveling] that doesn't want to teach you, or doesn't want to help you,
> [then] you're not gonna have any motivation either. And I think when the
> kids get teachers that don't care, or that don't want [makes noise like crin-
> kling paper], or aren't like organized, it's how could it … they make students
> be organized?

Beliefs and Expectations

A common complaint against teachers was that they did not believe that
Black students could perform academically like White students. A related
complaint was that teachers expected Black students to behave differently;
they expected Black students to not pay attention in class and to not do
classwork or homework like White students. Parents and other adults in the
community shared these perceptions of teachers' beliefs and expectations.
An example of the parents' view occurred one day at a dinner with several
people in the community. One father reported an incident in which his
daughter was humiliated by her teacher. His daughter and her friend were
not doing well in this class and were not keeping pace with the rest of the
class. Apparently referring to his daughter and her friend the teacher told
the class that some people in the class were stupid. Then, directly looking at
the man's daughter, the teacher told her that she was stupid.

The perceptions that teachers did not believe that Black students could
perform well came up again and again during the discussion with high
school students. One student reported having had two teachers "that just
put you down so much that it makes you … feel really bad." Another student cut in, saying "I know. Like you can't do it."

In interviews several Blacks students reported that teachers did not expect them to do well. They made it clear that they were talking about teachers in general, that regardless of race teachers had more negative expectations about how Black students would behave in class. Such expectations inevitably had negative effects on their academic performance. Students' perceptions of the lowered expectations increased by school level. They were minimal at the elementary school—only one elementary school student we interviewed reported that teachers expected Black students to do worse than White students. She did not mention an actual case but described a hypothetical situation:

Anthrop: Do you think that [teachers] sometimes have expectations of what Black students are gonna be like?

Student: Mh-hmm. They'll try ta, no they'll expect you to do worse than, 'cause just by the past and what has been goin' on. Some of them would expect you to, 'cause they'll look at a test and say, "Oh, this is so and so." They'll, even if they [Black students] miss an answer, [teachers will] mark an answer wrong, thinking that it's wrong, not knowing that it is not wrong. I mean, cause they'll [teachers] be a, they could be a real nice teacher and just [assume/expect] that [as a Black student] you're gonna kind of do bad on the test 'cause they'll probably [think] it's ... a hard test. And they [teachers] kind of end up marking [Black students] down.

We did not observe any such incident or record an actual complaint of such an incident at the elementary school. Neither did we see situations where teachers overtly showed lowered expectations of Blacks. This does not mean that some teachers at the elementary school did not have low expectations of Black students, but what we found was that teachers had low expectations for individual students, Blacks and Whites, because of their past performance and reputations.

There were more reports of low expectations from middle school students. All the Black students interviewed there reported that teachers believed that they could not perform like White students, did not do classwork and homework and, in general, did not behave like White students. However, none of the students described his or her own encounter with such teachers' beliefs and expectations. They usually talked about hypothetical incidents that might occur as a result of stereotypes or reputations of Black students. The stereotypes included general misbehavior in class, not paying attention during lessons, and not doing classwork or homework. Another stereotype was that Black students performed less well academically than White students.

Some students speculated about how these stereotypes might shape teacher expectations. One said, "[teachers] probably like to think the Blacks are gonna act rowdy in class, and not pay attention and don't listen." Another student agreed, saying, "Um, sometimes, 'cause sometimes when a teacher can look at the way a student, um, acts in the class, and they can figure out what their destiny is gonna be … a good or a poor student." There were students who explicitly stated that teachers' negative beliefs and low expectations adversely affected Black students' academic performance.

All but one high school student we interviewed thought that there were Black and White teachers who believed that Black students were less capable of performing academically than White students and therefore did not expect similar attitudes and behaviors in class. Unlike middle school students, the high-schoolers gave examples from personal experience. Equally important was that high school students believed that teachers' lowered expectations were a part of lowered societal expectations for Blacks as a group. One student provided a link between societal expectations of Blacks people and teachers' expectations of Black student.

> I think to a certain extent, yes. You know. I think there's teachers who, they just … it seem like they just have lower expectations of maybe, you know, [of Black students]. And which is unfortunate for the student 'cause, you know. If you walk into classes and a teacher's not expecting an A from you, what are the chances you're gonna work for that A … And like, I don't necessarily think there are teachers who are outright racist, but it might even be like a subconscious thing, like that's just what they expect, you know, just how society expects that you know. That's what they, the pattern has been with their Black students. So why should they expect any more from these [students], you know. So I think that's that. It's an expectation thing maybe.

One perceptive student pointed out that teachers were people, too, and were inclined, like anyone else, to stereotype people. But he noted that not all teachers at Shaker, White or Black, had low expectations of Black students. It depended on the teacher's background and personal history.

Anthrop:	When Black students come into the class, do teachers have any sort of assumptions or expectations of them?
Student:	Yeah, that's what I thought you were asking. Um, I think it goes back to, uh, the history of the teacher … where they were brought up and what sort of mentality they have, in their

bringing up ... What their environment has done to them in terms of their assumptions. But we all have assumptions, we all um, tend to prejudge each other and um, mainly for the color of our skin. So, I'm sure it happens. [teachers] don't, they don't express that feeling, but I'm sure that does happen.

The next student talked about differences in expectations of academic ability for Black and White students:

Anthrop: OK, um, do you think that teachers have expectations about how well [Black students are] gonna do in the class?

Student: I don't think [the teachers], when they see you at first, unless they have prior knowledge of that person coming in the classroom [i.e., that the Black student had performed well in his or her previous class], I think they're generally thinking that the White people score a little bit higher than a Black person can.

Some Black students contributed to the lowered expectations by establishing reputations manifested in disapproved attitudes and behaviors. The following student was among those who blamed their fellow students for the problem:

Anthrop: Do you think that teachers have any sort of expectations or assumptions about what Black students are going to be like?

Student: Um, I think they do. Like a lot, depending on what kind of reputation you build up through the years. 'Cause I know it's not, you don't just come here and nobody know who you are, you know. If you have that type of reputation. Like teachers know me that I have never had [a bad reputation] in my life. They're like, "Well, you're a good student," or like "Oh, you have a nice GPA." Like a counselor said that to me (laughs). I was like so surprised. She was like "Oh, yeah, you have such a nice GPA." I was like "Oh my God" (laughs). But then like, at the same time, [there are other] kids who are in like [the Minority Achievement Committee], like the potential scholars I know, that the teachers know like what they got in their old school, or what they got in the middle school. And I'm sure that it has something to do with it. I mean just because I see what happens when you do good. I mean like well what happen when you do bad? You know, of course they know.

According to the students, some teachers went beyond low expectations to punish bad behavior with low grades; that is, the grades a teacher gave to a student were based on the student's behavior in the class and not just on performance in the course. To some this was a problem in addition to lowered expectations. Teachers' lowered expectations caused Black students to do less well than White students; in addition, teachers might give grades that were still lower because of bad behavior in class. One student illustrated the issue of grading behavior with her own experience. She had a teacher who "would give you an F in a test regardless of how well you did if you're bad during class. He'll just choose whatever he wants to give you, even though you done good. This happened to me. The teacher, he just gave me an F because of my bad class behavior."

Because Black students collectively faced lowered teacher expectations, those who did well were treated as exceptions and different from other Blacks. Several students were concerned about this. They believed that because of lowered expectations teachers and other school personnel were usually surprised or would begin to pay a Black student more attention when he or she did well in a class. In the following case the student did not say that the teacher expected her to do poorly; nonetheless, the teacher was surprised when she did well because she was Black:

Anthrop:	And what about when, like you've seen when students do well, what do [teachers], what do they say, or what do they think?
Student:	Its like "Great job!" Its like you're an exception, you know. 'Cause like most Black students don't do well so, you get, you know, this one Black student who is getting an A or something. And its like "Wow!," you know, "you're really smart. Move up to an honors class." Or something, you know.
Anthrop:	Do teachers give you a lot of attention when you do well?
Student:	Yeah … me in particular?
Anthrop:	Mh, hmm.
Student:	Yeah, I think so. Like even my English teacher, she's Black. And she, you know, she was just thrilled that I had an A the first quarter. It was like "Great!" I don't know that she necessarily expected me to do bad, but she was, you know, very happy for me that I got an A. And, you know, she was just very happy, you know.

Were some students using low teacher expectations as an excuse for not doing their schoolwork and for not making good grades? That indeed was indeed the case, according to some students in the high school discussion group. In a mimicking voice, one student described how other students use this excuse: "The teachers, they don't want me to do well, 'cause I'm Black." Or, "You know, 'cause I'm Black, they gave me a (sic) F. Now if I was White, this—." They blame everything on skin color.

In general, students at the middle school and high school believed that teachers, regardless of race, did not believe that Black students were capable of performing academically like White students, but they also believed that the attitudes and behaviors of some Black students were partly responsible for the teachers' low expectations. Black students thus hurt their own performance.

Some students developed interesting strategies for handling the teachers' negative beliefs and low expectations. One strategy was to strive to prove to the teachers that they were wrong. Students who used this strategy were determined to break the stereotypes about Black students by performing better than expected. One student described his approach this way: "Um, I don't care. 'Cause I just think if I do well, then I'll just prove em wrong." Another strategy, which we describe in the DISCIPLINE section, was to maintain a good relationship with school authorities.

Classwork

In chapter 6 we presented several cases from our classroom observations. Here we comment briefly on teacher expectations on the basis of those observations. Some researchers have reported that teachers call on Black students less often than they call on White students during lessons; furthermore, they make more negative comments on Black students' answers to questions (Leacock, 1985). In our observations of honors and AP classes we did not see differences in teachers' calling on Black and White students during lessons. What we found was that Black students did not raise their hands as much as Whites students did. In the skills and college prep classes where Black students were the majority, they dominated class discussions. We did not observe negative comments specifically directed at Black students' responses during lessons.

Suggestions were made during some class discussions that in the past the school curriculum did not include Black experiences. Indeed, public schools curricula excluded the experiences of all minorities and lower class Whites or presented the negative side of their experiences (Elson, 1964). We did not make a systematic study of the exclusion or inclusion of Black experience in Shaker Heights curriculum. We describe in the next chapter one incident in the Department of Theater that suggested that little effort was made in the past to include Black experience in its curriculum, but we want to point out that during our study we found materials on Black experience in some social studies and literature classes. In those classes Black students participated more actively and showed more knowledge of the contents of the materials than White students.

On the whole, it is difficult to say that there was a differential treatment of Black students in the classroom and that the differential treatment contributed to their academic disengagement and lower performance. Of course, there were differences in the treatment of students in honors and AP classes, which were predominantly White, and the treatment of students in the skills and college prep classes, which were predominantly Black, but the differences were not necessarily along racial lines.

Homework

The issue of homework came up repeatedly when we talked with middle school and high school teachers. Teachers who met with us were particularly concerned that they did not get back homework assignments in the skills and college prep classes. The situation was different in the honors and AP classes, where homework was given regularly and where both students and teachers treated it seriously. Homework was usually integrated with classroom lessons.

We now use our observations in two classes to show the difference in teachers' homework expectations in honors and AP classes, on the one hand, and in skills and college prep classes on the other. In an AP class with one Black male out of 25 students on the day we observed, both the teacher and the students regarded homework as an integral part of the lesson. Homework assignment was a part of the overall lesson, and what students learned from doing their homework was tested by the teacher. Thus, when one student apologetically asked the teacher if she could turn in her overdue homework the teacher told her and the rest of the class to keep the homework to study it for a test he would give the next day. In contrast, in a college prep class with mostly Black students, one student more or less bragged during a class discussion that he didn't do homework, didn't take notes, or follow class rules. The teacher reacted as if he tolerated this type of behavior. Furthermore, the teacher told the class in a manner hardly disguising his criticism of his colleagues, that he had heard of "teachers who deliberately failed students because they didn't do their homework regardless of whether or not they were learning." Apparently, this teacher and his students did not regard homework as a part of the lesson or knowledge to be tested.

There were teachers, however, who treated homework as very important at all course levels, especially in mathematics. One teacher explained the importance of homework in mathematics by saying that math was a subject that required constant attention and practice. If students did not do homework or received no homework, then the knowledge and skills they learned in class would not be reinforced much. In his view, students at every course level would do homework if the teacher demanded it. As he put it, "If you expect to get homework back from students as a teacher you will get it." However, from our observations that was not necessarily the case. Students in some college prep and skills classes refused to do or return their homework even though teachers expected them to do so.

Grading Practices

In spite of complaints about teachers' beliefs and expectations, we found few actual complaints that teachers graded Black and White students differently. When such complaints were made, there were also questions about students blaming teachers for their own failure to do their work. Our overall impression was that throughout the system there was no strong feeling that teachers were unfair in the way they graded the work of Black students. Elementary school students believed that they were graded by teachers the same way that White students were graded for the work they did. Most high school students who were explicitly asked about teachers' grading practices said that Blacks were graded fairly. Students seemed to take responsibility for their academic performance, as can be seen in their answer to a question specifically about who was responsible for the type of grades they made. The overwhelming response was that they themselves were responsible.

There were, of course, some exceptions to the acceptance of personal responsibility for their grades. We came across one student who reported receiving poor grades not only for academic performance but also for bad behavior. Furthermore, a few students were said to come to school with the belief that, because of racism, the system was against them; therefore, White teachers would not give them passing grades. A case in point was a high school male student who said that his father told him that White teachers would do everything they could to make sure that Black students did not succeed academically. This was how he phrased his father's message:

> My dad told me that um, most White teachers want you to fail out [of] their class. I don't know why he said that. I guess that's from his past experience or somethin'. But he said most White teachers want you to fail out the class. And every little thing that they, that you do they'll count [it] against you know. 'Cause most White teachers might uh, grade you half of the time on effort, and you uh, your acting in class, like if you say, like maybe, couple of words that are [bad] all the time. They might, they're more lenient towards Whites.

This student then went on to complain about discrimination against Black people in society at large:

> Student: If a Black and a White person'll start at the same position in the uh, big corporations, I think the White person'll do well fast.
>
> Anthrop: Do you think that that is, OK, for yourself, for example, knowing that, is that a sense of, does that make you frustrated, or does that give you strength?
>
> Student: I think, it make me frustrated.

We do not know the proportion of Black students and parents in Shaker Heights who felt this way about White teachers or U.S. society. We think, however, that this type of belief would have an adverse effect the academic striving of students who felt this way. To reiterate, Black students did not complain that teachers gave them lower grades than White students received. We heard, however, as we reported in chapter 2, that there was a time when Black students before entering the ninth grade received more social promotion than White students.

School Authorities on Expectations

There was also some concern among school authorities over teacher expectations. Teacher expectations constituted a major theme in a talk given by a well-known national figure invited to speak at Teachers' Conference Day. Other school personnel also went to hear the speaker, who urged teachers to have high expectations and hold a standard of excellence for Black students. In a conversation with one teacher after the conference, he

said that he agreed with the speaker on the importance of high expectations and high standards for Black students. The teacher said that he himself was a product of an educational environment in which a standard of
excellence was considered necessary and was fostered. He went on to say
that he wanted Black students in Shaker Heights to have a similar experience. This was the same teacher who said that Black students would do
classwork and homework if teachers expected them to do so. However, as
we commented then, we observed that this was not necessarily true. In
Shaker Heights the problem of teacher expectation was more complicated
than our informant saw it. It was also more complicated than the literature
usually presents it. In more than 100 classroom lessons we observed, there
were many instances in which it was difficult to say whether students
were unwilling to do classwork or homework or whether their refusal to
do so resulted in low teacher expectations. We were not sure which came
first; however, students' own accounts of their schoolwork and homework attitudes and habits both in group and individual discussions as
well as in interviews outside the classroom suggested that in some cases,
at least, teachers' lowered expectations were held partly in response to
students' attitudes and behaviors. When students repeatedly failed to do
classwork and failed to complete or return their homework, lowered
teacher expectations would be a predictable consequence.

Classroom Observations

We observed some 110 classroom lessons. These included general, skills,
and college prep classes in which the demands for students to perform were
minimal. A case in point was the algebra lab we described earlier. We reiterate that when students felt little or no demand to perform they might not
develop a good understanding of the relationship between the effort they
made and the grades they received. They also might feel that they were doing well or that they were "good students" when, in fact, they were not.

DISCIPLINE

Almost every study of Black students' relationships with school personnel
and among themselves has found that lack of discipline or disruptive behavior is a major obstacle to teaching and learning (Fordham, 1996; Foster,
1974; Hanna, 1988; Levy, 1970; Payne, 1984; Polite, 1991). By *disruptive behavior* we mean verbal and nonverbal behavior that interferes with teaching and learning. In a previous study conducted in Oakland, California,

(Ogbu, 1998), we recorded more than 10 such behaviors, including fighting, defiance of authority, profanity, vulgarity, and so on. In the Oakland study some of these behaviors were also found among Whites, Mexican Americans and Latinos, Chinese, and Filipinos, but to a much lesser extent. It is surprising that the problem of disruptive behavior, especially in the classroom, has not received a systematic treatment in the research community (Hanna, 1988). In Shaker Heights, discipline was a major factor in students' academic disengagement. In this section we describe the problem and show how it became increasingly detrimental to academic engagement, from elementary school to high school.

Elementary School

At the elementary school we saw only one disorderly classroom. It was disrupted by two White male students. This does not mean that the school did not have discipline problems. There was in the same school a dingy-looking room for keeping students with disciplinary problems for an extended period of time, sometimes for a whole day. The teachers considered this better than suspension or expulsion.

Differential disciplinary treatment of Black and White students was apparently not an issue at the elementary school. In our classroom and schoolyard observations we did not see differences in treatment based on race. Individual students, Blacks and Whites, were punished for misbehavior. Those who were punished often—again, both Blacks and Whites—were individual students who developed "reputations" associated with misbehaviors. In the cafeteria at one elementary school there was a table reserved for teachers, and another table nearby was reserved for students on punishment. There was a Black girl among the students who sat there regularly. One day she sat alone at the students' table. A teacher asked her why she was sitting there and she replied that she was not on punishment that particular day. The teacher concluded and we concurred that she was sitting there out of habit. In our observations in this cafeteria on several days we did not find that Black students were disproportionately represented at the punishment table. Just as elementary school students believed that punishment was based on individual misbehavior, they also believed that students treated more leniently were teachers' pets, not because they were White. The pets could be Black or White.

The only incident of differential treatment at the elementary school occurred outside the classroom. This was in a fourth-grade program on race relations, Student Group on Race Relations. Students participating in the program came from different schools with a White high school student in charge under a teacher supervisor. During the meeting one White student was continually disruptive by speaking out of turn and drawing attention to himself. A Black student was similarly disruptive. The White student leader repeatedly told the Black student to stop misbehaving but never asked the White student to stop misbehaving. After the meeting the supervising teacher told us that it was typical of the White high school student leader to reprimand Black but not White students for misbehaviors during the meeting.

Middle School

Disciplinary problems emerged as a racial issue at the middle school. They were often discussed by students, school personnel, and parents. They were also obvious in our observations in the classrooms and other settings. It was at the middle school that parents complained during ordinary conversations and formal discussions that their children were unfairly and differentially disciplined because of race. A typical complaint occurred at a tutoring session in the community for middle school students. One mother complained about her son's suspension for a week because of fighting with a White student. She said that her son was not a troublemaker and had not meant to get into the fight. She said that she was aware of the school district's rule that fighting automatically resulted in suspension; however, she felt that her son should have received a shorter suspension. She believed that if her son was White he would not have been suspended for a whole week. She and other Black parents present thought that there was a racial bias in the way students were disciplined.

All the Black students we interviewed at the middle school believed that Blacks were disciplined more than White students. Some of these same Black students qualified their belief by explaining that students were more likely to be punished for misbehavior. Others agreed that more Black students misbehaved but still maintained that there were racial differences in the students' punishment.

We do not discount entirely the beliefs of Black students and their parents that Black students were disciplined more than White students. However, as at the elementary school our impression based on our own observations was that middle school students were disciplined because of individual misbehavior rather than because of race. We observed both

Black and White students, when they misbehaved, sent to the office of the assistant principal for discipline. In these observations there were more Black than White students sent to the assistant principal's office. Furthermore, almost invariably, when we passed by the assistant principal's office we saw more Black than White students there.

Also, the large number of middle school Black students who were being punished came from basic skills and college prep classes. These were classes with the most discipline problems, and the majority of the students were Black. As could be seen in the cases described in this chapter on effort and attitudes and behaviors during instruction, these students did not always pay attention or follow rules. They also behaved in a similar manner during tutoring sessions and other special programs at school and in the community to help them improve their academic performance. Adults in charge of these programs often worried about the students' disruptive behaviors.

High School

Our observations of discipline problems at the high school began with two instances of student detention. All the detained students were Black. One was a classroom detention with about 5 students. They were expected to do their homework during the detention but were not doing so. The other detention was in a small auditorium. The students sat quietly, with their heads down, reading.

Often when we were in the hallways between classes we saw White students hurrying to their next class in time. This was not the case with Black students. An incident that took place in the hallway during the first day of our visit to the high school will illustrate the racial differences in hallway behavior. This incident caught our attention because of the presence of several security guards.

As we walked through the hallway with a school official who was showing us the campus, the bell rang, indicating that it was time to change classes. The school was on a shifting period system, so that all students would not be in the hallways at the same time. The students were given 4 minutes to go between classes. We asked our guide if 4 minutes was enough time for students to get to their next class. He assured us that it was more than enough to travel from any part of the school to another. After the chime, there were several students still walking in the hallways. Our guide asked us to note who was still in the hallways. Although he did not state it directly, it was apparent that he wanted us to take note of the fact that they were mainly African American students. He asked two of them who were talking loudly to be quiet as they walked by but did not attempt to hurry them out of the hallways. Possibly this was the role of the security staff. About nine minutes after the first chime, the hallways were virtually empty. Of approximately 10 students still there, only one appeared to be White; the rest were African Americans. In a conversation later a security guard told us that he would not have a job at the school if it were not for the misbehavior of Black students.

Racial differences in discipline at the high school constituted a real issue for parents, students, and school authorities. The discipline problems were discussed on several occasions at school and in the community, and we also observed them in and outside of the classroom. The behavior problems at the high school resulted in widely held stereotypes of Black students among Black and White students, Black and White parents, and school authorities. At the center of the stereotype was that it was mostly Black students who got into fights. The extent of this belief was demonstrated during a class discussion of a fight in the hallway. The teacher who witnessed the fight began his lesson with a discussion of stereotypes. He then asked how many students thought that the fight he witnessed was among Black students. Several Black students and a few Whites raised their hands. Next, he asked how many of their parents, on hearing of the fight, would assume that it was among Black students. Again several students raised their hands, suggesting that their parents believed that it was mostly Black students who got into fights at school.

On a number of occasions, different people, including students, commented on the disruptive behaviors of students in basic skills and college prep classes, where most of the students were Black. On the other hand, they said that discipline problems were minimal in honors and AP classes, where the majority of the students were White. Students knew that there were differences in teaching and learning between the two categories of classes and that discipline problems contributed to the differences. This was pointed out by a Black male at a class discussion. He said that in skills and college prep classes teachers spent a lot of the lesson period addressing discipline problems, whereas in honors and AP classes they spent the whole lesson period teaching their subject.

The consensus among Black high school students we interviewed was that Black students got into trouble more often and were disciplined more often than White students, but there was some disagreement as to whether the greater punishment was fair or justified. The majority be-lieved that there was no racial bias in the administration of discipline. Among this group of students, Blacks were disciplined more often be-cause they misbehaved more often. The view of the following student is representative:

Anthrop:	OK, do you think there's a difference in the way kids are disci-plined? Do Blacks get disciplined more or less or the same as Whites?
Student:	Parental?
Anthrop:	Disciplined here at school.
Student:	Well, I really do.
Anthrop:	Do they get into trouble more often?
Student:	I mainly see a lot of Black people getting in trouble.
Anthrop:	OK.
Student:	Every time I pop up, it's—you rarely, rarely do you ever hear of a fight in the hallway with White people ... I don't remember hearing one. Maybe one, and that's it. But basically maybe ev-ery week or every other week, you hear, "Oh, so and so was fight in the hall; two Black boys or two Black girls."
Anthrop:	Now, do you think they're disciplined more often because the behavior is worse or they are disciplined differently by the school [because they are Black?]
Student:	From my experience, I would have to say it's their behavior.

Other students did not attribute the disproportionate discipline of Black students to additional factors. According to some, these other fac-tors were (a) the stereotype or beliefs of school authorities that Black stu-dents misbehaved, and (b) cross-cultural misunderstanding. Because of the stereotype held by school authorities, even a minor behavioral infrac-tion by a Black student attracted more attention from teachers and other school officials than would a similar infraction of behavior by a White stu-dent—that is, because school authorities usually assumed that Black stu-dents would misbehave, they more often noticed it among Black students. Because they did not assume that White students would misbehave as much, they failed to notice misbehavior among White students, even when White students misbehaved. The differential expectation and treatment were noted by the following student:

> *Student:*   It's stupid stuff but it's like weighs on like what happens later, I guess. Cause I know like if a White guy walks down the hallway the security guards he'll be like "Oh, Hi," like that. And if a Black guy walks down the hallway, "Don't you have a pass? What class are you going to?" Or, like, even sometimes like they'll be [thinking] that the White kid is going to class. But if the Black kid is going down the hallway they'll be thinking that he is skipping class.

Several students described their personal experience or the experience of someone they knew as examples of what they considered unequal discipline. Here is one example of personal encounters with unequal disciplinary treatment:

> *Anthrop:*   And how about discipline? Do you think that Blacks get disciplined more, or suspended more?
>
> *Student:*   Yeah. I think they do. I think maybe ... I don't know why it's like that. But I had an altercation back in the eighth grade, with a White guy. He like broke into my locker and stole my coat. And we got in a fight. And I got expelled for that but he didn't get even suspended. But recently, like when me and that White girl had got into it [i.e., a fight], ... we both got suspended. But I know some other people that got into it with like White girls and White guys, and they got in a fight and they [Blacks] got expelled.
>
> *Anthrop:*   And nothing happened to the White person?
>
> *Student:*   No.

Cross-cultural misunderstandings also contributed to the disproportionate discipline problems of Black students. The case we report here involves cultural differences in jokes. The two racial groups in Shaker Heights, as elsewhere in the United States, have been socialized into different jokes and joking behaviors. As children, Black and White teachers learned different jokes and joking behaviors that remained with them as adults. This resulted in cultural differences in teachers' interpretations of students' jokes to the disadvantage of Black and White students. Black students at Shaker High reported that at Shaker High a White teacher would identify with the jokes of White students in his or her class and so might not punish them, but he or she would label the jokes of Black students as misbehaviors because she did not identify culturally with their jokes. They correctly observed that the opposite was true of Black teachers. The latter would identify with the jokes of Black students and would not punish them, but he or she might not identify with the jokes of White students and would punish them in the belief that their jokes constituted misbehavior. The following student was among those who provided an example of this cultural explanation:

Anthrop: How about discipline? Do you think that Blacks are disciplined more or have more discipline problems at this school?

Student: Cause some Black people just tend ta act a little wild sometimes, [just] like the White people … They act wild, too. [But] since it's a White teacher, [the teacher] can relate to how [the White students are] actin'. But like if a Black [student] act wild [White teachers] can't relate to the Black people. He'll still interpret it as misbehavior and punish them. [For example], like the teacher … last year … in [my] English class and the Black people, they would like act wild, and [the] Black teacher, the teacher was Black too, so she act with us, too. But like [when] we go to like another class and like [Black students would] act the same [wild] way, and the [White] teacher couldn't like handle [relate to] it or tolerate it or whatever. But if like [a] White person would like crack some corny joke, and like [the White teacher] she'd laugh at it. It's just the way you relate … like how you, like their culture … the way you grow up and stuff.

Some students developed strategies for staying out of trouble or getting lighter punishment when it is unavoidable. One strategy was establishing a good relationship with school authorities. Students who used this approach were careful not to misbehave too often. When they misbehaved, they usually received less punishment than they would otherwise get. The following student explained why he resorted to this strategy and described some of its advantages.

Anthrop: What do you mean that it depends on what kind of kid you are?

Student: You get in good with your assistant principal. I know all my teachers. I know all my teachers from the past 4 years. I still go in and say hello to them and so I get a little bit more slack. And if I mean, they're a lot of kids like that—who have like good friends in the school who are their teachers and who are their administrators. And [such students are] not gonna get Saturday school right off the bat [i.e., will not be punished heavily] for something little that they did. But it does not matter what race you are. You'll see kids are suspended everyday both White or Black.

We did not formally interview teachers and other school authorities about discipline. Our impression was that more Black than White students at the middle and high school were punished, for three reasons. First, Black students probably misbehaved more. This conclusion is based on our observations, interviews with students, and informal discussions with parents and some school authorities The second reason is the stereotype and expectations school authorities held regarding Black students, as reported by the students; the third reason was cross-cultural misunderstandings of jokes. The issue of race and school discipline is a sensitive one. Our main concern in describing it in Shaker Heights is that it seems to us that the disproportionate number of Black students involved in discipline problems adversely affected teaching and learning in classes with mostly Black students and thus contributed to the academic disengagement and the achievement gap.

III

Community Forces

8

Opportunity Structure: Schooling and Getting Ahead

EDUCATION AND THE AMERICAN DREAM

In chapter 3 we described the public school system as a delegate agency. In this capacity it prepares young people for the job market by teaching them knowledge, skills, and attributes required in the workforce and by credentialing them to enter the workforce (Ogbu, 1983). For the education system to function effectively as a delegate agency it must teach and credential people, and those whom it trains and credentials must believe that they will enter the workforce and receive the expected rewards—and for some, people they must have experienced the promise of the reward. In other words, how people respond to the schools as delegate agencies depends in part on their past and present experiences and future expectations in the labor market or other designated domain of life. It depends on what they believe about getting jobs and wages that are commensurate with their school credentials. People will believe more strongly in the school as a delegate agency and put more effort in pursuit of school credentials if, as a group and as individuals, they are usually rewarded with jobs and wages or other benefits commensurate with their education than if they are not.

According to the "American Dream," the public school system is expected to provide all children, regardless of their background, with an equal opportunity to acquire the knowledge, skills and credentials that will enable them enter the workforce and obtain jobs and wages based on a merit system (Ogbu, 1983; Warner, Havighurst, & Loeb, 1944).

Blacks, Education, and the "American Dream" Before 1960

Historical and comparative research suggests, however, that until the 1960s the American education system did not function effectively as a delegate agency for Black Americans because of discrimination. Before the 1960s there was a job ceiling against Blacks that prevented them from getting jobs and wages that were commensurate with their education. It has been suggested elsewhere that, for this reason, they did not develop and believe as strongly as White Americans that education would enable them to achieve the American Dream, although they wished they could do so (Mickelson, 1990; Ogbu, 1978). According to Mickelson (1990), the reason White Americans believe strongly that they can achieve the American Dream through education and hard work is that they have historically actually achieved the American Dream through education and hard work. She characterized White beliefs as *concrete*, because they are based on actual experience in the opportunity structure. In contrast, the beliefs of Black Americans are *abstract*, because they are not based on a history of actual achievement of the American Dream through education and hard work because of discrimination. We suggest that the beliefs of Black Americans are more or less wishful thinking, because they are not based on actual experience. We can conclude from this analysis that White concrete beliefs and Black abstract beliefs will have different influences on the academic attitudes and effort of the two groups.

The Job Ceiling and Black Response to Education

The discrimination against Blacks in the labor market before the1960s created a disconnection between their educational preparation and their treatment in the job market (Katz, 1967; Ogbu, 1978), a disconnection in their thinking about how to prepare educationally for specific jobs. Another consequence is that the uncertainty that education will pay off probably discouraged many from pursuing education beyond the legal age requirement or even encouraged some to drop out before the age limit. Still another consequence is that it prevented them from developing a good understanding of the connection between different levels of schooling. By this we mean the extent to which children at the elementary school understand how their performance will affect their schoolwork at the middle school, and how children at the middle school understand how their performance will affect their placement and performance at the high school, and so on. It was our impression that because Blacks did not experience a strong connection between their schooling and their chances in the job market, they were discouraged from developing a strong norm of academic pursuit, in spite of their aspirations. Therefore, many generations of a lack of connection between school success and success in adult life probably resulted in skepticism about the real value of schooling. This skepticism undermined their academic engagement. Shack (1970) summed up the difference between Whites and Blacks in the development of persistent academic pursuit when he contrasted Black and White maxims. For Blacks, the maxim was "What's the use of trying?," in contrast, to the White maxim of, "Once you try and you don't succeed, try again." Finally, lack of equal opportunity structure in the mainstream labor market or the American Dream resulted in the pursuit of self-betterment in alternative opportunities and through alternative strategies that do not require school credentials. We discuss this later in the chapter. We note here, however, that this too must have further undermined Black students' academic engagement. Readers should keep in mind that, unlike immigrants, Black Americans did not choose to become minorities in order to achieve the American Dream through education and hard work,—that is, by adopting the strategy that works for White Americans.

On the basis of comparative studies, Ogbu (1978, 1983; Ogbu & Simons, 1998) has suggested that members of a given minority group, such as Black Americans, share beliefs about the connection between schooling and the job market or mainstream opportunity structure. Minority students form their image, or social construction, of the connection or lack of it between school success and success in adult life from the beliefs, attitudes, and behaviors of people in their community. This image is also based on their observations of the experiences of the adult members of the community, the textures of their parents' lives, and the experiences of older siblings (Luster, 1992; Ogbu, 1974). Protests and other activities of civil rights advocates, and the portrayal of the employment "problems" of minorities in the media, provide minority students with further materials for the construction of their social reality in the job market.

Even before they are old enough to understand the weak connection between education and jobs through observations, children hear about it from family discussions and begin to internalize the beliefs of their family and community. Furthermore, minority parents and other adults may teach children the abstract beliefs about the importance of education, yet their own educational practices may convey contrary messages. In practice, children may observe very little cultural emphasis on striving to do well in school or to get good credentials. The emphasis may, in fact, be on breaking the barriers in education and in the opportunity structure rather than on practicing the behavior and attitudes that are conducive to school success. Under these circumstances, minority children do not see their parents and other adults in their community as role models for professional and other jobs or positions as being based on school success or school credentials; rather, they see them as role models in the collective struggle against the system.

Changes In the Opportunity Structure Since the 1960s

The civil rights movement of the 1960s brought significant changes in the connection between minority education and opportunity structure. The specific reasons for the changes included civil rights legislation; affirmative action; and various federal, state, and local programs for equal opportunity in education, the labor market, housing, and so on. These factors have enhanced the connection between school success or educational credentials and adult opportunity in the job market. We assume that because of these changes Black Americans beliefs that they can achieve the American Dream through education and hard work have become more concrete and stronger. Although we did not study the changes in the opportunity structure in Shaker Heights suburban community, what was important for our purpose was how Black people, particularly students, in Shaker Heights perceived these changes both locally and nationally.

The Polyanna Effect

The *Polyanna effect* is the belief that discrimination is a past phenomenon, something that happened in the days of one's parents and grandparents. According to this view, discrimination has been eliminated because of civil rights legislation, affirmative action, and other special programs to promote equal opportunity for everyone (Mickelson, 1990).

There were Black students at every school level who believed that Blacks and Whites now have equal opportunities for education and in the job market. These students admitted that their grandparents, and perhaps their parents, had experienced discrimination when trying to get a job or promotion. However, things had changed; it was now up to the individual "to make something" of him- or herself. One elementary school student, while admitting that things might be different "outside Shaker Heights," emphatically denied that there was job discrimination in Shaker Heights.

Affirmative Action and the Polyanna Effect

A few middle and high school students also believed that Blacks were no longer denied employment on the basis of race because of government policies prohibiting racial discrimination. They mentioned affirmative action, which they said encouraged employers to give preference to qualified Blacks where they were underrepresented because of past racial discrimination. The same students, however, feared that White opposition to affirmative action threatened the emerging equalization of opportunity between Black and Whites. They explained that White people opposed affirmative action because they did not understand the extent to which Blacks endured barriers in the opportunity structure. It was because of the extent of past discrimination that affirmative action was instituted, and affirmative action was still needed because of the residue of discrimination and the effects of past discrimination.

Persistence of Unequal Job Opportunities

From elementary school to high school, the majority of the students believed that Blacks in Shaker Heights and in the entire United States still lacked opportunities equal to Whites'. They believed that Blacks continued to face racial barriers when applying for jobs or job promotions. The belief was most pervasive and strongest among members of the older age groups. Only a few elementary school students mentioned job discrimination in interviews and informal discussions. At the middle school, however, most students believed that Blacks faced racial barriers and thus had more problems than Whites in trying to get ahead. Whites and Blacks were not treated equally in the business world and in the job market. One student summed up this perception this way:

Anthrop: Do you think that Blacks have, um, more problems getting ahead than Whites in the United States?

Student: I think they do, sometimes, because Whites—since they created the United States or whatever, they usually get like more jobs or they'll get paid more [than Blacks]. And Black people be doin' the same things but they won't get paid as much, or they won't even get hired.

The high-schoolers expressed the strongest belief that Blacks did not yet have equal opportunity with Whites. Blacks experienced difficulty when trying to get ahead because of "their color." Ten of the 13 high school students we interviewed believed that racial discrimination in the opportunity structure still existed, that U.S. society continued to give preferential treatment to White people, thereby making it more difficult for Black people to succeed when they competed with Whites. The views of the following students are representative of the perspective.

Anthrop: In general, would you say that Blacks have more difficulty getting ahead in the United States than Whites?

Student 1:   I think so, just because of the total climate of the United States. Like how um, subconsciously, you know, [the employers] always have preconceived notions about who it is comin' to get that job interview, or who it is comin' to apply to that college. Like it's always a type of thing [i.e., this preconception can be seen in White reaction to programs] like the affirmative action thing. It's like, "Well, I'm gonna hire these Black people even though I don't think they can do a good job." I mean that's the way I see it [because White people do not believe that you, Black employees are qualified] … You're always working to prove yourself [i.e., prove to the Whites that you are qualified]. Whereas if you were a Caucasian person trying to get ahead, its sort of like they welcome you more. It's like you're one of them, so they're gonna help you get ahead, whether you're the best or not.

Anthrop: Do you think that Blacks have different problems in trying to get ahead than Whites do in the United States?

Student 2:   Well, I mean, you could say that. Most Blacks, um, they usually … wanna change their life [i.e., get ahead]. Sometimes they feel they can't and they feel that that's where they're supposed to be [i.e., they know that they have no chance of upward mobility]. But most Whites, they want to succeed. They know they will.

High school students were more aware of the long history of the discrimination against Blacks in the opportunity structure. They pointed out that it was because of this historical discrimination that Blacks still lagged behind Whites in education and occupational status in spite of affirmative action and related programs. It was also because of this historical discrimination that affirmative action should continue to enable Blacks to catch up with Whites. In other words, the long history of discrimination justified affirmative action. The following student was among those who made the

connection between the history of discrimination and the need for affirmative action:

Anthrop: What types of special issues do you think that Blacks are facing
            in getting ahead, like in the United States?

Student: Probably overcoming the boundaries [i.e., discrimination],
            like we were discussing in class ... Like how they said we're
            trying [to be] equal. But really we not [equal] because uh, you
            know, our ancestors, when they were also locked up [i.e., not
            allowed equal opportunity]. White people still have stuff to fall
            on. [This is because] they had their great, great, great, great
            grandparents, you know, [who had the opportunity to accu-
            mulate wealth] and pass it on to other generations. But we re-
            ally don't have that [i.e., such a long history of opportunity to
            accumulate wealth]. We might have [had about] two genera-
            tions. But we really don't have [more than] two generations
            back or three generations back ... you know, [compared to]
            Whites who have had like six.

Anthrop: Mh-hmm.

Student: So, we're still tryin' to catch up even though they say we're
            equal. But we're still held down ... by society ... really ... That
            is why you need affirmative action.

Racial discrimination in the opportunity structure was spontaneously
brought up at student interviews and was extensively discussed at meetings with Black and White high school students.

Blacks Worked Twice as Hard For the Same Reward

We reported earlier the case of a student who complained that Black employees worked hard to prove to the White employers that they could do
their job because White employers did not believe that Black workers were
qualified. This was an important issue among middle school and high
school students. In both group discussions and at individual interviews
they reported that Blacks were expected to work twice as hard as their
White peers to satisfy White employers, to earn the same wage, or to be promoted on the job. Even though Black employees had the same qualifications, as their White co-workers, White employers still expected them to
prove themselves. Black workers generally knew that White people had
lower expectations of them, and for that reason Black workers felt that they

had to prove themselves. The following excerpts are taken from interviews with students who expressed this belief. The first excerpt is from a middle school student, and the other excerpts are from high schoolers.

Anthrop:	OK, what about sometimes they say that Blacks have to work twice as hard in order to get a good job. Do you think that that's true?
Student 1:	Um …
Anthrop:	Like twice as hard as a White person?
Student:	Maybe, 'cause of pressure … people say that.
Anthrop:	What kind of pressure do you mean?
Student:	Like, um, like people may not expect for [Black] people to do as good as White people. And uh, that's like a lot of pressure on people, so they have to work extra hard to um, do what they want.
Anthrop:	Now, some people say that Blacks have to work twice as hard to get the same job as a White person. Do you think that's true?
Student 2:	I think they're checked a little bit more than White people. Like they'll check their records or whatever a little bit harder than a White person.
Anthrop:	OK, now have you ever heard it said that Blacks have to work twice as hard, or be twice as qualified for a job to get it?
Student 3:	Yeah.
Anthrop:	OK. Do you think that that is true?
Student:	Um, yeah. I think that is true. Like you have to try twice as hard just to be like as good as whoever, I mean as a White person.

A few students did not necessarily disagree that Blacks had to work twice as hard or be twice as good but said that nowadays Blacks should not feel that they have to prove themselves to White racists. They noted that some White people were not racist and Black people should go to work for Whites who were not racist. The student below shared this point of view.

Anthrop: Do you think that that's true, that Blacks have to work harder sometimes they say that Blacks have to work twice as hard to get the same job ... that sort of thing. Do you think that that sort of thing is true?

Student: Um, well, a lot of the paying positions, CEOs you know, the managers and directors of companies are held or controlled by White ... White males, I guess, you know, predominantly [White]. And some of them are racist, so you might not get the job [you want]. Um, but there are other places to go, instead of having to prove yourself. There are a lot of White people that aren't racist, and you can go to them for a job. So, it depends on where you look. Um, but I don't think that having to work twice as hard as Whites is an excuse. I don't think that that's a really good theory that Black people have to work twice as hard as Whites because that's not true.

Anthrop: Do you think that a lot of people use that as an excuse?

Student: Yes, a lot of people use that as an excuse.

Most students believed otherwise. They had heard that Blacks had to work twice as hard as White people from family discussions of their parents' experiences and those of other significant adults around them.

Even though a student did not know from personal experience that Blacks had to work twice as hard as Whites, he or she had probably been told of it by someone in the family or by a relative or heard it in a discussion. In the case of the following student, it was his aunt who made him aware of it:

Anthrop: OK, now have you ever heard anyone say that Blacks have to work twice as hard or be twice as qualified to get a job?

Student: Yeah, my auntie has told me that a lot.

Anthrop: OK. And what do you think about that?

Student: I don't know. I haven't been put in that situation yet, but they [his aunt and other relatives] said I need a ... if I wanna get a good job, if I wanna get that certain job, and if it's a White person goin' out for the same job, I have ta have twice as much um, education, as him. I have ta go ta school and work twice as hard. I have ta [prepare myself for] the job twice as much, you know. If I was average, they say if I was average, if we have everything the same [just as qualified as the White applicant], they said I wouldn't get the job. So they said I have ta have more than him. I have to be better than him to get it.

It is obvious that from elementary through high school Black students in Shaker Heights believed that Blacks still faced some obstacles in getting ahead because of their race. Furthermore, they believed that for Blacks to compete successfully with Whites for the same job, wages, and on-the-job advancement, Blacks had to be twice as good as their White peers and had to work twice as hard as the Whites. Although these beliefs were based on the experiences of their parents and other adults in the Black community, they affected the students' thinking about their own future. This can be seen from their frequent reference to affirmative action and White opposition to it.

Opportunity Structure and Schooling

Students talked about the impact of racial barriers on the academic orientations and efforts of Black students. Although the impact on academic effort might not be serious in the early grades, it became more serious as students got older and began to think that they, too, would have difficulties in the opportunity structure, like their parents had, just because they were Black. It was said that older students became more discouraged from striving for academic pursuit; they become disengaged from schooling. The following female student described quite well the academic consequence of students' perceptions of their limited chances in the opportunity structure.

> I think that a lot of [older] African Americans don't feel that they need to achieve or to strive. [But] you know, this wasn't always the case. At a young age everyone wants to learn and so on, but when you get to a certain age, a lot of African Americans realize that they don't have the [chance] to succeed in life [i.e., in a mainstream way], and that's because of the society in which we live. [Older students say] "What's the point in doing well? What's the point in being in [an AP or honors] class? You're not gonna be able to go to college. You know, you're struggling in school. Your parents are struggling … If they're [drumming it in] you: "You can be something. You can make it against all the barriers and whatnot," you're not gonna feel [certain] that they [really support] you, until you try.

While not disputing that students' perceptions of limited future in the opportunity structure had an adverse impact on their academic orientation and effort, another student cautioned about using this as an excuse to not strive to make good grades.

> *Anthrop*   (calling on another student): Do you think that Blacks have
>   special problems in trying to get ahead?

Student: I do because of society. But [it is not to the extent] to make it hard to succeed. It is not to the extent to cause such a large percentage, or such a large margin [between Black and White students] and to lead to hopeless. That would be an excuse for failure. But to [return to] the point if you're not … a minority, you really can't exactly understand, um, some of the barriers. But I hate to use that as any type of excuse because everyone can succeed.

There was no difference of opinion on the matter between students from affluent and nonaffluent families. They all felt that they didn't have the same opportunity as their White peers.

At a Minority Achievement Committee (MAC) meeting one scholar admonished potential scholars that "as Black men" they should be concerned because it would be difficult for them to get a job because of discrimination. Another scholar told them that it was important for them to be "right up there with the White man, and even [to be] better" in order to succeed in the larger society.

We now return to the interview materials for some insightful comments relevant to this issue. A student we interviewed noted that the mere existence of affirmative action was an indication that Blacks still did not have an equal chance for free and fair competition in the opportunity structure in the larger society.

Anthrop: OK, um, now tell me in general, in the United States, do you think that Blacks have different problems getting ahead than Whites?

Student: Yeah. Otherwise there wouldn't be any form of affirmative action … from that standpoint.

Anthrop: And, um, what types of problems do you think that Blacks have to deal with?

Student: Um, educationally and then like the, um, business world because like I'm looking at becoming a doctor and like the smallest percentage is Black females. Like looking at percentages and numbers, it just kind of throws me off like looking at schools. I'm thinking like, "Where did everybody go?" And I know its not because they didn't wanna go … but because opportunities weren't open to them.

Whether at interviews or in discussion groups, the general belief was that White people opposed affirmative action because they did not understand that Blacks still faced discrimination because of the color of their skin.

It was difficult for a White person to understand the obstacles faced by Blacks. They seemed to think that only a Black person or minority person could understand these difficulties, as the following student pointed out in the discussion group.

Anthrop: OK, now do you think in general in the United States, do you think that Blacks have more difficulty getting ahead?

Student: Yes, I do. Because I think that people try to pretend like it [discrimination] doesn't [exist], but it does. And that's one reason we need to get White people to understand that. And I don't think White people do. It's like they think that because we had the civil rights movement, everything's perfect, and all this other kinds of stuff.

ALTERNATIVE STRATEGIES

Sports and Athletics

In his book *Darwin's Athletes*, Hoberman (1997) argued that sports divert Black Americans from academic pursuits. Without endorsing all of Hoberman's argument, we can say that in our own research experience we have encountered instances where some Black students invested so much time in sports that they had little time for their academic schoolwork (see also Harris, 1991; Solomon, 1989, 1992). In Shaker Heights the competition between sports and academics was visible and was discussed by students at group meetings, at interviews, and during class lessons; the subject also came up in our discussions with some school personnel as well as with parents.

At a meeting with a high school student group it was reported that one alternative for Blacks, because of a long history of discrimination in White establishments, was to start their own businesses. However, most students believed that the best and most viable alternative strategy was in sports. Blacks went into sports because they perceived limited opportunity to get ahead through education and merit in the mainstream economy.

For some students, playing sports was all that mattered. Recall the case of one student we mentioned in chapter 2. At our interview he talked about several colleges that were trying to recruit him. He was considering some colleges in Florida or California, but had not made up his mind. He would be consulting with his agent about the colleges over the weekend. He considered himself a good student, although his self-reported grade-point average (GPA) was 1.9. He admitted that his GPA could be better if he worked harder. What mattered to him was playing baseball, and he was happy as long as he played baseball. Sports seemed to be very important to him, and he attributed his popularity in school to his achievements in sports. We should point out, however, that not every student involved in sports abandoned their interest in and effort toward academic pursuit.

Both male and female students had active interests in sports, but with different emphases. The males more often looked at sports as an alternative to academics. In fact, on several occasions female students cautioned the males about the risk of putting too much hope in sports. The contrasting views of male and female students on sports and academics can be seen in the following discussion at a middle school meeting.

Anthrop:	How are you gonna make your …?
Male Student 1:	I'm gonna be a basketball player.
Female Student 1:	How you think basketball players got to where they are today?
Male Student 1:	Um, playing basketball. (other students laughing and talking).
Female Student 1:	Well, they had to have a good education. (Other female students simultaneously): They had to have education. A good education.
Female Student 2:	I bet they do.
Male Student 1:	No, they don't.
Anthrop	(Calling on a student) Yeah. Go ahead. Go ahead.
Female Student 2	(to Male Student 1): But what if you, but what if you break your leg?
Anthrop:	(clapping to get students' attention): Quiet please. (Calling on a student:) Yes.
Male Student 2:	If he was a good basketball player or somethin' like that or somethin', you gonna bring money in.

CHAPTER 8

Female Student 2:	Well wait. OK.
Anthrop:	OK.
Female Student 3:	I've got something to say.
Anthrop:	Yes.
Female Student 3:	It's good ... (drowned by students' talk.)
Male Student 1:	What are you going to say?
Male Student 3:	You're gonna have a contract if you get kicked off the team.
Anthrop:	How will you understand your contract if you don't know how to read it, if you don't study English?
Female Student 3:	Oh! OK, hold on.
Male Student 1:	(answering Anthrop): [the agent] will sign it for you.

At MAC meetings, scholars and potential scholars discussed their involvement in basketball, football, tennis, soccer, and wrestling. They were usually advised by adult and student leaders to budget their time so that they would do their schoolwork and homework while involved in sports.

Some teachers, especially Black teachers, occasionally explained to students the risks in professional sports. In some cases teachers used themselves as examples to drive home their point. They told the students why they did not go into professional sports but instead had pursued academic success. One teacher spent a considerable part of a college prep lesson period talking about professional sports. He warned students against relying too much on success in sports for their future. He compared athletics to life. He told them that looking at superstars such as Tupac and Charles Barkley as role models was in the wrong direction. They had a better chance in life by working hard in school to become doctors, lawyers, or having some other good job than of getting into professional sports. He himself was very good in sports, but he had decided not to go pro.

Entertainment and Drug Dealing

Entertainment and drug dealing were other alternative strategies for making it. We take up entertainment in ROLE MODELS section. Here we briefly discuss drug dealing, which was said to divert students' "smartness" or "intelligence" from academics. Students did not think that playing sports necessarily required "smartness." For example, the middle school student who wanted to play basketball said that his agent would read and explain his contract to him if he were not literate enough to read and understand it. As we reported earlier in our discussion of internalized White beliefs about ability, some Black students in Stockton, California, believed that Blacks were good in sports because they had "brawl" but were not good in math because they were not "smartness."

Drug dealers were different: The students regarded them as very smart or intelligent Blacks who, because of barriers in opportunity structure, diverted their smartness away from academics into drug dealing. One male student explained this diversion:

Anthrop:	What about those who come from families whose parents have made it? Do they still feel that they don't have the opportunity.
Male Student 1:	OK. I think that it is definitely not true [that Blacks have more opportunities now]. But the problem is that many Blacks are used to directin' their intelligence and their intellectuality in the wrong direction [i.e., away from academics.] For instance, drug dealers. I mean, you can't be stupid and be a drug dealer.
Anthrop:	That's true.
Male Student 1:	Anybody knows that. But that's the wrong direction. More percentage of Whites than Blacks are in the right direction with their intelligence. So that's the problem, and that statement [that Blacks have unlimited opportunity] is not true. White people as a whole are not smarter than Black people.
Anthrop:	Why do Blacks not direct their intelligence towards academics? Why towards the wrong direction, such as drugs? Yeah. You want to finish answering that?
Male Student 2:	It all depends on the environment they've grown up in. Again, like everything that has been said here, your family, like one day you're living in a two-parent home, and another day in a one-parent home, or [with] some other person. That affects the issue, and any other person [or thing] that teaches you,

whether it be TV or radio or school, if you're enrolled in school. All of that collectively makes [up] that environment for you, and that's what teaches you what direction you go into drug dealing.

We have some evidence from research elsewhere to support the students' perception that Blacks who were involved in drug dealing were smart. Among the Black youths jailed for drug offenses in San Francisco and Santa Rita in California, one 15-year-old had an organization of 40 people working for him, and one 17-year-old youth made over $300,000 in his business. The youngsters knew the penal system very well and how to behave in order to get light sentences from the judges (Ogbu, 1981). During our research in Oakland, California, in the early 1990s we had a group discussion with some self-identified drug dealers and relatives of drug dealers in jail. The reason for the discussion was our concern about students who were working as "runners" in the families we were studying. We were quite impressed by the "business skills" of the participants (Ogbu, 1998). Our other source of data came from a conference on drug problems organized by the Black community in Oakland during our study and our own work with the Baugherside Neighborhood Improvement Association in Stockton (1968–1970). As members of the board of directors of the neighborhood association, we were at the center of the discussion of Black and Mexican American youth drug problems and efforts to address them.

One very important point made during one of our discussions with Shaker High School students was that expanding opportunities for Blacks (since the civil rights movement and affirmative action) would eventually have positive effects on students' academic efforts. The anthropologist had suggested that perhaps students who came from professional families might be in a better position to believe that they would become achieve professional success if they had a good education. In their response, the students implied that the changes in the opportunity structure in U.S. society at large had not eliminated the need for the alternative strategies that arose in the past but would eventually have some positive effect. However, at no time in the discussion did any student mention that any Black student from Shaker Heights was involved in drug dealing. Neither did we come across such information throughout the study.

ROLE MODELS

A *role model* is somebody a person wants to be like. It is a person a child wants to be like when he or she grows up. In the context of this study a role model is somebody a student wants to be like in adult life. It is also a person parents would like their children to be like when they grow up. The attributes or qualities of a role model usually become a part of the values underlying the aspirations and behaviors of the student as well as those of parents in raising their children. In Shaker Heights, as elsewhere, people found their role models in the family, community, and society at large. Regardless of where the role models were located, it is significant that Shaker Heights students had not chosen them because of their educational success, their professional success based on education and hard work, or because they possessed attributes conducive to school or professionals success. Indeed, these qualities were not central in the discussion of role models.

Locations and Types of Role Models

Working-Class Families. We consider role models in working-class and middle-class families separately to bring out their similarities and differences. What students emphasized about working-class families was the importance of male role models for Black males. Fathers were considered more effective role models because they were male authority figures in the home, and boys were more likely to listen to them than to their mothers. Students believed that "kids looked up to people like themselves." Male students, they emphasized, often did not listen to their mothers about school. In the following discussion with students, both male and female students emphasized of the importance the father as a role model in the home.

Female Student:	Other people in the family might not care, so I think that's the reason why most of 'em [i.e., male students] just don't go to school and just don't do anything, because there is nobody to really tell them. You know what I'm saying, ... [to] lead 'em the right way. Tell 'em what they should do. Cause a boy listens to their mom, but they really don't listen to their mom the way they would [listen to] their father.
Anthrop:	OK. Yes (calling on a student).
Male Student:	I can see what she's talking about, because it's easier to relate to somebody who you feel is more like you. And like, um, say my uncle's coming over to our house, to try to help, you know; to set up a positive like role model image. I also think that when there's the complete family group [i.e., two parents and extended family], that the males kind of work together. It's not

just a singular effort anymore. 'Cause, I know, I know with my dad, it's not just him. It's his dad, his brother, and I mean, even his sister helps a little. But if it were just his sister I could see, you know, the impact on me not being as great.

Not all males were good role models for Black males. One male student gave his uncles as examples of bad role models because their behaviors were not ideal. Therefore, he did not look up to them as role models or take seriously what they told him. His own father was also not a good role model although he was at home.

Male student: Uh, well, in my case my father's at home, and I guess he's pretty interested in what I'm doin'. But (laughter from other students) my uncles! My uncles ..., they like far away, and when I see 'em, well, they're my uncles. But I might not really relate to 'em as much as though. If they try to like tell me somethin' I might look at them and then compare it with what they doin', how they actin'. They'll say like, "You not doin' this." How you goin' to tell me to do somethin' you yourself did not do? You know what I'm sayin'? And so, I really just might listen to 'em, absorb the knowledge, then I might just (after prompting from another student:) go the wrong way or somethin'.

Anthrop: OK. So here it seems uh, your uncles were not really making it on their own. It's a good example of people who are not good role models. Therefore, if he talks to you, it doesn't have much effect because you see through them.

Male student (quietly): Right.

Anthrop: That he's not living that way of life. Like the preacher, you know, who tells you what to do but does something else himself.

Male Student (quietly): Right.

In some working-class families, children preferred to listen to their peers rather than to their parents because their parents did not understand contemporary teenage problems. One female student used herself as an example:

Female Student 1:	Um, I want to make a comment about what Mallisa and somebody else said … I don't relate to my mother. She tries to relate to me, [but] like Mallisa says, [it] goes in one ear and out the other. And I do exactly the opposite. I find myself copying off my cousins, because they're around my age, and I find them to be my best friend. Because, you know, they went through all the stuff that I'm going through. And they tell me what I should do since they've been in that predicament. They tell me, what I should do, and what not to do. My mother, … I'm just afraid to talk to her, because she can get so hysterical sometimes. And my father, he just get loud. And I don't want to hear any stuff like that. He's *around* (emphasizes word), but he's just not really there. He's there physically, but he just not there for, you know, to like, help me or whatever.
Female Student 2:	(quietly): He's not there mentally.
Female Student 1:	Huh?
Female Student 2:	Mentally, he's not like really with you.
Female Student 1:	Yeah. He's not mentally there for me. I mean, I love him. I love my parents, but they just, they just not there.

It is significant that students were aware that some Black males became successful in life without living with their fathers in the home. They also knew of some males who became successful in spite of living with a father whom they rejected as role model. In these two situations the male children decided and made concerted efforts to be different from their fathers. A female student speculated on how such individuals responded to their situations and thereby became successful:

I know some males that come out perfectly fine without having that male role model in the home. The reason is because their father may have died when they were little, or whatever … or … it maybe their father left their mother. They don't want to end up like him maybe out in the street somewhere. So they say [to themselves], "You know, I have to achieve. I have to strive, because I don't want to be like my father. He was no good. He wasn't there when I was little, or whatever the case may be. So, I don't want to end up like him. That kind of thinking can make, I mean, that can turn somebody's whole life around [That can help a person become successful, whether the father is there or not].

How did working-class boys think they would perform as role models for their children? Some of them promised to be a better role model for their own children than their fathers had been for them. In the words of one student who did not have a father:

> I'm seein' what went through like with me. Not having a father I'm going to be a father to my child, if I do have one. 'Cause like, you know, if you don't have no father, you don't have nobody to look up to. And then you don't have like my mother, she tell me stuff, but I don't be goin' through one ear and out the other. (Laughter began to well up in students but was held back.) I'm serious. I mean like, she try to preach to me and stuff like that, but I don't even want to listen.

Middle-Class Families.   Inquiry into role models in professional or middle-class families was prompted by students' remarks that some students from such families did not necessarily look up to their parents as role models. Instead, they chose athletes, entertainers, and drug dealers as their role models. During the discussion, the students implied that Black professionals in general were not particularly effective role models both for their own children or for other Black youth. They attributed this to the media, which have made athletes, entertainers, drug dealers and their success, wealth, or reputations more visible than Black doctors, lawyers, and other professionals. This invisibility of Black professionals in the media was discussed at length by students in response to the anthropologist's questions.

> *Anthrop:*   What about those kids who live with two parents who are successful as lawyers, doctors, real estate agents and so on? Why is it that some of them still don't do well? Or, [is it] as somebody said, that they are only telling you, "Do as I did,"? or "Do better than I did?" and so forth? Um, in fact, I thought that Shaker would be a place where students would see a link between educational effort and professional status. Then, why is it that the next generation is not making the same effort? Why is it that the next generation you are not heading toward the same direction of professional status? (Calling on a student) Yes.

> *Male student:*   OK. (mumbling, light laugher). Um, you spoke about middle-class parents, and some people [who] are not being, are not successful in their academics when they have role models. But you must understand that you don't just learn only from your parents. As I, as I said before, you learn from television, news magazines, uh newspapers, books, everything. Everything

takes an equal factor. Your peers. Everything has an equal factor. Obviously, there are some who do have a wonderful home, a wonderful environment where they reside to grow up in. But there is some other aspect of their life that has failed. Some other aspect in their environment. This happened (a) [even] when they have good parents, good role model parents. Yet they're picking the wrong friends. (b) Some have good parents and they be picking the right friends. But then, they're watching bad, they're watching bad, violent um shows on television. It's, one of those factors that is not helping them to succeed.

Anthrop: I think it's a dilemma that I'm going to take up with parents this afternoon, because uh, there are some minority groups where parents have more effective influence on their children than it seems among Blacks. Um, sure enough, you can have bad friends, or watch television, where your parents can control or make sure that your friends are the right friends, and that you watch certain kinds of, programs on television. I know families where they control what their children watch. And if there are programs coming at prime time for their children's homework, they tape them. They tape the programs. Uh, but it seems that among Blacks, the relationship between parents and children seem to be of a different kind.

The Community. The Black community was also a source of role models, especially for students who lacked them in the home. One female student explained how it worked:

Female student: Well, I was gonna say um what was related to what we were just talking about. I was gonna say that I don't think it's just the um, the immediate family that counts as far as the male role models is concerned. If like you have neighbors and stuff that are involved. Because my dad is like an active role model in my life, but also I look up to my next door neighbor, Mr. Washington. I look up to him (some laughter from a female in audience), and I go over there and like listen to his stories and stuff … Sometimes you need somebody else who's not just your parents. I mean other people. Other accessible role models in the community to look up to. I don't think it's just the fact that parents aren't involved. I think it's the fact that communities aren't as involved as they used to be according to what Mr. Washington and also what my parents have told me.

Anthrop: OK. So the community has something to do with it. (Calling on a student) Yes.

Society at Large.   Athletes, entertainers, and celebrities were influential role models in the lives of Shaker students. Some students chose rappers from Cleveland ghettoes as their role models over their professional parents (lawyers, doctors, teachers, etc). Looking up to athletes, entertainers, and celebrities had two adverse effects on students' academic striving. One effect was that emulating these "heroes" diverted students' attention and effort from academic work. The other effect was that students did not have the opportunity to observe how athletes and entertainers actually worked to achieve their success or fame; that is, they did not observe the process through which they had succeeded and gotten to where they were as portrayed in the media. Most of what students knew about "their heroes" was their success, wealth, and fame. The following student spoke to this missing piece of knowledge. As she put it, athletes were not good role models for academic success, but the media played them up. The media also did another thing wrong: They did not show the work the celebrities had had to do to succeed.

> I think um, going back to the role model point,.... I think athletes are, can be, uh serve as examples [of some other type of achievement], but not as role models for school success. And I think role models have to come, um, or have to be somebody that you see in ... that you see in their everyday life, um, not just you see on TV every week or when they show up to a game or something. So that you see the intricacies of ... every day. And they have to be someone close to the person that looks up to them, and not just see them when they're performing. But, you know, sort of you see like the behind the scenes, um atmosphere. And I think that's probably the most important, and one of the most important item. In that way [students] can sort of uh relate to what the hard work and everything that goes into it making the celebrities successful. And [they can] learn from the role models as opposed to just seeing examples.

The School: MAC Scholars.   MAC scholars were generally admired as good role models. One student spoke passionately about the importance of these students as role models for other students:

> Well, I think [MAC] is the answer. But I wanted to say that it is important that, um, in regards to the role models and the peers and what we can do to better the situation. I saw the video [of a MAC ceremony] that they presented, and it was wonderful. It almost brought me to tears. I think that it's a really important thing for everyone to see [the video], because here are (sic) a group of young Black gentlemen who are doing really well, and [are serving] as role models for younger kids. [They] are well respected by their peers, and

they're having a positive influence on not only the African Americans in the school, but on everyone. I think that it's really important that Black, White, you know, old people, young people, in Shaker and without, to see the video and hear from these students. We've all heard of MAC, MAC, MAC, but I didn't really know exactly what it was [until I saw the video]. I think that it's really an important, um institution that ... if everyone learns about it, we will thus be enabled to be more supportive and understanding about what goes on. And I'm glad that the MAC sisters are being started also.

Both students and adults attending MAC meetings also served as role models. They were sometimes held up to potential scholars as concrete examples of role models. On one occasion the younger scholars were asked why education was important. They cited learning, getting a job, not being stupid, and not killing people. When they finished, a veteran scholar began to lecture the young scholars about the role of education in building adult leadership skills. He used the adult leader at the meeting as an example. He described various things that the leader had accomplished because of his education. He concluded by telling the scholars that with a good education, they, too, could accomplish the same things.

SCHOOLING AND THE FUTURE: MISSING PERCEPTIONS

In this section we turn to two connections missing in the students' perceptions of their schooling and their future. The missing connections appear to be the result of Black people's historical experience in the opportunity structure.

Schooling and Adult Future

There was a relative lack of an instrumental or pragmatic attitude toward schooling among the students from low-income and affluent families. By lack of an instrumental attitude toward schooling we mean that students did not view their present schooling as a preparation for their future participation in the adult opportunity structure. That participation would include getting and keeping a desirable job that paid well. Rarely did students make the connection between their school career and what they wanted to be in adult life. This missing link was discussed at length during one of our meetings with high school students, because both the students and the researchers thought that the absence of this connection provided an important clue to the students' academic disengagement.

The students discussed various factors that contributed the lack of connection and, hence, to the academic disengagement. Among them was historical lack of equal job opportunity after school graduation. Some students noted that employment opportunities had improved because of affirmative action. What had not changed was that some students were not making the appropriate connection between their academic performance at Shaker and their adult future. For some students their family background prevented them from making the connection. These were students from poor families in which they saw no tangible benefits of education in their parents' jobs or life situations. Others, especially those from middle-class and professional families, did not make the connection because they believed that they would "make it" with or without doing well in school because they came from affluent families. These students apparently had not considered that their own parents had achieved their middle-class or professional status because of good education and hard work. If they wanted to achieve the middle-class or professional status of their parents, then they would have to succeed in school and work hard. We next reproduce a large part of our discussion with the students on this point because it provides a clue as to why even middle-class Black students in this school district are neither academically engaged nor performing at their expected level. The following male student stated the problem quite nicely:

Anthrop: (to a male student): OK. Let's begin with the earlier statement you made that some people are not doing well in school, right? Uh, what are the reasons?

Male
student: OK, um, well, I think the first reason is that um, many Black students don't understand the importance of succeeding in school. They don't understand that [school success] is the basis for the rest of your life. [Because of] lack of [Black people's] experience, they don't know the importance of succeeding in school.

Anthrop: You know, that almost throws my theory out of the window, because (student laughter, which the researcher joins) I'm told, and I'm impressed that Shaker is a very middle-or-upper class community. Somebody complained that we couldn't find a place to park our car this morning, because most of you drive to school. Where I come from students walked for miles to get to school. Hey! What a luxury you have. So, if you come from such an affluent background, how can you say that the kids don't know what getting a good education means? Okay, let him continue.

Male   Okay, well, um, (a) I think because we're kids, we have a hard
Student: time sometimes to grasp those realities. That's the first prob-
               lem, because of our lack of experience. And um, sometimes,
               uh, in some situations (b), our parents are of, most of us are of
               the upper middle class. We, we seem to think [it is] another re-
               ality from here. Um, we seem to think that whatever we do, we
               can just, we'll be just as good as our parents, or better.... So—

Anthrop: You mean without good education?

Male   Excuse me?
Student:

Anthrop: You mean without good education?

Male   Yeah. That's the, that's what I mean; some of us ... are saying
Student: that. Some of us don't. And that's just one of them, um; that's
               one of the perceptions of being upper, upper middle class. And
               that ... even if you don't do, whatever, to just get by, you're do-
               ing just as well as your parents, or you'll be better.

Anthrop: That's new to me. (Calling on a student): OK. Go ahead.

Female   I think I agree with what he's saying. I think a lot of minority
Student: students in this school that I have come across, you might say,
               don't realize how important it is to get a good education. And
               what I mean by that is that they don't know that's what you
               need to do anything in your life. I also think there's lack of mo-
               tivation— it's personal thing, too, where you have to be moti-
               vated. You have to have some motivation and things like that.
               And a lot of students don't have that. And I think that might
               also be a problem.

To reiterate, students from affluent families, like those from poor families, did not make the connection between their present schooling and
their future. Students from affluent families did not imagine that things
would be different for them as adults than they were for them as children.
Some naively assumed that regardless of how they did in school they
would end up in or inherit the socioeconomic status as their parents. This
apparent assumption can be seen in the following segment of the dialogue
between the anthropologist and the students.

Anthrop:	OK.
Female Student:	Well, I think it's kinda like, most of the time you think it 's just like whatever your parents have, it's almost like a given. Like they think (imitating a dull male voice:), "Oh, well, I'm one of those people who will make it all right. I'm gonna go to college. You know, I'm goin' out there," and all that. Duh, duh, duh, duh, duh. And if I don't like it, it's, ok." So definitely, you don't think about where I'll [go]; [you don't think], "What if I grow up and I'm not gonna be as wealthy as my parents, and my kids are not gonna be as lucky as I am.? They are not gonna grow up the same way I did." You think it's almost like the way I grew up, it's gonna exactly be for them. That's the way my life gonna go. The same way I grew up." This is the way students from affluent families are thinking.
Anthrop:	But, do they know why their parents have the jobs they have? The positions they hold? The role of education? That's what I'm trying to get at. (Calling on a student:) Yes.
Male Student:	I think, I think that's where we're lacking. I just don't think that [students] question it. Some have heard their parents say, "We had, you know, [to do] this and this, so we could get here." But a lot of students, think that they their parents just did it. They take it for granted. They don't think of school and their future, towards [getting] ahead … project ahead and [how] you get there. They don't plan ahead with a goal in their mind. I really believe some of us do plan, but some of us do think that way [i.e.; they don't plan]. And my answer to your question is that the reason, why we don't [plan, make the connection], and we don't know how education helped our parents get their positions is because of the way we're thinking.
Anthrop:	Okay, let me tell you one incident that happened to a friend of mine, and then you think about your parents in relation to your future. My friend is a stockbroker who makes a lot of money. His son wanted to be a garbage truck driver. You know one of those trucks that come to collect garbage in your yards. Kids get excited when they see those trucks. So my friend asked his son the things he wanted in life. The son listed them. Then his father told him how much money he would be making as a garbage truck driver . He asked his son how far would the truck driver's wage go in acquiring the things he wanted in life. From their dialogue the son realized that being a garbage truck driver was not enough. So, if you want all these things you now enjoy in your affluent families, what do your parents tell you

> about how you can get them? I want to know the kind of communication that goes on between you and your parents that makes you feel that you can get what you want without having worked hard for it by getting good education.

Apparently, the students had not had such communications with their parents. The discussion ended with several students saying that they would study more and make better grades by making appropriate connections between their present schooling and their future.

We observed the same lack of connection in a class discussion we referred to earlier at the high school. During that discussion, several students said that they would think about careers "when I grow up." The teacher reminded them again and again that they were already grown up. He told them that in some countries people of their ages were married with children and adult responsibility.

Educational Qualification For Jobs

The other missing connection was the idea that certain jobs or professions have their own educational requirements, some of which start with courses at the precollege level. For example, students aspiring to become engineers need an appropriate math background from high school. Students wanting to become medical doctors should start developing their science knowledge and skills in the high school. Many Black students in Shaker Heights did not have an idea of the type of courses or education they should get at the present phase of their schooling to prepare them for further education leading to the careers of their choice. Indeed, some students who wanted to go to college did not know how their present school behavior and performance affected their chances of going to college.

Course Sequence for Higher Education and Future Social Mobility

On a number of occasions students explained that participation in academic enrichment classes at the upper elementary school was a good background for honor and AP classes at the middle and high schools. We do not know if many Black students knew this but avoided honors and AP classes because they did not want to do the amount of work required in these classes, as some reported. On the other hand, it was likely that some students did not take the honors and AP courses at the middle school or high school because they missed the appropriate background courses for doing well when these courses are taken at the level they are offered. As we discuss in chapter 11, many Black parents did not seem to know the requirements for taking the honors and AP classes.

9

Collective Identity, Culture, and Language

The study of collective identity is important for understanding the issues of cultural and language differences in minority education. Without this concept, it is difficult to explain why minority groups whose cultures and languages are more different from mainstream White American culture and language are better able to overcome the cultural and language differences and perform better academically in public school than minorities whose cultures and languages are less different from mainstream White American culture (Ogbu, 1995a, 1995b). As we suggested in discussing the framework for this study, the reason for this is the type of collective identity associated with the cultural and language frames of reference of the minorities. The collective identity and the cultural and language frames of reference are properties of the minority group qua minority group. Children, of course, acquire them as they grow up and bring them to the public school or other settings. At school these attributes may be modified by school-related and other factors. It is important to bear in mind that one does not grasp the full nature of the collective identity or the cultural and language frames of reference of a minority group by studying them only at school among students. In this chapter we describe the collective identity and cultural and language frames of reference within the Black community of Shaker Heights. In the next chapter we examine their implications for academic disengagement.

WHAT IS COLLECTIVE IDENTITY, AND WHY DOES IT MATTER?

For members of a minority group, *collective identity* is a sense of who they are, the "we" feeling or feeling of belonging. Collective identity is a product of the group's history and experiences. It gives individual members a sense of self-worth. For an involuntary minority group such as Black Americans, collective identity is more or less oppositional, because it was forged under oppression. In education, oppositional collective identity is associated with affective dissonance in the domains of curriculum (culture), language (standard English), and relationships with teachers and the school system. Involuntary or nonimmigrant minorities perceive and experience the school culture or curriculum and language as an imposition by the dominant group and its schools. The minorities feel that they have to endure the imposition because they have no choice. In addition, involuntary minorities often experience the school curriculum and language negatively, because the dominant group uses both the curriculum and language to communicate to the minorities the message that they are inferior. As several authors have shown, the U.S. school textbooks, curricula materials, and language are replete with such messages (see Carpenter, 1941; E. M. Clark, 1971; Fell, 1990; Haynes, 1985; Holt, 1972). For these reasons, it is difficult for involuntary minorities to separate the issue of the school curriculum and language from that of their overall and historical relationship with White Americans. Under this circumstance, they view with suspicion what is taught, and they question the motives of White Americans who control their education. They experience their relationship with teachers and other school authorities as one of indifference, of "not caring." The way minorities perceive and experience schooling is affected by the way they respond to schooling.

In Shaker Heights schools, and elsewhere in the United States, the interlocking issues of collective identity, culture, and language are better understood from a comparative perspective—that is, the responses of Blacks as a nonimmigrant minority group are compared with those of an immigrant minority group. As an involuntary minority Black Americans developed their collective identity under oppression and in opposition to the sense of the collective identity of their White oppressors. In school this oppositional collective identity is characterized by affective dissonance in the two ways indicated earlier: (a) perception of school culture or curriculum and school language as an imposition, and (b) their negative experience with the school curriculum and language because Whites use them to communicate the message that Black people are inferior to White people. For these reasons, the minorities have difficulty separating the affective meaning of displacing their identity, culture, and language and the instrumental value of acquiring knowledge, skills, and credentials for future adult positions in the opportunity structure. The minorities are, therefore, suspicious of the motive behind what public schools teach and of the implementation of the curriculum and language requirements by teachers. Given the origin of their minority status, these minorities lack the pragmatic trust of immigrant minorities who evaluate the school curriculum and language in terms of their instrumental value and who consider teachers and school authorities experts in useful knowledge, skills, and language for school success and later success in the job market.

Because they interpret school curriculum, language, and even the classroom pedagogy as White and as impositions, minorities may consciously or unconsciously resist them. Some label and reject as "White" certain pedagogical beliefs and behaviors that are conducive to making good grades. As we discuss in chapter 10, on peer pressures, some Black students at Shaker High accused other Blacks of "acting White" because they behaved in "White ways," such as speaking standard English, enrolling in honors or AP classes, "hanging around too many White students," or making good grades (a prime indicator of behaving like White people), even though the students accused of doing these things did not necessarily reject their Black identity.

In this chapter we present data showing the existence of Blacks' collective identity, provide examples of how Shaker Heights Blacks expressed their collective identity, and examine the role of collective identity in Blacks' interpretation of the cultural and language differences between Blacks and Whites. We examine the influence of collective identity on schooling in chapter 10.

BLACK COLLECTIVE IDENTITY
IN SHAKER HEIGHTS

Blacks as a Category With "We Feeling"

Blacks were easily identified as a separate and named category in Shaker Heights. The most important identification symbols were skin color and membership recruitment. Membership was by birth; even biracial children affiliated with Blacks, as some students pointed out. Furthermore, during a community discussion of the group membership everyone agreed that children born to a Black couple were Black and children born to a mixed or biracial couple were also Black. Biracial children were identified as Black because society automatically classified them as Black. Someone explained that, unlike California, there was a "one-drop rule" in Ohio. "One drop rule" was the rule that children born to Black/White parents had to be labeled Black and had to affiliate with Blacks. This rule prevailed until the United States Census of 2000 when biracial children were officially allowed to chose their racial category, Black or White. (Rockquemore & Brunsma, 2002.) Another person jokingly added, "We [i.e., the Black community] don't exclude anyone. We take everyone."

Expressions of the Sense of We Feeling

Regardless of how an individual was situated in terms of residence, church membership, friendship network, and professional status, he or she shared with other Blacks a sense of "we feeling." Adults as well as students identified themselves as Black Americans. Consider the case of one student we interviewed. She was a successful student and talked about her family background, lifestyle, and priorities. She criticized Black students for cutting classes and other misbehaviors. When asked about White students, however, she said she did not know how to respond, "because I am Black, not White." She was conscious of and very clear about of her identity as an African American, even though she distinguished herself from other African Americans.

There were several ways Blacks in Shaker Heights expressed their sense of the "we feeling" or collective identity. Some expressed their Black identity by shopping in Black-owned stores, some by their choice of dress. Some parents wanted their children to have only Black dolls or dolls that reflected Black identity. One informant was unhappy that her mother-in-law had bought a White, blond, and blue-eyed doll for her daughter. To make matters worse, her daughter was very fond of the doll. The informant's solution to her dilemma was to let her daughter play with the doll at home but not in public. She would let her daughter take the doll when they went out but would insist or convince her to leave the doll in the car to "take a nap" or because the doll was "too tired."

Shaker Blacks also expressed their collective identity in their collective feeling about representation in the White news media. Both adults and students believed that Blacks were misrepresented in the media. They complained that Whites often highlighted and generalized to all Blacks an offense committed by one Black person.

Blacks had a different cultural model of social reality; that is, they interpreted the same event or phenomenon differently than Whites. Their interpretation of Princess Diana's death serves as an example. It was evident that the people at a middle-class social gathering used the discussion of her death to express their collective oppositional identity. To begin, the participants saw "something more" in Princess Diana's death than the reasons given in the White media. (We did not interview Whites about their explanation of Princess Diana's death, but we assume that if we did they would not say that she was killed in a car accident to avoid having a child with a non-White man.) In their version of the account of Princess Diana's death, Shaker Heights Blacks believed that she was killed because she was dating "a brother," an Egyptian. The latter was definitely not White but a Black brother. When asked if Egyptians are really Black, they answered unequivocally that Egyptians are Black. It was their view that, Diana was the future queen of England and was a potential mother of a Black man's children. To prevent that from happening, to avoid racial mixing in a White royal lineage, White people plotted to kill her.

Another expression of their collective identity showed up in Shaker Blacks' feelings about the school district's plans for events in Black History Month and the location of the classroom where a Black history course was being taught. They wanted the events and materials for the history month to reflect Black identity and culture. They complained that a course on Black history (taught by a Black teacher) was in a room in the basement. They felt that locating the class in the basement reflected the school district's lack of regard for Black dignity. They were unaware that the teacher preferred the basement room for his own purposes. The complaints of the community were examples of how Blacks view things differently from Whites. There were also differences between Black and White students that showed up in their participation in the Black history course. Most of the students in this course were Black and were usually more eager than their White classmates to express their opinions and feelings about events in Black history. Their willingness to express themselves among other Blacks was a good indication of their collective identity.

Quest for Recognition

Black students pressured the schools, especially the high school, to give their cultural identity more recognition. An incident in the Department of Theater illustrates this. There was apparently a misunderstanding between a theater teacher and Black students over play production. It appeared that the theater department had not made a significant effort to produce plays based on Black experience and had not encouraged the participation of Black students. For these reasons Black students put up their own production reflecting Black American experience. It was described as very well attended and appreciated by Black students and their families. Our informant concluded with the comment that Shaker High should realize that it was "OK to be Black and it was OK to be White."

Even Blacks' reaction to the *Shakerite* article on Black academic performance was an expression of their collective identity. Black adults and students alike agreed that all the information in the Shakerite article was correct but complained that the publication more or less intended to make Blacks look bad.

COLLECTIVE IDENTITY AND CULTURAL FRAMES OF REFERENCE

The Black Way Versus The White Way

We asked students if there were cultural differences between Blacks and Whites. What did they consider White, rather than Black, cultural behavior? What did they consider "White" in the behavior of other Black students? Students at all school levels reported that Black and White students behaved differently. Lower elementary school students were less sure that there were cultural differences and less explicit in identifying the differences; however, some students at the upper elementary school were more explicit. As can be seen from the following interview excerpt, students at this level mentioned speaking standard English and talking intelligently as examples of White behaviors.

Anthrop: OK, like have you ever heard the term "acting White"?

Student: (Laughs affirmatively).

Anthrop: What types of things, ... what does that mean?

Student: What, acting White?

Anthrop: Acting White.

Student: Oh, well, some—I say, sometimes I meant he'll be like talking all proper and intelligent. And its just, people just talk about 'em. I don't really know.

Middle school students defined "acting White" as behaving in a way that other Black students did not consider normal. They criticized Blacks who did not behave "normally"; that is, those who behaved like White students. They called them "oreos" (i.e., Black on the outside, White on the inside). The "White behavior" most often singled out for criticism was "talking proper." We will discuss the language issue in the next section.

Black students at the high school were accused of acting White for dressing like White students, having mostly White friends, participating in sports and extracurricular activities traditionally dominated by White students and teenagers, and for talking properly.

Some parents reported that their children were criticized because of the way they dressed and their general appearance. One man reported that his daughter was accused of acting White because she wore her hair naturally and had pink hair streaks. Apparently the reason his daughter wore her hair naturally was that she often went swimming. By wearing her hair that way she did not have to worry about the weather, but to her Black peers this was acting White because, like White people, she did not have to worry about processing her hair. She was also criticized because of the way she dressed and for talking "proper." Her father ended with a remark that Black students at Shaker were inverting the meaning of Black hairstyle. Not long ago, Blacks used to wear their hair natural, but now they processed it. This meant that they were changing the definition of Blackness. Another parent said that his daughter was also accused of acting White because she played tennis and went skiing, activities generally considered "White." His daughter, who was present, said that she was criticized more for going skiing than for playing tennis. Her Black peers considered skiing "more White" than tennis.

On several occasions there were discussions of racial differences in sports at the high school. "White sports" included golf, lacrosse and, as already mentioned, tennis and skiing. Not everyone agreed that it was bad for Blacks to play White sports. However, those who played the White sports were criticized and did not appreciate the criticism.

Anthrop: Mh-hmm. Now those sports that are typically White or considered white, um, what is the reaction from other Blacks when some Blacks do take part in those sports?

Student 1: Um, it's a shock. It's a shock. But um, I don't think it's so much of a shock whereas they have to put you down or try to bring you down in some way ... Um, because I'm kind of on the golf team and a lot of people were shocked about that. But it wasn't that big of a deal.

Anthrop: For you in particular, or for all of the Blacks that might be doing that sort of thing? Is there any criticism about … ?

Student 1: Well, you know at first there's some criticism. They'll say, "Why, why are you doing that?" You know, but they do look up to you for that … breaking some sort of barrier or what not … So its, it's a shock but it's a good shock.

Student 2: It's like a couple of Black people on the lacrosse team. It's not as, its not as much as like two or three [i.e., there were not more than two or three Blacks].

Anthrop: Now what happens when some Blacks go into those sports that are typically White?

Student 2: Then you get, like I did …

Anthrop: I mean, is there any, did anyone give you any kind of hard time?

Student 2: Yeah, they think I'm White 'cause I play that sport.

Anthrop: Who, the Whites or the Blacks?

Student 2: The Blacks, I mean, cause I think Whites will accept you more than Blacks will …

Anthrop: OK … you mean doing things that aren't typically …

Student 2: Yeah.

Anthrop: OK.

Student 2: 'Cause like if a White person plays basketball, then their friends won't be like, 'Oh, oh, you're acting like a Negro now … a Black person.'

Anthrop: Mh-hmm.

Student 2: But, if you play, 'cause I know when I started playin' lacrosse in the eighth grade, we had to wear our jerseys for game day. And I didn't wanna wear my jersey 'cause it had lacrosse on it and everybody was makin' fun of it. But then after awhile I just got [used to the criticisms] and I didn't care anymore. I just wore it, cause that's the sport I play.

Hanging out with "too many White friends" was another behavior of which Black students disapproved. It was considered bad by 7 of the 13 high school students we interviewed. Two students explained the criticism this way:

Anthrop: Would you say that acting White is along the same line as being an oreo?

Student 1:   Yeah.

Anthrop: OK, so what behaviors can someone do to be considered acting White or being an oreo?

Student 1:   I guess its uh, company that you keep or whatever. It depends, you know, on the company that you keep ... and it is based on the way you act towards everyone.

Anthrop: OK, do a lot of Blacks and Whites here at the high school, do they have friends of different cultures than themselves, or do they pretty much hang out with their own races?

Student 1:   I mean yeah. They have friends of different cultures.

Anthrop: OK, so the Blacks that have friends of different cultures, because the company that they keep, is that why they are considered acting White?

Student 1:   Nah, it's like, all right you have like people that are, you know, friends, but its like, OK, like say if I was to have friends that's Black and White you know, and we hang together, it's like some that are Black but prefer only to hang with White people and vice versa.

Student 2:   (responding to the same question): Um, I think as we've gotten older, we don't say it as much, like the term oreo and that kind of stuff ...

Anthrop: Uh-huh ...

Student 2:   Like in the fifth and sixth grade[s], that kind of stuff, and not, I really haven't heard it like that, like for the longest. But I do still hear comments like directed towards me about ... the number of White friends I have, like a lot of, um, a couple of Black kids I come to school with, I've heard like, one said like 'Well, I don't know any White kids, at least not as many as you do." Something like that. Its just ... its kind of played out in different ways now.

COLLECTIVE IDENTITY AND DIALECT FRAME OF REFERENCE

Speech Community and Bidialecticalism

A *speech community* is a population that shares both a common language or dialect and a common theory of speaking or cultural rules for conducting and interpreting speech acts (Hymes, 1967). A person is considered a competent speaker in a speech community if he or she knows both the language per se (i.e., phonology, morphology, syntax or grammar, and vocabulary) and the cultural rules for using that language, such as when to speak (speech situations), which speech event is appropriate (e.g., conversation, lecture, or debate), which communicative code (verbal or finger-pointing), and what style to use (e.g., confrontational or conciliatory, etc., Hymes, 1971). A child grows up in a speech community to become a competent in that community by learning both the language per se and the cultural rules of speaking it (Hymes, 1967, 1971).

A speech can have more than one language or dialect, as in the case of the Black community in Shaker Heights. In such a community, each language or dialect has its own cultural rules for speaking it; that is, there are separate cultural rules governing speaking (a) Black English, and (b) standard or proper English within the Black speech community. During their language socialization, Black children learn Black English and the cultural rules for using it as their mother tongue; they also learn standard English and the rules in their speech community for using it. The rules for using standard English in the Black speech community are not necessarily the same rules for using it in White speech community or at school.

The relationship between coexisting languages or dialects, such as between Black English and standard English, may be characterized by *diglossia*, as in Shaker Heights; that is, each dialect has a separate function or is used for different purposes (Ferguson, 1959). People in the speech community know this and accept the separate functions. In the Shaker Heights Black American speech community, standard or "proper" English is used for education, jobs, and communication with "outsiders."

Black English, or the mother tongue, is used for everyday life in the family and community (Fishman, 1967; Ogbu, 1999). Sometimes the diglossia relationship between the coexisting languages or dialects is more or less oppositional or equivocal. When this is the case members of the minority community are ambivalent or even oppositional toward learning and using the language of the dominant group (e.g., proper English), even though they know that it is important to learn it for education, jobs, and communication with outsiders. The point we want to emphasize is that Black students in Shaker Heights schools came from a bidialectical speech community in which Black English their mother tongue; at the same time, they accepted standard English as the language for education and jobs.

The Bidialectal Black Speech Community

We found evidence both in the community and at school that the Black speech community in Shaker Heights is bidialectal or bilingual. Within the community, speech style was an important identity marker. We were told on several occasions that Blacks and Whites definitely talked differently. In a social gathering we attended of a dozen or so middle-class Black professional residents, their communication was often done in Black speech style. People were conscious of the fact that they were expressing their collective identity in their speech behavior.

At one point during this social gathering, someone jokingly observed "How we are all talking at once [rather than taking turns like White people], and talking kind of loud. Yet, we all hear [i.e., understand] each other." Another person responded, "This is part of the comfort level that Blacks folks enjoy with one another." A third speaker began to elaborate on how Black people talked. He added that Black people learned to switch between the way they talked and the way White people talked. When Blacks were among themselves they were relaxed in their manner of speech and talked Black. But when they were around White people they tried to pay very close attention to the way they talked because they knew that White people were judging them by their speech. The speaker went on to say that *ebonics*, or Black English, was a separate dialect and gave examples of how Blacks created the vocabulary in ebonics. Some words, according to him, dated back to Elizabethan English.

Cultural Rules for Using Black English and Standard English

Rules for Black English.   Like the adults, Black students used Black English among themselves, in the family and community. Almost all the students we interviewed formally, from elementary through high school, answered our questions in Black English. Most Black students in discussion groups as well as in informal discussions used Black English. Students participating in tutoring sessions in the community and in some programs at school often talked with one another in Black English. It was not uncommon on those occasions for anyone who spoke proper English to be noticed. They were self-reports by students who were criticized by other Black students for "talking proper." Some Black parents also reported that their children were teased by other Black students for talking proper English.

Rules for Standard English.   Most students understood that they should speak proper English at school, especially during lessons. This was indeed the case in our classroom observations. In other words, students followed the rule of using Black English in the community and among themselves and proper English at school. The following students explained this the rule of code-switching:

Anthrop: Do you think that when Black people come to school, um, as some people say, there's a problem with language differences and that Black people don't learn to use standard English? Or, is it that they don't want to use standard English?

Student 1:   Um, like when you're talking to your friends, like what's the purpose, you don't talk proper. If you was on a job interview or talking like [to] a teacher, then you talk proper.

Student 2:   (responding to the same question): You know I talk different when I make a speech in class or in front of a group of people, than when I'm with my friends. You know it's natural.

Other evidence that Shaker Heights Black students recognized the separate function of standard English came from their performance in the state's reading proficiency tests. They did less well on these tests than White Shaker students, but they did better than other Blacks in the state. Even more significant, they did better than White students in the state outside Shaker. In 1995–1996, the passing rate of fourth-grade Blacks in Shaker

Heights was 90% in the state reading proficiency test, compared to 60% of fourth-grade Blacks in the rest of the state and 86% of the White fourth graders outside Shaker Heights. However, in the sixth grade Shaker Heights Blacks had a passing rate of 70%; to Whites in the state outside Shaker Heights had a passing rate of 78%. From that point on, Shaker Heights Blacks, while maintaining their lead over other Blacks in the state, consistently performed lower than their White counterparts in side and outside Shaker Heights (Whittington, 1996, pp. 4–10).

We are not suggesting that Black students in Shaker Heights consistently spoke standard English in the classroom or other settings where they were expected to speak it. For example, it was reported that at a Minority Achievement Committee ceremony one student talked in a manner that raised some concern. A student "who spoke perfect standard English" suggested to the organizers of the ceremony that the student should be allowed to use Black English in order to establish rapport with the younger and potential scholars. What needs to be stressed is that Black students generally recognized standard English as important, that they understand was required at school, and that they tried to follow the rule of its usage.

When Rules Are Broken

Using Black English Out of Place.   Students criticized others who spoke Black English where it was not appropriate to do so. There were two kinds of students who broke the rule and were criticized for using Black English out of place. One group consisted of students who talked in Black dialect and used it in their writing because they were apparently not competent in standard English. The following student explained the situation of such students:

> *Student:*   "I think there are a large number of any Blacks, they've grown up without knowing how to talk proper. I guess you could say it's like that, you know. They don't know standard English. So they're not goin' to talk proper."

The second group of students who broke the rule were transfer students. Some of the transfers came from school districts with less strict rules about English use during lessons. The transfers who spoke Black dialect out of place were teased by other Black students. One transfer student who had not completely learned the rule during our study described how he was teased and made fun of by other Black students.

Student:	It's like, here, you, they probably can speak standard English. But it'll take time [for a transfer like me to get used to it] because like when I first came here, I spoke a lot of ebonics, a very lot. And they used to like make fun of me. But now it's like ...
Anthrop:	Who made fun of you?
Student:	Like people [other Black students], when I ... first came here in my classes.
Anthrop:	The other students?
Student:	Yeah ... And it was like, uh. Now when I go back down where I used to live [Cleveland], they ... talk like the way I [used to talk]. But now when I go back there [my former schoolmates tease me that] I talk like I'm from Shaker.

Speaking standard English out of place.   Talking properly at home and in the community amounted to breaking the cultural rule of standard English and was criticized by some Black people as acting White. Middle school and high school students also criticized those who talked properly among themselves. They often equated talking properly with acting White; to many students, acting White had something to do with how a Black student talked. One student explained this.

Anthrop:	OK, now what about um, how do they get classified as acting White?
Student:	Acting White. Right now if other Black people were in this class, I would be classified right now as acting White.
Anthrop:	What do you mean if other people—you mean in this room?
Student:	Yeah. Right now in this room, if they were to hear me speaking, they would classify me as acting White. I've been classified as acting White for a very long time because I choose not to say "ain't" and "fittin" and "duh." I wasn't raised up, I wasn't raised to speak like that.

Students who used proper English outside the classroom complained that they were subjected to criticism from other Black students. These students knew that they were breaking the rule and found it to be a dilemma. On the one hand, they wanted to talk properly—not because it was White but because it was important for school success. On the other hand, they were criticized by their peers who considered their speech "White" and not "normal."

Opposition to Standard English?

No adult or student said that he or she was opposed to proper English. Opposition to talking properly occurred primarily when it was done out of place. Sometimes, however, students spoke Black English to teachers not because they were opposed to speaking standard English but out of frustration; they felt that they would receive a poor grade in the class even if they spoke proper English. An example was given by the following student:

Anthrop: Is language ever something that prevents students from doing well? Whether not being able to, or not electing to speak standard English in the classroom?

Student: Yes, because there are some guys that I know who would not talk proper in class. And it irritates me because they're bright people, you know, just bright. But they don't do the right thing. They're like, "She's gonna flunk me anyway."

10

Peer Pressures

UNIVERSAL BUT VARIABLE INFLUENCE

Students' peer groups and peer pressures are found in almost every school with adolescents, but their influence on students' academic engagement and performance varies even among students of the same racial or ethnic group. For example, in his study of Hightown Grammar in England, Lacey (1970) found positive peer pressures on academic achievement as well as peer pressures against school success. Willis (1977), also in Britain, found peer pressures among working-class boys against academic success. In that study, some lower class boys preferred manual labor that did not require academic success. The coeds in North Carolina studied by Holland and Eisenhart (1990) developed a peer culture, the goal of which was "to catch a man" or a fiancee, instead of pursuing their initial academic and professional goals. In a personal communication, Elena Yu (August, 1985) reported that among Asian students in Chicago peer pressures promoted academic engagement and success; the students who were more or less ridiculed and ostracized were students who were not doing well academically. Our own ethnographic findings among Chinese students in Oakland, California, support Yu's observation in Chicago. However, some studies of other minorities have found negative pressures toward academic achievement (Fordham & Ogbu, 1986; Kunjufu, 1988; Luster, 1992; Matute-Bianchi, 1986; Petroni, 1970; Petroni & Hirsch, 1972). The point we are stressing is that not all peer pressures are against academic engagement and good school performance. Indeed, as we show later in this chapter, White peer groups in Shaker Heights were not perceived to exert negative peer pressures on White students' academic engagement to the extent that this happened among Black students.

Characteristics of Black Peer Groups

Peer pressures among Black American students are likely to be negative toward academic engagement for two reasons: First, as we noted in the last chapter, Blacks tend to interpret school curriculum and language as White impositions; they also experience the curriculum and language negatively because White Americans have historically used both to communicate to Black people that they are inferior. Some researchers have noted that Black linguistic and behavioral responses appear to be a rejection of what they perceive as White people's attempt to define "White ways" as the "right ways" to talk and behave and "Black ways" as the "wrong ways" (E. M. Clark, 1971; Haynes, 1985; Holt, 1972; Luster, 1992; Nesteby, 1982). From this perspective it seems, for some Blacks, that to accept the White definition of the right way to talk or behave is to accept White judgment that Black language and cultural identity are bad and should be replaced by White language and cultural identity.

Fordham and Ogbu (1986) found that some Black high school students in Washington, D.C., avoided certain attitudes, standard English, and some behaviors because they considered them White. They feared that adopting White ways would be detrimental to their collective racial identity and solidarity. Unfortunately, some of the attitudes and behaviors labeled "White" and avoided by the students were those that enhanced school success.

Other researchers and the media have misinterpreted the Fordham–Ogbu (1986) article to mean that the reason for the academic achievement gap is that Black students refuse to make good grades because making good grades is "acting White" (Ainsworth-Darnell & Downey, 1998; Carter, 1999; Cook & Ludwig, 1998; Ferguson, 1998; Kunjufu, 1988; O'Connor, 1997; M. B. Spencer, Noll, Stoltzfus, & Harpalani, 2001. Some researchers have "challenged" the so-called *Fordham–Ogbu thesis*, using data from various national longitudinal studies (Cook & Ludwig, 1998) or qualitative interviews (Carter, 1999). They usually conclude that they did not find a support for the "thesis." This is not surprising. Fordham and Ogbu did not claim that rejecting certain White attitudes and behaviors was the main reason Black students fail to make good grades or perform like their White peers. As we have indicated in the preceding chapters, there are many other factors that might adversely affect the school performance of Black students. Equally important is that there are many other factors than the fear of acting White that cause peer pressures among Black students. Furthermore, not all peer pressures are directed against making good grades. Before we take up these issues, we compare peer pressures among Black and White students in Shaker Heights from the perspectives of school authorities and Black students.

RACE AND PEER PRESSURES
IN SHAKER HEIGHTS

Peer Group Formation

Peer groups in Shaker Heights were based primarily on race, especially at the middle school and high school. Our observations throughout our field-work confirmed reports by school authorities and students themselves. We began to collect data on peer group pressures and academic disengagement after someone at a meeting with a group of school personnel suggested that peer groups in the school district were based on race and appeared to have different impacts on academic engagement. He then went on to suggest why the formation of Black peer groups in the Black community might have some implications for academic engagement:

> At the high school level, uh, I think one of the most dramatic contrasts that I've noticed over the years here, is the closeness the of the Black peer group. Black guys will talk about "my boys." And Black girls will talk about "my girls." Now that is what I've found relatively nonexistent among White middle class kids. There's not that absolute um, bond. And I think in relation to what you're saying is, unfortunately, I think many of our African American kids learn consciously and unconsciously that they need to have a defense network. I know it's true in the neighborhoods. In … the tough neighborhoods of the city you better have your boys there or you're in trouble. But I'm afraid [this happens] in Shaker as well, due to the unfortunate fact that, uh, we still are not able to see past color.

Black peer groups were described as more cohesive and oriented toward physical self-defense than White peer groups.

Black students had a different explanation of the formation of their peer groups. They said that they formed separate peer groups partly because they did not feel welcomed in White peer groups. They also said that leveling or tracking segregated Blacks and White students, thereby limiting the chances of the two races to interact informally. When a class was mostly White, the White students did not include their few Black classmates in social activities and conversations. As a result, Black students did not feel that they belonged socially. This feeling of a lack of social belonging could be seen in the experiences one elementary school student and a high school student in our discussion of the reluctance of Black students to enroll in honors and advanced placement (AP) classes.

Race, Peer Pressures, and Academic Disengagement

School authorities and Black students agreed that there were racial differences in the influence of peer groups on schoolwork. White peer groups studied together, or at least were not observed to discourage one another from doing their schoolwork. In contrast, doing schoolwork together was not the usual activity for Black peer groups. Someone reported at the meeting with school officials that he had observed this difference over the years:

> Now ... what I do see on a daily basis ... here at the high school is when I walk into school I have to step over kids who are sitting in the hallways studying together. Now those groups are almost invariably (brief pause) White. Uh, ... and if I go into the cafeteria, I'll see a table of kids studying together, and that, unfortunately, is *consistently* (repeated with emphasis) a White phenomena *(sic)*.

Black students also reported that Black and White peer groups had different norms and different degrees of involvement with schoolwork. According to them, Black friends did not study together; instead, some influenced one another to do poorly in school. In contrast, White friends encouraged one another to do well in school. This difference was described during interviews with Black students:

Anthrop: What about um, things like related to school? Do you think that Blacks and Whites put different pressures on each other? Or, do they pressure each other to do well?

Student: I mean its kind of like, I think everybody has that pressure to fit in more or less. And it's like, in the White community it's like that's how you fit in. Most, ... the majority of them do well in school. So it's like if you're gonna fit in [their group] you do well in school too, even if you're not actually saying to yourself, "I'm gonna fit in, I'm gonna do well in school." Like you might not actually think that, but it's kind of what you do.... That's why you know it's like, that's just how it happens. And I think it's the same way in the Black community. It's like you know, you're not doing well in school, but who cares because neither is anybody else you know [doing well]. For the most part, there might be those few Blacks who are doing well in school, but you know, they're an exception.

This student's perceptive analysis of racial differences in peer pressures on school performance was supported by other students at a discussion with high school students. One female participant described White peer pressures as encouraging enrollment in honors and AP classes as well as hard work. She believed that among Whites "all their friends work hard" and all the people around them worked hard. For that reason, "they're gonna work harder." In contrast, most Black students took less difficult skills and college prep classes. In spite of that they still did not make good grades, because they and their friends did not work hard. All their friends were not doing well. "So, they're not gonna do well." Another student, however, reminded the group that "The picture is not so dichotomous." There were some positive peer pressures to do well in school among Black students. Examples of positive peer pressures described for us at interviews included the following:

Anthrop: What about peer pressure, how important is that to how well a student is doing, or how poorly a student is doing?

Student: Um, it depends upon how the ... person was brought up because we all have different um, levels of ... vulnerability to peer pressure ... Um, some people just shrug it off and some people are really affected by it.

Anthrop: Mh-hmm.

Student: But ... I do think it in some way it does have, like you know, the most minute effect on us ... So um, if, you know, you hang around people that are doing well in school, you're gonna have a tendency to do well in school. If you hang around people that are the opposite, you might do bad. So, it does have some sort of effect on us. There's pressure that we can apply upon other people. Then, if you're in the case where you're doing well, and other people aren't doing so well, um, you know, you might [influence them] to bring their grades up. So it does work both ways.

WIDESPREAD NEGATIVE PEER PRESSURES AMONG BLACKS

With few exceptions, peer pressures among middle school and high school students were described as having a negative effect on students' academic striving. This was particularly true of Black males. School authorities often commented on the effects of peer pressures on Black males, and their comments were borne out in our observations in the classroom and other settings.

One day a teacher showed us an essay question he was going to give to his class to find out the extent to which peer pressures affected their school performance. He said that the question was not specifically about Blacks or Black males, but he hoped to learn about them from the essays that Black students would turn in.

The prevalence and negative influence of peer pressures were discussed at several middle school and high school Minority Achievement Committee (MAC) meetings. On one occasion when a teacher asked students what deterred them from doing well in school, the overwhelming response was distractions by the presence of friends and talking with them on the phone. Friends made students forget their homework and shift their priorities from schoolwork to other things. The students said that they understood that schoolwork should come first but that their friends made them reverse their priorities. At another MAC meeting a student emphasized the fact that everybody wanted to do well in school but that they might not want to show this openly because their friends might accuse them of being "nerds." The same speaker advised his fellow scholars "to do it for yourself"—that is, to ignore the distraction from peers and strive to do well in school. The school staff who initially organized the MAC program believed that one reason the program was working was that the scholars "learned to invert the meaning of studious behavior among Black students." The scholars learned to attach positive meaning to academic engagement and success. They came to prefer being on the Honor Roll as a result of hard work than to achieve popularity among their peers for nonacademic activities. The scholars eventually began to feel proud of themselves that they were on the Honor Roll because they worked hard, and when they didn't make the Honor Roll they were openly disappointed. So, for the scholars, working hard to do well became a goal worth pursuing. Eventually, as at the time of our study, MAC scholars also enjoyed popularity because of their academic success.

The negative influence of peer pressures was also discussed in other programs, like *CORE* (Committees on Racial Equality) and the Student Group on Race Relations. During one CORE meeting a teacher talked to the students about how to handle peer pressure. He asked them to think of an instance in which they had been subjected to peer pressure or in which they themselves had pressured others not to do their schoolwork. They then proceeded to suggest things one could do in such a situation.

There were classes where smart Black students did not show their intelligence by raising their hands to answer teachers' questions. Instead, they played dumb, remained silent, and did their classwork. We got several self-reports by students who played dumb during lessons. One high school student who believed that he was smart told us that on more than one occasion he did not show his intelligence in class or do his schoolwork. Sometimes when we observed him during lessons he appeared to know the answer to the teacher's question but made no effort to answer it. Parents also reported negative peer pressures on their children. One father whose daughter was taking mostly AP classes reported that the daughter was criticized because she was with White students most of the school day and befriended them in her classes.

SCHOOL LEVEL AND PEER PRESSURE

As would be expected, peer pressures increased with age or school level. At the elementary schools they were not very noticeable and had limited effects on students' schoolwork. Of the three students who discussed the problem of peer pressure during the interview, one denied that there were racial differences. Another had a positive mutual experience, saying that her friends did their schoolwork together.

> *Anthrop:*   OK. Do you think that there's some Black students that pressure their friends to do well in school?
>
> *Student:*   Mh-hmm, yeah. When they're like good friends, they'll like tell you "come over." And we'll help like do our homework, we'll do our homework and work on it together, cause I have friends that do that.

The third student explained how he handled his peer group so that his schoolwork would not suffer:

> *Anthrop:*   Do you um, have any friends that'll try to pressure you maybe to not do well in school?
>
> *Student:*   Mm-mmm (negative). They know better than that because I mean, I don't listen to them. They can't, I mean they really can't do it.
>
> *Anthrop:*   Do you think that that is ever a problem for some Black students? That sometimes their friends are um, try to get them to

do other things besides maybe do their homework or things like that?

Student: Yeah, cause they'll go out and play. They'll say "come on, let's go play." And then the homework doesn't get done. Or they're in a special class and they'll like do other things, not concentrate and that really. Cause this boy [who] sit next to me in class and does that. And it's irritating.

Elementary school students seemed generally enthusiastic about their classes, and many actively participated during lessons. They also did things to gain teachers' approval. We even found some instances where Black students were competing with one another to do well. An example of the latter was an occasion when four Black girls were doing a group project. One was apparently smarter than the others; she got all the answers to the assignment right. Two others competed with each other to come up with the right answers first. Only the fourth girl appeared content, waiting for others to find the right answers; she then copied them. The three who competed for the right answers covered their papers to prevent the fourth girl from copying them.

We did not come across any elementary school students during the study who were rejected by their friends for doing well in class, but at the high school we found some students who recalled that they had been rejected by their peers at the elementary school because they were good students. One described how she was teased by her classmates when she left her to go to academic enrichment classes.

Anthrop: Do you think that peer pressure is important [in doing well in school]?

Student: I think … there's a lot of negative peer pressure towards … Black students doing well even at the elementary school. I don't know if it's still [so] now. But like, when I was in elementary school, and um younger, like I would leave class to go to the um, [enrichment] class, like high class or whatever …

Anthrop: Mh-hmm.

Student: And um, people used to be like, "Oh, going to her smart class," or whatever. I mean, I got teased a lot.

Those who remembered being teased at the elementary school also reported that students who went to remedial classes also were teased. One was teased in the sixth grade when she left the regular class to go to a remedial reading class. In other words, teasing at the elementary school was directed at both good and poor students.

Increased peer pressures and teasing, as well as their adverse effects on academic engagement and performance, were evident at the middle school. Several middle school students admitted that peer pressure affected their own schoolwork or the schoolwork of other students they knew. Friends sometimes supported one another's academic goals, helped with homework, and competed among themselves to make good grades. For the most part, however, middle school students said that negative peer pressures were pervasive and led to disengagement from schoolwork. Some were able to avoid the peer pressures with the help of their parents. We discuss the role of parents and other strategies for dealing with peer pressures later.

Peer pressures reached their peak in high school. Here they had much greater influence on student enrollment in honors and AP classes and academic performance. Our conclusion is based on formal and informal interviews with students as well as our own observations. Students admitted in interviews that their friends had a lot to do with the classes they chose to take, their attitudes toward school, and their academic performance. The views of the following two students are representative of the high school students:

Anthrop:	What are some of the reasons that students don't do well, why Black students don't do well?
Student 1:	Um, I would say peers, 'cause that has a lot do with um, doing well and doing poorly. A lot of kids are .... After you're with a certain group of friends for a long time, they're afraid to um, not do the behavior that they've been so accustomed to. Like if they really do want to go out and do well, but their friends aren't, they don't wanna make them feel that they're better than them, or stuff like that.
Anthrop:	How important do you think people's friends are to how well they do in school?
Student 2:	I think very important ... Because like if you hang out with people that, you know, get straight As and all this and that, I mean, that's gonna motivate you know. It's gonna help you. I mean it's gonna make you feel like, "Well, they get straight As, I should, you know, apply myself. And, you know, force myself to do good." But like most of them [students] talk probably be about schoolwork and all this stuff, but they don't do as well,

you know. They'll be ready to hang out instead of do homework and stuff like that. So it takes away a lot of your time and
your study time.

It was apparent at the high school that the older the students got the
greater the peer pressures they experienced, and this influence was generally in the negative direction. The problem was minimal at the elementary
school. Middle school and high school students in particular strongly felt
that they had to "fit in." There was a consensus among informants that
Blacks more than Whites believed that they had to conform, to "fit in,"
even when this meant not doing well in school. Although individual students did not usually admit that their own schoolwork suffered, we observed instances to the contrary. Take, for example, the behavior of one
12th grader. When we were looking for students to interview in one class,
he eagerly volunteered. But during the interview he was concerned that
his friends might find out. He spoke quietly and pretended to be disinter-
ested in the interview.

PEER PRESSURES AND ACADEMIC
DISENGAGEMENT

It should be obvious by now that peer pressures had a negative impact on
the academic engagement of Black students. Teachers, counselors, and
students themselves were fully aware of this. One school counselor reported that even at the elementary school "social pressures discouraged
students from doing their schoolwork." Some elementary school students
reported being teased there, but it was at the middle school and high
school that teasing was related to academic engagement and that their impact became noticeable or a serious problem.

Poor academic performance at the middle school and high school was
partly due to the achievement norm of peer groups. It was not merely a
matter of ability, bad teaching, or low teacher expectations leading to academic disengagement. A transfer student who had experienced peer
achievement norms in her former school district believed that White peer
achievement norm at Shaker might be more conducive to school success
than the Black Shaker peer achievement norm.

Um, I think that your friends have a lot … to do with it. When I was in kindergarten and first grade I lived in another community. I didn't know a single
Black person in my school…. I can remember one thing: People were too involved in their schoolwork. I don't even remember if it was because it was a

good school; probably it was a good school. Then when I came back here for a semester, I went to one inner city Cleveland school. I remember all of a sudden being at way top of the charts. All of the sudden [I was] so much smarter, you know, than everybody else. And then I came to Shaker, and all of the sudden it was like in my first school: I was mixed again, but I still liked to do well because I've always remembered my friends doing well, when I lived in my first school district, you know, in the White school. And it's just like you do well, because you see what your friends do, at least when you're younger. And so my friends had always been White, and the White people seemed to always do well. I did well.

TYPES OF PEER PRESSURES AGAINST ACADEMIC ENGAGEMENT

There were two types of peer pressures that adversely affected students' academic engagement. The first type arose from students' interpretation of certain school requirements as acting White; the other pressures were not related to this interpretation.

Peer Pressures Against Acting White

Contrary to what critics think, Black students in Shaker Heights and probably elsewhere did not reject making good grades per se because it entailed acting White, yet they were disengaged from academic work. What these students seemed to reject were certain attitudes and behaviors that they perceived or interpreted as White, but that were conducive to making good grades. The behaviors and attitudes that some Shaker Heights Black students rejected included speaking standard English, enrollment in honors and AP classes, being smart during lessons, and hanging around too many White students. Before high school, most Shaker students did not equate making good grades with acting White, although they criticized other Blacks with White attitudes and behaviors conducive to making good grades. The reasons given for the labeling had little to do with collective identity.

Use of Standard English

Speaking standard English could be seen as requiring Black students to cross dialect boundaries and potentially diminish their dialect identity. Perhaps for this reason some Black students resisted it. This, no doubt, adversely affected their school performance. However, we did not come across many students who did not want to use standard English. As we saw in chapter 9, Shaker Heights students recognized the importance of standard English. Many seemed to follow a definite rule for using it in their schoolwork and with school authorities while speaking their own dialect at home and among friends. Those who did not speak standard English in appropriate settings were criticized by their fellow Black students. This does not mean that Black students did not have language problems that affected their school performance, but they were socialized in the two English dialects, with Black English as their primary dialect or mother tongue. Some parents and grandparents spoke mostly Black English, which was all that the children had heard and learned before they started preschool or regular school. Thus, some might begin school lagging behind their White middle-class peers in standard English. As a result, their late start in standard English would affect their performance, at least for awhile, in courses requiring standard English. Some children needed assistance to learn and use standard English.

The students, like the rest of their community, did not want to give up their dialect in exchange for the standard English that was required for school success, because their dialect was a part of their collective identity. Some solved the language problem by choosing to speak standard English most of the time and in appropriate situations; some chose to switch between their own dialect in the community and standard English at school. Some students did not speak standard English at school because they did not know how to speak it. A few refused to speak standard English because they did not think that speaking it would help them succeed in school.

Enrollment in Honors and AP Classes

It was repeatedly pointed out by students that Blacks avoided taking honors and AP classes because they were "hard" and that most of the students who took them were White. Often the avoidance was due to pressures from other Blacks. As can be imagined, peer pressures to avoid "difficult classes" (i.e., honors and AP classes) resulted in few Blacks taking these classes, while they constituted the majority in the easier classes. The few Black students in the honors and AP classes did not always fit in socially with the majority of White classmates. In addition, Blacks in these classes were often subjected to criticisms by other Black students who accused them of trying to be White. Because students wanted to fit in, they avoided enrolling in the honors and AP classes and avoided striving for high grades. One female high school student explained how this happened:

Oh, OK. Um, what I'm saying is that you got to think about [your friends] influencing you … I think that has a lot to do with it. I mean, if Black kids see a lot of the [other Black] kids not doing well, they can do it. Nobody wants to be an outcast and then like they do label people as acting White. I see one Black student who does do well and, of course, they say they're acting White, because the majority of Black students aren't achieving like that. They see that the White students are the ones doing well, so they label it as acting White. I mean basically, that's what the problem is. You want [to do well but you don't because your friends don't]. But I think it's an individual thing. It's like your personal mentality. You have to, if you want something bad enough, you have to try for it. I mean, you don't [depend on others]. It's basically your own personality. I mean you can't let all these people influence you: and you'll say, "I'm not gonna do this, because everybody else isn't doing it." You have to go for it and get it yourself. You can't worry about what other people are gonna say.

Students' concern about fitting in socially in the honors and AP classes came up several times during formal interviews. The social integration of Black and White students in these classes appeared to be a problem. Although in the classes we observed, Black and White students participated more or less equally in discussing the subject matter and in interaction with the teacher, there was not much interaction between the two groups of students. According to the following students, the social relations between the two groups in the classroom were uncomfortable.

Anthrop:	OK, do you think that there's any effect on kids, um, when they're moved to different classrooms for certain subjects? Like is there any impact on kids that are leaving, and also the kids that are staying?
Student 1:	Definitely, cause in the fifth grade, I was the only one in my [academic enrichment] class. Leaving the room to go to the upper level, class was like, I don't think, no one left to even take a lower level, everyone just stayed in the room. I was the only person. And so, it kind of felt like as the year wore on, like I didn't have the same chemistry with [White classmates] as they all did with each other. So, that's kind of difficult.
Student 2:	I've experienced being in AP classes. Uh, being the second Black person.
Anthrop:	Mh-hmm. And what was that like?
Student 2:	It … was difficult because I could not relate to them as far as socially. Now when it came to dealing with the work that was as-

signed to us, then I could relate. But when we had a lot of social time, I was in the corner to myself.

Anthrop: OK.

Student 2:   And that's basically how it stayed. I didn't, like that. I didn't like not being able to participate in conversations because their topics were different, their situations were different. I didn't hang with them. So, what they decided to do after class and what happened on the weekend, I knew nothing about. So it was, I mean, I did it because I knew that I wanted the challenge and I could do it, but as far as socially, I didn't like it. I didn't like it at all.

On the other side, although Blacks in the easier classes would fit in socially, their work often suffered from the norm of minimum effort and discipline problems.

Being "Smart" During Lessons

That the accusation of acting White was about fitting in and not about making good grades is further illustrated by the treatment of smart students in and outside school. *Smart students* were defined as those who paid attention during lessons, raised their hands to answer questions, always got the answers right, and did their schoolwork and homework. These students experienced pressures against acting White by answering teachers' questions during lessons or behaved in other smart ways in class. We heard from several students who had been subjected to the peer pressures to prevent them from answering questions in class or doing their schoolwork. A good example of this type of pressure was reported by a school counselor who described the experience of a "very bright" student who never volunteered to answer questions during lessons:

School   He was very bright. And I go and evaluate classes all the time.
Counselor: He sat in front of me in one of our science classes. The teacher asked a question. He didn't put his hand up. I heard him mutter under his breath the right answer. I poked him, and said, "Hey. What's going on here? Why don't you put your hand up?" "Oh, duh duh, I don't know, duh duh." The class was over. He's walking out, and I said, "Come to my office. I know you're smart. I've seen you in the office. I've seen you in class. Why didn't you answer any questions?" He said to me, "You don't understand." I said, "You're right. I don't. That's why I'm asking you, so I, so I could understand."

Anthrop:	You're an anthropologist (laughs; general laughter by other school personnel).
School Counselor:	He said, "You don't have to ride home on the bus like I do." I said, "You're right. I don't." "You don't have to play in the neighborhood with all the other kids." I said, "You're right. I don't understand." He said, "I don't want 'em to know I'm smart. They'll make fun of me. I won't have any friends." I said, "So you'd rather sit there and pretend that you don't know than face kids who might say you're smart." And he even said, "Worse than that." I said, "Well, what's worse than that in your world?" He said, "Where I live, they're gonna say I'm White." I said, "Oh!" I said, "Now I think I understand. I don't agree with you, but I, now I hear what you're saying: I don't want 'em to call me names." "I want 'em to think I'm just like everybody else, and if that means sitting in class and not raising my hand, and not doing better in school, I have to live here. And that's my world. So don't think that you can say, "Oh, you should be proud of being smart," he says. "I am, but I can't let anybody know that, and that's coming from one of the, one of the fourteen year old youngsters."

Thus, peer pressures prevented smart students from performing according to their ability. Those who refused to conform might make good grades, but they suffered socially for it. Some of the dreaded penalties were noted by the counselor, such as being "picked on" for getting As or for answering the teacher's questions. The following male student explained the dilemma of the smart student:

I think when kids choose their friends, a lot of times they're your friends. You think they're you're friends. [Later you realize that they, in fact, will be the first ones to discourage you. They'll] say, "Man, look, I ain't takin' the test." And then you'll say, "Man, you ain't gonna take that test, man." "What man?" You know what I'm saying? And they do that. And then when they don't pass, they're like he said, they got that attitude .... And they gonna bring you down with them, 'cause you know … they don't want you to be different from them. Also, we might say, "Every Black kid in Shaker, they want to be good students." They want to be good, man. I don't care. They want to be good students. It's just that, you know, maybe they're not gettin' it from home or whatever; that it's probably they really, you know, they don't want to embarrass themselves by goin' to all of their classes and makin' As. 'Cause like uh we said, they don't want to get picked at by their friends. You know, nobody wants to get picked on, you know.

Hanging Out With Too Many White Students

It was not acceptable to hang around with or have too many White friends. This was not obvious at the elementary school. At that age, most of the students did not link doing well in school with having White friends or realize that either of these was a "bad" thing. It was at the middle school that the notions began to emerge that good grades were White and that students who made good grades were "acting White," "hanging around too many White students," and behaving like White students. These accusations probably stem from the fact that Black students who were hanging out with White friends were often the ones in honors and AP classes with mostly White students and were in those classes because they were making good grades like White students. One student suggested this during an interview:

> You'll see some, I mean very few Black kids with White [students], you know, acting like [a] White group. And they be like the only Black kid in the White group. Those [Blacks] are the ones who be gettin' good grades with them. 'Cause, you know, White people like ... to learn and stuff like that. You know what I'm sayin'? So, like if [Black kids] hang around with them, then they be gettin, you know, the education they need.

Good grades themselves were not stigmatized, but acting White, such as hanging out with Whites or behaving like White students (who got good grades) was. Note that students were also accused of acting White for hanging out with Whites in situations other than those related to striving for academic success.

WHY THESE ATTITUDES AND BEHAVIORS WERE LABELED "ACTING WHITE"

We inquired at the middle school and high school why students labeled behaviors conducive to making good grades as "acting White." These students explicitly distinguished "White behaviors" from "Black behaviors." The reasons for the labeling included the following.

Success in White Establishments and Bona Fide Black Identity

The students said that it was inappropriate [i.e., not normal] for a Black person to behave like a White person because it implied renouncing Black identity. However, in some situations some students did just that. Therefore, some pressures were used to keep peers behaving like Blacks and not like Whites. The peer pressures had serious consequences for students' academic engagement and for Black people in other White institutions or establishments. We describe here students' perceptions of the collective identity status of academically successful students in the school district and professionally successful Blacks in a White establishment. Both successful students and successful professionals were accused of abandoning their racial identity. We therefore inquired whether it was true that they abandoned their racial identity. If they did, why and how they did they abandon their collective identity? If they did not, why were they accused of abandoning their racial identity?

School Success and Bona Fide Collective Identity. We asked the students if Blacks who made good grades, took honors and AP classes—in short, those who were academically successful— gave up or rejected their collective racial identity. By giving up their racial identity we meant not only adopting White attitudes and behaviors that enabled them to succeed academically but also adopting other White attitudes and behaviors that were not related to academic or school context. Did such students, for example, take up White extracurricular activities, such as going skiing, playing tennis, having a White hairstyle and hanging around mostly White students?

To reiterate, the idea that school success made a Black student less Black was nonexistent at the elementary school. Elementary school students did not accuse their schoolmates who made good grades of giving up their Black culture, dialect, or identity. Rather, they teased students who got poor grades. One of the two students who reported teasing poor students explained it this way:

Anthrop: Does anyone ever get teased for the grades that they get?

Student: No, because that really not in this class. The teacher doesn't allow that.

Anthrop: OK. What about if you have to look at the whole school. Would you say that there are some cases where Black students might get teased for doing well or not doing well?

Student: Yes. I do.

Anthrop: And what do they get teased for?

> *Student:*   Um, it's for like if they don't understand something. And they just give a super super-, um, superficial answer. And they just, um, write anything down. And they'll probably get teased for that. Say, like, you know, don't know how to study and stuff.

Most middle school students we talked with did not believe that Blacks abandoned their cultural or racial identity when they became successful students. The next two students provided representative views of their peers:

> *Anthrop:*   Now, sometimes people say that um, Black people who go to school give up their culture and their language and their identity when they start to do well in school, when they start to move up. Do you think that that's true?

> *Student 1:*   Well, that's all from one person's opinion or perspective on how a Black person is really supposed to be ... I'm pretty sure if a Black person had all White friends, then they would act the way that their Caucasian or White friends act. And if a Black person had all Black friends or anything like that, they would act like their Black friends act. So I'm not really sure, really certain that a Black person loses their culture because school isn't their whole life. They have family issues and everything like that. So it doesn't really take up all their time and how they're supposed to act.

> *Student 2:*   No. Because there are a lot of strong Black, smart people. I mean, you don't have to live up to any stereotypes. That'll be dumb not goin' to college unless you give up your culture. I think you should keep your culture and go to college , so that you can be one of those role models for other Black people.

In contrast, several high school students suspected that some Black students who made good grades, and some adults who had higher education or were successful as professionals in White establishments, did indeed give up their culture and identity. The majority were not sure that this happened; there were only two students who downplayed the issue, explaining that it was not important. In the words of one of them:

> *Anthrop:*   OK. Um. Do you think that it's a common thought that Blacks who do well in school and go on to college, feel that they're giving up their culture or identity?

> *Student:*   No. I think if they do, they're ignorant, so ... I've heard very few people in Shaker Heights who ever say that.

Anthrop: OK.

Student: And the kids that do say it , are young, they're not going to
              class, they are smoking weed and they're not coming back to
              school. So I really can't speak on that anyway because it's just
              ignorance, period.

Some knew other Black students and adults who believed that school
success had a negative influence on Black collective identity. However,
the informants said that they themselves did not believe this. They knew
students who were accused of giving up their culture or identity because
they were doing well in school or taking high-level classes. From their
point of view, the accused students did not, in fact, give up their culture
or identity. The following excerpt is from a conversation with two students who did not believe that academically successful students abandoned their Black identity.

Anthrop: Tell me whether or not you think education makes Black peo-
              ple give up their culture and identity.

Student 1: I don't think that it does, but I think that um, Black people who
              aren't achieving or who don't feel that education is important,
              will try to make you believe that [it does], and make you feel in-
              ferior to your culture for being smart.

Anthrop: Some people think that Blacks who do well in school, go on to
              college, etc ... uh, give up their culture or identity. Um, do you
              think that ... well number one, do you think that that's true?

Student 2: No. I remember people used to say that. 'Cause I was tryin' to
              do well in school they said I was tryin' to be White or what-
              ever. And that used to upset me so much because, just because
              you do well in school, why does it mean that you're no longer
              Black?, You know. And, um, that used to really bother me.
              Like I used to, um, have lots of problems with that. They think
              you're an oreo, and that used to upset me really a lot. But now,
              I mean, I don't care. I'm doing well in school so I can go on and
              do whatever I want. And I don't think that I'm any less Black
              or anymore White. I don't see why like, how well you do in
              school is linked with the color of your skin ... I just don't un-
              derstand.

Professional Success and Bona Fide Black Identity.   It was only at
the high school that students reported that some highly educated Blacks

and successful Black professionals in White establishments and institutions gave up or abandoned their culture and racial identity. Nearly half of the high school students we interviewed believed this. They gave two reasons why this might happen. One was acculturation, which started during public school education. At this point in their school career, some very ambitious Black students would take honors and AP courses; hang around too many White students; and learn to think, talk, and behave like White people. When they got to college they took more difficult courses; hung around more White people; and got more into the habit of thinking, talking, and behaving like White people. Through such acculturation they lost their racial identity, because they no longer knew how to behave and talk like Black people, and they no longer interacted with other Blacks. One student described this process of one-way acculturation among ambitious Blacks:

Anthrop: OK. Um, do you think that going to school and doing well in school or going on to college makes some Black people give up their culture and their identity?

Student: Mm, sometimes.

Anthrop: Like in other words, do they start acting White when they start getting higher in education or becoming successful [after finishing school]?

Student: Yeah.

Anthrop: And how do they do that ?

Student: I mean, I guess, they get the status. But I mean they work hard for it [i.e., to be successful]. So they deserve it. But you know, they just forget about their heritage. Like they be getting into [mixing with] the White people, I guess. 'Cause the Black people that take AP history or AP whatever, they just begin to hang around that class of people [i.e.,Whites]. So I guess that in that way they begin to act like Whites.

Anthrop: OK. So it's mainly the people they hang around ...

Student: Like socializing themselves with them.

Anthrop: OK. Um, how can a Black person not do that, I mean, do you have any suggestions for how a Black person can avoid losing his or her culture and still do well?

| *Student:* | I mean it's ... I think it's alright to, you know, like, uh, excel in education. But don't forget where you came from ... you know. And don't look down on like the people that's not in AP classes ... you know, 'cause that could be you. |

Another explanation was that some Blacks professionals might give up their cultural identity and embrace White cultural identity as a survival strategy. This might happen because Black professionals in a White establishment had to learn to fit in with highly educated White colleagues. Under this circumstance, the Black professionals were more or less forced to adopt White people's attitudes and had to behave and talk like them. The problem of fitting in for Black professionals in White establishments was described by one student as follows:

Anthrop:	Do you think that education makes some Black people give up their culture, language and identity to be like White people?
Student:	Yeah, in a way....
Anthrop:	In what ways?
Student:	Like sometimes they've pushed [worked] so hard that they tend to like just push everyone else aside. And usually they are like the most educated people in this society [who] are White people. So [the educated Blacks] tend to go like be with them. It's not necessarily their fault that they lose [i.e., cultural identity], or that they push it away. They have to make the change or else they're not gonna be able to fit inta like the White society. So they just end up being with the educated White people. And then, they take on some of [White people's] habits and speech patterns and stuff like that.

Ambivalence About Success in White Institutions and Establishments

Black students who took honors and AP classes and successful Black professionals were accused by other Blacks of abandoning their Black cultural identity for the same reasons: Black Americans as a group were ambivalent toward other Blacks who were successful in White institutions and White establishments. Therefore, Blacks were ambivalent toward their fellow Blacks who were successful in White institutions or White establishments in regard to whether they had abandoned their racial identity. This explanation was offered by high school students when they were asked why Black students were underrepresented in the honors and AP classes. According to them, Black people usually welcomed a certain level of success from other Blacks in White institutions and establishments. However, once individuals exceeded the level expected of them, other Blacks in the community would begin to criticize them.

This ambivalent attitude was present among Shaker Heights students. Some admired and praised Black students who were doing well for setting good examples and for making other Blacks proud. At the same time, however, Black students in the honors and AP classes, and those who made good grades, were criticized and accused of acting White. The following student reported on the Black cultural attribute of ambivalence toward success.

> *Anthrop:* OK. Um, let me ask you a general question about education. As Black people get more educated, do you think that, do some Blacks think that, um, they give up their culture and identity to do so?
>
> *Student:* Um, I think when African American or Black people are first starting to branch out [i.e., move up or succeed], I think everyone is just down for the cause. Everyone says "More power to you." But once you start reaching whatever the level is, some type of upper level or higher education, somehow, that coincides with losing a connection with the community. This usually either means you're moving out [of the neighborhood] because you have a nicer house [elsewhere], or because you have more money. It means that physically going away from the community. Somehow Black people have come to make the connection that moving up in society or moving up in an intellectual alley is being farther away [separating yourself] from your heritage or something, which is not good. Not like, I don't think anyone likes to see anyone do bad, especially fellow African Americans, for that type of matter. No one. I mean no one wants to see anyone doing bad. But if you're doing bad yourself and you see someone above you, you kind of tend to be spiteful for whatever reason. Because they're doing better you might lose, um, focus of what they're really trying to do. And even if they come back into the community, they come back and say, "Here's me, I've gone through 8 years of school, I've got lots of money, and I'm back," or whatever. So you know, [they'll say] "You're a sellout. You left us." Or I mean, I can [understand] those feelings. But I think the most important thing is that we not look upon education or getting higher education as bad in any type of way.

As we have already noted, the idea that a Black person gave up his or her identity because of school or professional success was not widespread until high school. A few middle school students reported that some Black students were accused of giving up their cultural identity or labeled as acting White because of their school success. The middle school students were not afraid that they themselves would be accused of abandoning their culture if they did well in school. In fact, they felt very comfortable with and looked forward to doing well in school. The situation at the high school was different and complicated. High school students knew more about the prevailing belief that good grades in the public school, higher education, and professional success made some Blacks give up their culture and identity. Although some believed that this happened, many provided interesting explanations of why some Black people held these beliefs.

Inadequate Knowledge of Blacks' Struggle for Education

The third explanation was that some students equated making good grades with White behavior because they did not understand the history of Black people's struggle for education. Black students who were not aware of the extent of Blacks' struggle for access to education, to equal education mistakenly believed that only White people developed the cultural value of hard work to make good grades in school. These students assumed that making good grades was not a part of Black culture but an aspect of White culture. Furthermore, they might think this way because they did not know that even when Blacks were prohibited by law to learn to read or write during slavery, some Blacks defied the law and learned to read. This showed that Black people, like White people, development the cultural value of getting an education and making good grades. In the words of one student,

> It is uninformed students who don't want to make good grades because they think it is White. But uninformed students don't want to because they don't know. They don't know that doing well in school [being a good student] is not a White thing. They don't know that their ancestors who, you know, were the part of the struggle. They defied the law and learned to read.

Black Opposition to the White Establishment

The fourth explanation was that equating good school performance with acting White and rejecting academic and professional success were a part of Black Americans' general opposition to White society, or their anti-White-establishment tendency. One student's explanation is worth reproducing in full because of the way this informant (like others) linked Black educational attitudes and behaviors to other features of Black experience in history and society at large.

> I had a comment that was kind of connected to both questions [asked by the anthropologist]. Um, one thing is [that we] Blacks, it seems like, we always want to go with the anti-establishment. [That is], we [want to] go against society. Traditionally in American society, it has seemed like we have been under oppression. For example, there were laws simply to oppress Black people .... So (because of this [oppression] Black people came to believe that it was always good, you know, if you could find some way, just somethin' small, you know, just to annoy society. [You do this] ... just ... so that you could go against society. That would make you feel good. And so that's why a lot of times even drug dealers will [say], "Well, [i.e., White people] say it's wrong. So, you know, [I don't feel bad]; I feel like ... I'm gettin' [at them], you know ... The cops are chasin' me and everything. And so ... that's good." And [drug dealers] want to do that [i.e., go against society]. And the same thing with education [i.e., in students' attitude toward education]. Because, you see all these White people get up on the stage and talk about education this and education that. And you [as a Black person] just gonna [i.e., say to yourself], "Well, I don't care what you [got in mind],." And so you don't [you don't behave like White people to make good grades].

Thus, because of their marginal position in U.S. society and in White institutions, Blacks developed anti-establishment beliefs and behaviors, which were partly expressed in peer pressures against the school norm of achievement.

A Ploy by Failing Students

The fifth explanation was that equating making good grades with acting White was a ploy by low-achieving students to discourage their friends from striving to make good grades. Students who were not doing well or not interested in school usually used this tactic to discourage their friends from doing schoolwork and making good grades. One student described the peer pressure this way:

> I think when kids choose their friends. A lot of times, you think they're you're friends. Later you realize that they, in fact, will be the first ones [to discourage you]. They'll say, "Man, look, I ain't takin' the test." And then you'll say, "Man, you ain't gonna take that test, man? What man?" You know what I'm saying? And they do that. And then when they don't pass, they're like he said. They got that attitude .... And they gonna bring you down with them. 'Cause you know, they don't want to be different from their friends. Also, we might say, "Every Black kid in Shaker, they want to be good (students)." They want to be good (students), man. I don't care. They want to be good

[students]. It's just that, you know, maybe they're not gettin' it from home or whatever [i.e., not supervised by their parents]. That it's probably the reason they follow their friends. They really, you know, don't want to embarrass themselves [before their friends] by goin' to all of their classes and makin' As. 'Cause like, uh, we said, they don't want to get picked at [by their friends]. You know, nobody wants to get picked on.

Teasing

Finally, the accusation of acting White was a form of joking relationship among students. In the joking relationship, teasing was not necessarily linked to school performance. For instance, a Black student in an honors class, and therefore, a good student, might accuse another student of acting White, as in the following cases.

Anthrop:	OK, um, have you heard the term "acting White?"
Student 1:	(raising her voice) Yes, I have.
Anthrop:	OK … How does someone get accused of "acting White"?
Student:	Well (laughing), I'm not gonna lie. I can't say I haven't used that term myself before, but … um,
Anthrop:	Mh-hmm, it's OK.
Student 2:	Uh, lets see, ok. Um, you want me to actually give you the details and everything like that?
Anthrop:	Yeah, I mean if you want to.
Student 2:	Well, its all about, it revolves around the question that you asked about a Black person losing their culture depending on who they hang around with. Um, like for instance, it's kinda hard. Um, if OK, well, of course. You've seen, um, the movie "Clueless," right?
Anthrop:	Uh-huh.
Student:	Well, if you see a Black person, um, or any other person, um, walking around and acting like that, saying "Oh yeah," like you know, like totally cool, man, you know, and stuff like that. I don't know. It kind of strays from the point, but you know you can tell that they're acting different just in front of their friends instead of the way that they would normally act.

Looking at the overall situation from the point of view of the students, elementary school students did not associate getting good grades with acting

White. Neither did they think that it was bad to make good grades. Middle school students did not criticize Black students for getting good grades; they did not stigmatize good grades. Instead, they criticized them for hanging out with White students, thereby behaving like them, including talking properly. The White behaviors they criticized were, however, those that are conducive to making good grades. It was at the high school that making good grades itself was most often equated with acting White and criticized.

Other Pressures Against Academic Engagement

"Cool" Status

Our analysis of the reasons for academic disengagement included the status symbol "cool." It was not cool to work hard in school or to be academically engaged. Peer pressures to be cool were detrimental to academic engagement. One strategy of achieving the status of coolness or of "a cool guy" was not to do one's schoolwork. Others strategies included avoiding difficult classes, cutting school, cutting classes, and not doing homework. Being cool was mainly a male affair, but our best descriptions of the practice of being cool came from two female students. The first informant also pointed out some of the negative effects on schoolwork of being cool.

> I think that part of the problem with the Black people in this school is a lack of respect for academic striving, because of being in, trying to be part of the crowd. Trying to be with the cool people (cough drowns out some words). That is not to say that everybody's like that. [But some don't want to be put down by the crowd]. [They know that] it's hard to sit as minorities in AP and honors classes. So they gonna try to [be in class with] all minorities. We may not be minorities in school any longer, but we are in [AP and honors] classes. That's where we are the minorities.

According to the second informant, although some students believed that making good grades was not cool, this attitude was not entirely free from self-doubt about the ability to succeed like White students:

Female
Student 2:   Some students feel that being successful is not cool. It's like, um, I don't know, their priorities are kinda, uh, mixed up. You know what I'm saying? It's just—. It's just peer pressures, and it's just that they don't have the strong foundation laid to want to um succeed as much as a lot of the White students do. You know, their friends—. I mean, you know their friends, they don't have a lot of the same aims as a lot of the White students. And Whites, their friends have, like going to college and stuff.

That's really, you know, that's really a big thing to a lot of White students. And it is to some of Black students, too, but um to some other Black students that's not a big thing, that's not their aim. They just, it's just a whole different mind set, kind of. But not all students are like that, but the ones who aren't achieving, I think that's why they think like that.

Anthrop: So it's first of all, one, lack of self confidence. They don't feel they can.

Female Student: Right. They don't think they can. And because they're Black, they feel that being smart, doing well in class, is something that they're not supposed to do. That's for White students. That's for the bet—, you know, I'm, you know, they think that their skin color means that they have to act into the stereotypes that are put on them. So that's why I think.

Anthrop: OK.

Quest for Popularity

Being cool was not the only way to achieve popularity among peers; one could also become popular and admired for wearing nice clothes, expensive shoes, and having other expensive material possessions. Some students were driven to acquire these things at the expense of doing their schoolwork and striving to make good grades. We should point out that students who reported the pursuit of material goods for the purpose of peer popularity and admiration at the expense of their schoolwork did not usually describe their own personal experience.

Keeping Friends

Some students were disengaged from their schoolwork because they wanted to conform to what their friends wanted them to do; otherwise, they would lose their best friends. Two students explained this fear of losing friends as a factor that contributed to academic disengagement.

Anthrop: What are some of the reasons that students don't do well, why Black students don't do well?

Student 1: Um, I would say peers, 'cause that has a lot do with um, doing well and doing poorly. A lot of kids are.... After you're with a certain group of friends for a long time, they're afraid to um, not do the behavior that they've been so accustomed to. Like if they really do want to go out and do well, but their friends aren't, they don't wanna make them feel that they're better than them, or stuff like that.

Anthrop: How important do you think people's friends are to how well they do in school?

Student 2: I think very important … Because like if you hang out with people that, you know, get straight A's and all this and that, I mean, that's gonna motivate you know. It's gonna help you. I mean it's gonna make you feel like, "Well, they get straight A's, I should, you know, apply myself. And, you know, force myself to do good." But like most of them [students] talk probably be about schoolwork and all this stuff, but they don't do as well, you know. They'll be ready to hang out instead of do homework and stuff like that. So, it takes away a lot of your time and your study time.

Nonacademic Priorities

We noted in our discussion of academic disengagement in chapter 2 that there were several nonacademic activities that took priority over academic ones. We briefly note one factor that greatly affected on academic disengagement: consumerism. Middle school and high school students persuaded their friends to take on part-time jobs with too many hours rather than strive to take difficult classes or study to make good grades even in easy courses. A middle school student provided some insight into the effects of the competing priorities on students' schoolwork:

But most Blacks, they think they um, wanna be popular and stuff like that. And they don't focus on their schoolwork. They just focus on just goin' to school and tryin' to be hard [cool] and stuff like that…. They focus on popularity more than their schoolwork. They worry about what people might think of them or stuff like that. And they don't really wanna do bad. I mean some people care about education, but it's the friends, the people they hang around with. That just make them different.

Ghetto Lifestyle

Another explanation for the academic disengagement offered by a male student was that some Black students believed that their root was in the ghetto, where the lifestyle does not include academic engagement. Therefore they wanted and pressured their friends to act like ghetto kids.

It seems to me that um, when we sit here, it feels … almost … like Black students in the ghetto. The fact that we go to Shaker, which is a fairly affluent community, ... [Black students still] worked like [they're] going back to their perfect roots or something, you know. (Other students laugh.) Like, people [seem to] talk and act as ghetto as possible ... , as much of the time as they can. And I think that um, that's a lot of the problem. (You can observe this attitude and behavior in class. You'll be sitting in class and they say [things]; the people will just leave, or [act] like we're [playing games] in class. And [when] the teach handed a test to somebody the student will act like,"Here, you can have it back." But I mean like [think] that's just ridiculous. I mean ... it's [there's] no reason for that, but, I mean, [it seems that the only reason is that] they're trying to make a scene; [they] like to show theirself *(sic)*, you know. And um, I think that's a big problem: you're over there trying to learn, but other people aren't.

COPING WITH PEER PRESSURES

We can see from several accounts given by the students that some did not succumb to negative peer pressures. In spite of peer pressures, some students enrolled in honors and AP classes, worked hard, and made good grades. How did these students handle the peer pressures that probably prevented others from doing so?

Two things minimized the negative impact of peer pressure on these "good" students; that is, students taking honors and AP classes and those making good grades. One was family upbringing and support. Some parents not only instilled in their children the importance of making good grades in school, taking honors and AP classes, but they also supervised their schoolwork. Their parents or guardians monitored their work and screened their peer group membership and thereby ensured that friends did not distract them from their schoolwork and homework. Here was how one student explained how this type of family educational strategy:

> Anthrop   Mh-hmm. So what gave you the strength then, to resist peer pressures, because that ... seems to be something that comes up a lot; and that's peer pressure. So, what gave you the strength to avoid that?
>
> Student: I guess it's, I don't know really. It's just something I knew I had to do ... I guess it maybe, like traditions and stuff that have been instilled in me by my parents ... stuff like that.

The second strategy was a student's own device. In this case, a good student handled the negative peer pressures by choosing his or her friends from other Black students who also were good students. For example,

Black students taking honors and AP classes or making good grades chose other, similar Blacks as friends or chose White classmates as friends.

Furthermore, the good students usually interpreted peer pressures as distractions from their goals of school success and, therefore, took necessary steps to avoid them. One student explained this interpretation quite nicely. She said that it depended on individual students: A student who really wanted to succeed in school would strive to do so, take honors and AP courses, and study to make good grades. He or she would not cave in to peer pressures. She concluded, "You can't worry about what other people are gonna say."

11

The Family

Research on the role of the family in children's education falls roughly into three categories: (a) studies that examine and recommend ways to increase parent involvement in school or improve family–school relationships (see Epstein, 1995; Hoover-Dempsey & Sandler, 1995, 1997; Lightfoot, 1978; Lombana, 1983; Sheppard & Rose, 1995), (b) those that focus on the relationship between families and schools (Curtis, 1988; Diaz-Soto, 1997; Shannon & Latimer, 1996) or how to empower parents in that relationship (Miramontes, Nadeau, & Commins, 1997), and (c) those that examine how families manage their children's education and what results in academic success or failure (R. Clark, 1983; Ford, 1993; Gutman & McLoyd, 2000).

Our study of the family role in Shaker Heights does not fit any of these three research categories. We did not look for ways to increase parent involvement, examine the relationship with the schools, empower parents, or academic management in poor Black families. What we wanted to know was what Black parents did or did not do about their children's education at school and at home. We defined this as a study of their educational strategies or how they went about to implement their educational aspirations for their children. We looked for such implementation in terms of what they did at school and at home. It was necessary to study parents' involvement with their children's education at home because our comparative research had suggested that in some minority groups the influence exerted by parents at home had a strong positive influence on their children's education, even when the parents were not particularly involved with their schools. In this comparative perspective, parent involvement was not determined by socioeconomic status. Our findings in Shaker Heights are presented in two parts: (a) educational involvement at school, and (b) educational involvement at home.

SHAKER HEIGHTS EDUCATION AS A GOAL

The Black community, like its children, believed that the Shaker Heights public school system was the best in Ohio and one of the best in the nation. For many parents the graduation of their children from the Shaker Heights school system was a goal in itself. Some working-class families moved to Shaker Heights, willing to work at two jobs or more to pay the high school taxes so that their children would graduate from the district. Several students described the struggle or sacrifice of their parents to give them a chance to graduate from Shaker Heights. Indeed, the concept of struggling for their children to go to school in Shaker Heights was a frequent theme when students described the educational aspirations of their working-class parents. This can be seen in the following statement made by a female student at a discussion with high school students.

> I just wanted you to know [that] I definitely agree with what Mabel said, because people are always saying there are a lot of [rich Black] people in Shaker ... "They're all rich. They're all from a [wealthy home]." That's not true ... [for] most of us ... Our parents, they work hard for us to go to Shaker. So, a lot of times both parents do work two jobs, you know. Sometimes ... they don't have time to talk to their child ... because they busy workin' for their child to go to Shaker. So it's not always them, because people sometimes make [a decision] to go to Shaker, [even though] we're not like—[rich people].... My mother struggles just like everybody else. People can struggle. Sometimes they ... work hard. And they don't have time to sit down and tell you the things they need from you, because they've probably been workin' so that you can go here.

PARENTS' ACADEMIC EXPECTATIONS

Black parents expected their children to do well in school. Children at every grade level knew this. Many students reported that their parents had told them that it was important for them to succeed at Shaker and to go on to college. But for some parents the ultimate goal was for their children to graduate from Shaker High. Five out of six elementary school students interviewed recalled their parents explicitly telling them what grades they should make. Two were told to make As; two to make As and Bs; in the remaining case her mother wanted her to make As, Bs, and Cs; however, her mother was usually unhappy when she got a C. The expectations of middle school parents were just as high. Middle school students believed that their parents' expectations were important for their school performance.

High school students also were expected to make good grades, not just to graduate from Shaker but to go on to college. Eight of the 13 students interviewed said that parents' expectations were very important for school success or failure. For 3 students, getting good grades was mandatory in their families. For this reason, they developed for themselves the same high expectations their parents had for them. They did not have to be reminded that they should make good grades; it was taken for granted. This was how one female student explained why she made good grades.

Anthrop: OK, um, when a student is doing well, who do you think is responsible for that? Do you think it's the student, the parents, the teachers, the school, who is responsible?

Student: I really think it's the student. I mean, when they're doing well it's the student. I mean I think in some cases … I think the parent might have something to do with it. There are parents, you know, [who] put on a lot of pressure on their kids to do well in school, or threaten or whatever. "You better do well in school or else." You know what I mean. In my case, it's always been mean. Like my parents, they've never, they've never told me, you know, "You have to do well in school." But it's like a given, you know, why wouldn't I?

Other students said that their parents were happy as long as they did their best. Only two seniors said that their parents did not have high academic expectations for them, but they were nonetheless doing well. The mother of one of them worked most of the time and expected her son to be independent. The other student was frequently absent; he was suspended once for fighting during our fieldwork. In spite of a lack of high parental expectations and supervision, and in spite of his behavior problems, he was determined to make good grades. And, according to him, he did.

Anthrop: OK, now as far as grades, what types of grades do your parents expect you to get?

Student: Um, they expect me to get um, well they would love it if I would get straight As. But I think I'm harder on myself than my parents are. (Laughing) … 'Cause like um, as long as they know that I try as hard as whatever. 'Cause they know that, I mean I try in school. So as long as they know that I'm working hard and I'm trying then um, like whatever I get is OK. Like generally I don't, I've only gotten one or two Cs. But um, (inaudible) I don't get any Cs. When I got my first one, I was just so upset.

Students believed that the reason their parents expected them to do well in school was partly because their parents themselves did not have much education or did not have good jobs because of poor education. After getting her general equivalency diploma (GED) recently, one mother began to tell her son that it was important for him not only to graduate from high school but also go to college.

Anthrop: OK. OK, how far do your parents expect you to go in school?

Student: Um, college at least.

Anthrop: OK. And how often do they make that clear to you?

Student: Um, basically it's just been this last year, when my mother made it important to me; she never graduated from high school or whatever; she got her GED. So she made it important to me that I have to go to college.

There were parents who did not tell their children explicitly that it was important to make good grades while at Shaker or to go to college after Shaker.

Racial Differences in Parental Expectations and Supervision

Black students compared their parents' expectations with those of White parents. They generally concluded that White parents had higher expectations than their own parents. They explained that this difference was due to the fact that White parents were better educated. Some also attributed the higher school performance of White students to the higher parents' expectations. The following student represented the point of view that the higher expectations of White parents were due to their being more educated.

Anthrop: OK, do you think that Black parents have different expectations than White parents for their children ... as far as grades?

Student: Yeah. 'Cause a lot of Black people ... a lotta Black people like haven't necessarily graduated from high school or college. So, basically, just like the main expectation for them is to get through high school, and like if they can, get to college. And ... most White people, they've gone to college and they have their own businesses and stuff, that's what they expect their children to do.

IMPLEMENTING PARENTAL EXPECTATIONS

Although most students believed that their parents expected them to do well in school, they also believed that there was a gap between those expectations and what their parents actually did to ensure that they met the expectations. On the basis of reports by school personnel, students' reports on their parents' effort, discussions with parents, and our own observations, we now describe two aspects of the parents' endeavors, or lack of endeavor, to implement their expectations: implementation within the school system and implementation at home.

Parents' Involvement Within the School System

From school personnel reports of school authorities, interviews with students, discussions with parents themselves, and our observations we can confidently conclude that Black parents in Shaker Heights did not participate actively in school organizations and in school events and programs designed to enhance their children's academic engagement and achievement. Here are some examples of these organizations, programs, and events.

Parent–Teacher Organization (PTO)

It was reported both in the community and at school that very few Black parents were members of their schools' PTO; neither did they attend the PTO meetings. The principal of one elementary school attributed their low participation to the distance of her school from the neighborhood where most of the Black students lived. In this case Black parents would have to travel quite a long distance to the school. The principal also suggested another reason, namely, that the school was located in a predominantly White neighborhood. This might well be a factor, because we observed throughout the study that Blacks did not ordinarily go into predominantly White neighborhoods. However, their participation in the PTOs of schools within their own neighborhoods was not much higher. On the whole, very few Blacks were active members in the PTO in the schools within or near their neighborhood.

Organized Academic Programs

Their participation in academic programs organized by the school district was dismal, in spite of the fact that several of the programs were primarily for Black children. Notable among these are an early elementary school program and workshops for proficiency tests. Their participation in these programs, or lack thereof, was described by the school officials in charge of the programs. Our informants did not conceal either their discouragement or frustration by the low participation.

Early elementary school program for low achievers.   A first-grade teacher for 17 years in the school district recounted her unsuccessful effort to get Black parents to come to meetings about her program. The program was for children whose learning problems could be reduced or eliminated if treated early. She scheduled meetings with parents at different times of the day, including in the morning before school opened and after school; she also tried to communicate with them in other ways. She did this for more than 15 years and always tried to make herself "approachable." She did not have much success. She concluded by saying:

> *Teacher 1:*   And I'm very frustrated by that. And I don't know how we can change that. And I think that affects achievement from first grade on, when parents either don't come or help in a way that doesn't foster independence for their child.

Workshop for Parents.   We recorded parents' participation in three workshops. Two took place before our fieldwork, and the third took place during our fieldwork.

Parents' participation in a summer workshop before our fieldwork was very low. The teacher who organized it said that she found her experience just as frustrating as that of the first-grade teacher. The overwhelming majority of students who failed the state proficiency tests were Black. The workshop was specifically intended to show parents how to help their children prepare to pass the tests. Initially, some parents came, then attended irregularly or dropped out altogether. This frustration of this teacher can be readily sensed in the rest of her account:

> *Anthrop:*   OK. So parent involvement is a part of the problem. Um. Yeah, OK. Somebody else. (Calling on someone:) Yes.
>
> *Teacher 2:*   To dovetail on the parent involvement, and I'm saying that's a part of it. Not the whole, of course. But I work um, in a government supported program, and I work with fifth and sixth graders, and uh we, we have uh, low achievers. Let me back up and not say low achievers. We have children, the criteria for our program are children that score very low on standardized tests or proficiency tests. Now that's what places them into my pro-

gram. And uh, going back to the parent involvement. We had, we have offered three, uh workshops for our parents over the years. Over one school year. Say this school year in particular. And one was on proficiency achievement.

Regarding the school-year workshop prior to our fieldwork, the same teacher continued:

Teacher 2:   Another workshop we just had not too long ago was on ways that you can help your children through the summer. We had camps. We have a list of camps. We had uh tutoring available. Um, what other we had? We had about three or four different packets and things that child, ... they can do with their children during the summer. And uh, what was? ... Our first one is a dinner meeting that we have with our families. We provided, you know, offered them, uh, different types of food to eat, because it's in the evening. We know, you know, that a lot of families are getting their, uh, dinner for their families and they want to be together. And so, and we have, I guess, about over 100 families in our, um, ... in all of our classes. And uh, I guess [at] one meeting we had, maybe, 15. And then through, throughout the year the number dwindled. In our last meeting we had, we had, maybe, 10 families that came. And it really broke my heart, because we worked very, we worked very hard for all of our workshops, but this one really got me this last time. And uh, I have one White student in my class. And I guess in the whole program there might be, I guess it's like 98% percent are African Americans, and, uh, out of the people that showed up for this last meeting that maybe there were eight there. The White family was also, uh, present. And, uh, just kind of hurt me.

Teacher 1:   (Quietly) Uh huh. Uh huh.

Teacher 2:   I'm very discouraged.

There was a brief discussion of the differences among minority groups in school involvement. The anthropologist shared with the group his findings on parent involvement in another research project. He had interviewed teachers, parents, and studied the comments that teachers had written in the children's folders. In that study, the students ranged from kindergarten to 12th grade. In his analysis he noticed that teachers and parents interpreted parent involvement differently. He found that immigrant minority parents, such as the Chinese and Mexicans, did not participate actively in their children's school partly because they did not understand the U.S. public school system. They might also have emigrated from societies where the education system did not require parent involvement (Ogbu, 1974). This was not, however, the case of Black parents. Many Chinese immigrants could not help with their children's work, because they could not speak English. Yet their children did relatively well in school. Why was this so? One of the two teachers who spoke earlier explain the difference between Black and Asian American parent noninvolvement in the district:

> *Teacher 2:*   What I've noticed among, my um, Asian students who come
>   with, with very little [English] language or hardly any at all, is
>   that the parents know how to network. And even if they have
>   very little English, they seem to have a support network in
>   their community. And they will call another Korean parent, for
>   example, to help. And I know, it happens with parents of
>   high-achieving kids, and maybe that's part of the reason.

We observed one workshop during our study. This was organized by some Black teachers. It was on a weekend at the Woodbury Upper Elementary School. There were only 15 students, and their parents showed up, even though a larger number had been expected. The parents included a White couple. This was apparently one of a series of such workshops conducted during the year. At the end of each workshop parents received instructional plans about how to prepare for the next one. Among Black parents in attendance the day we observed only one had gone to the last session and therefore knew what was to be done that day. The rest came unprepared.

As already noted, the workshop was designed to teach children the skills they needed to pass the proficiency tests. During the workshop, parents were taught some games and other techniques to use to help their children master the skills at home. Parents were told that it was their responsibility as parents to help their children learn the skills. After explaining to parents how to help their children, the teachers gave the children some assignments to do with their parents. At the end of the session the parents and children received some practice worksheets to do at home. The teachers told the parents to ensure that their children did one exercise every day. They were also given plans for the next workshop.

Minority Achievement Committee (MAC) Scholars Program. According to one account, successful Black students who were the initial members of the MAC Scholars program told the organizers that their school success was due to their parents' support. This led the organizers to assume that students who were not doing well probably did not have such parental support. They believed, however, that all parents wanted their children to make good grades but that not everyone knew how to help his or her child achieve this goal. Although parents usually discussed their children's performance when they received their report cards, many did nothing else to foster better academic achievement. The organizers of the MAC program hoped to increase parents' support of schoolwork through the program, but that had not happened at the time of this study. In fact, many Black parents said that they had not heard of the MAC program and did not know how it was supposed to help their children. We even found that some Black parents employed by the school district at the middle school and high school who had not heard of the program.

A Math Lab Conference.   As we reported in chapter 6, some teachers organized a math lab conference for parents whose children were in basic skills math classes. The purpose of the conference was to explain to parents the difference between basic math and higher math and to show them how to help their children take and succeed in higher math courses.

Although most students in basic skills math classes were Black, only 20 Black parents attended. The 20 parents had a total of 12 children. Nine other parents had signed up but did not attend the conference. Nevertheless, the teachers considered the attendance a success beyond their expectation.

The teachers explained to those present how the method of teaching math had changed but not for the at-risk or minority students. In spite of the change, the method of teaching math to at-risk students continued to emphasize remediation. The remediation approach prevented students, especially Black males, from taking algebra and geometry in high school. Because the at-risk students did not take algebra and geometry in high school, they had difficulty in math courses in college. The teachers were trying to convince the parents that the math lab was good for their children, because students who enrolled in the lab approach were taught the thinking and problem-solving skills needed to do higher level math or algebra and geometry. Teachers discussed increases in pass rates in math proficiency tests to further convince parents of the benefits of taking the math lab. Parents were told that in 1987, before the math lab program was introduced, 21% of the students failed their math exams. However, after the math lab was started, only 9% of the students failed.

The parents were given a math exercise to do with their, children who had accompanied them to the conference. They were also asked to go over their children's folders containing their lab work . After parents had completed the exercise the teachers reviewed it and gave them feedback. The next activity was answering questions from parents. During this phase the teachers emphasized how the new method was better for their children.

When the conference was over, the parents seemed convinced that the math lab was better for their children. They collected signatures to petition some higher school authorities to provide more math labs.

Every parent was given a packet containing a "Spirit Pass." They were told that the Spirit Pass was given to students who demonstrated a lively spirit for his or her work. On the whole, the teachers made the parents feel welcome. They provided them with juice, fresh fruit, and bagels. After the parents left we commented that it was a nice conference. The teachers replied that it was really necessary to make the parents feel welcome and invited. They wanted them to go home with the feeling that the conference was really beneficial.

Open House. The dismal participation of Black parents during Open House at both the middle school and high school was another indicator of the discrepancy between their educational expectations and what they actually did to ensure that their expectations were met. We went to the Open House because some school officials had suggested that observing Black parents' participation would give us a sense of parents' school involvement. These officials believed that parent involvement affected parent–teacher relationships, especially at the middle school.

We decided to observe parents in the classes we had been observing during lessons. For comparative purposes, we describe our observations of honors and Advanced Placement (AP) as well as skills and college prep classes. Where possible, we describe parents' attendance in higher and lower level classes on the same subject or taught by the same teacher. All the names of teachers in the presentation below are pseudonyms.

MIDDLE SCHOOL OPEN HOUSE

AP English: Mr. Gaines

Most of the parents were White, and many seemed to know one another. There was only one Black parent among them. We gave her our seat because she came late and there were not enough seats. Mr. Gaines asked a student present to hand out several pages of information.

TABLE 11.1
Black Parents' Attendance at the Middle School Open House

Teacher	Course Level	# Black Parents
A	AP	1
A	CP	2
B	CP	3
B	Skill	4
C	AP	1

Note. AP = advanced placement; CP = college prep.

The teacher then proceeded to explain his high expectations and his grading scale. He gave an A for 92%, not 90%. He did this to keep students challenged, and to prepare them academically and socially for the "Big House," by which he meant the high school. He remarked that sometimes students in an AP class think that they knew it all. Admittedly, sometimes they were close, but he had found ways to ensure that they were challenged. He then asked the parents for their help. One parent asked a question, which the teacher answered. After this session, several parents went to introduce themselves to the teacher, while several more talked to one another.

College Prep English: Mr. Gaines

Most students in this class were Black. There were fewer parents in this group than in the AP class, and so there were plenty of empty seats. There was one mixed-race couple. Two students, both African American, accompanied their parents tonight. Mr. Gaines asked the students to hand out the information to parents. The wife in the mixed-race couple said that she didn't need the handout because her husband had already gotten one. It was not clear why she did not take a copy, because she did not appear to follow what was going on from her husband's copy. On the whole, this group of parents seemed less attentive to what was going on. Many however, were friendly; as new parents entered the room, most of the others already seated acknowledged them, suggesting that they were known to each other. During this session, the teacher explained the lesson topics on a board. He said that they were things he "hoped" to accomplish. His approach to these parents was in contrast with the one he used with parents of AP students. To the latter he presented things that the students accomplished, but to the parents of the college prep class merely told the parents that all the students "had potential." He went on to tell them that many of their children had "hidden skills" that were lying dormant. He was pushing them to reveal and develop those skills. One of his strategies for doing so was to require them to make a class presentation. At this point he solicited questions from the parents. One White mother asked about their vocabulary quizzes; she also asked if the children would have to use them in sentences.

College Prep Math: Mr. Kleinberg

Only 3 of the 18 parents attending this Open House were Black. Mr. Kleinberg dressed up this evening, although he was usually one of the more casual teachers. His teaching style also appeared somewhat casual. He admitted to the parents that his teaching style could be boring because it was very methodical. He then wrote down an equation on the board and said that the answer was easy and that everyone knew it. However, what was more important was the process of arriving at the answer. He proceeded to tell the parents that he had three objectives in this class. One was to prepare students for algebra, the second was to make them comfortable with math, and the third was to ensure that they passed their math proficiency test. He expected their children to do 30–40 minutes of homework every day, regardless of whether he actually gave assignments. He did not encourage the use of calculators; he wanted the children to be able to go through the thought process. He had rules for his class. One rule was that it was OK to blurt out an answer. He felt that this was fine, because someone could state an answer and do it with some level of anonymity. Another rule was that he scheduled conferences with parents only when students were having difficulty. He did not call home with disciplinary problems; he handled them in the classroom. After returning their graded tests, students could recover about half the points they initially lost if they corrected their mistakes. In closing, he invited the parents to come and observe his class anytime, with an advance notice.

Math Skills Class: Mr. Peters

There were only 4 Black parents at the Open House for this class, although most of the students were Black. Mr. Peters was late because he had another Open House session on the other side of the building. Before the teacher arrived we talked with one of the Black parents who appeared unsure as to whether she was in right class. She was looking for a basic pre-algebra class. When she mentioned her son's name, we recognized him. He was one of the brighter students in this class during our lesson observation.

There were two students with their parents at the Open House. When Mr. Peters finally settled down, he put an equation on the board; then he called on the students to solve the problem. The students did not respond. Mr. Peters remarked that it was not fair to call on them but still continued to question them. Finally they responded and got the answer right.

Mr. Peters told the parents that the objectives of the class were to improve the students' math skills, prepare them for algebra, and enable them to pass their math proficiency test. He had the same goals for college prep class. He told the parents that their children would be doing lots of story problems, because there were 40 stories on the proficiency test. They would be doing a lot of them in the class; they would analyze the stories or problem passages until they became comfortable with this approach to mathematics. He also told the parents that he did not give a lot of homework but gave no reasons for this. He wanted the students to do most of their work in class. Finally, he explained his rule about raising hands to answer questions in class. He did not want students to raise their hands when they knew the answer to a question, because students who raised their hands often knew the answer to a question and thereby set the class pace. In concluding, he asked them to call if they had a concern. He also told them to come and observe his class any time.

(Seventh-Grade AP) English Class: Ms. Dawson

There were only 2 Blacks out of 37 students in this class. One of the Black students was present tonight. Most of the parents were White. Most of the seats were occupied when we entered, so we had to sit on a table near the door.

When we entered, Ms. Dawson was commenting on her age. She remarked on that she looked young enough for some parents not to think that she was the teacher. She began to describe her class. The students were reading Tom Sawyer and would be doing a skit. The students were very excited about the project. She then talked about her expectations of the class, especially the skills she wanted them to demonstrate. Among other things, they would read, study grammar, and do some creative writing. Each student would also have an opportunity to make a speech. Ms. Dawson said this was important, even though she herself did not like it when she was their age. She told the parents to encourage their children to read outside of the classroom. Next she discussed her grading policy. Then she turned to homework, letting it be known that it was important. She showed the parents where she kept their children's folders. The work could be overwhelming sometimes, but students were given planners in order to organize their work. She asked the parents to monitor their children's progress by looking at their planners.

HIGH SCHOOL OPEN HOUSE

AP English: Mr. Answorth

There were 15 parents in attendance, including 1 Asian and 1 Black. On entering the classroom, the teacher, Mr. Answorth, handed out copies of *The Shakerite* issue with accounts of a fight and other events following a party. The teacher then began by telling the parents of his love of the Classics. He told them that he had discovered from class discussions that their children were amazingly conservative. They should ask them about the class because that would generate a lot to talk about with their children. As he named the books the class had yet to read, one parent asked "Are you going to read anything serious (books)?" The teacher chuckled a bit; then he told the parent that *Wuthering Heights* was quite a serious work as were others on his list. He added that the class would read parts of *1984*, just to give them a sense of what could happen because of current technological advances. He pointed out that the high school had just installed security cameras around the building. At this point several parents raised their hands to ask more questions. Responding to one parent, Mr. Answorth pointed out that they were very firm in what they expected of students in high school. For example, he expected students to turn in every assignment on time. This might not be the case when they went off to college. Returning to his method of instruction, Mr. Answorth said that he tried to get students to write in order to develop themselves. One parent requested printouts of the

TABLE 11.2

Black Parents' Attendance at the High School Open House

Teacher	Course Level	# Black Parents
D		1
E	AP	1
E	CP	0
Team	Math lab	2

Note. AP = advanced placement; CP = college prep.

reading list so that parents could discuss the books at home. Several parents chatted with one another at the end of the Open House. One father stayed behind to talk about the reading list. He asked for and got the teacher's home phone number. The teacher told him to call if he really wanted to. The parent said he would.

AP/College Prep Social Studies: Mr. Glenn

We were surprised that there was only one Black parent at this Open House session. We had seen this woman earlier in the evening. She seemed to know many of the White parents. Prior to the Open House we had observed this and other classes taught by Mr. Glenn. There were many Black students in each of the classes. Mr. Glenn began by talking about the history of the class and its significance. He said that it was not too long ago that the world remained silent while ethnic cleansing occurred. He gave several examples before focusing on the Holocaust. He said that morality was used to justify the Holocaust and that it was therefore important to understand mass movements. He said that people sometimes acted contrary to their religious beliefs and yet justified their actions in the name of the same religion. Next, he talked about some of the class textbooks. Then he described his philosophy of teaching. He didn't think that students should compete with one another but only with themselves. One parent asked how he graded students; she was concerned her child had not received any grade in the class. Mr. Glenn replied that he did not give grades; his goal was to develop the students as critical thinkers who would use their creativity to become unique individuals, not clones of himself. He concluded by saying that he believed that if you could teach one individual to make the world a better place, then maybe the world would become a better place. He hoped that his students would challenge some of the views of their parents. Finally, he invited the parents to come along with the class during a Holocaust field trip he was planning.

Second-Year Algebra Lab: Team of Three Teachers

When we entered this class, the teachers greeted us with handshakes and seemed pleased to see us. They greeted two Black parents who next entered the room in the same manner. The two parents sat on either side of us. The lead teacher said that it would take up to 1 hour to give parents a really good idea of what went on in the class but that that would not be necessary because the teachers were planning parent conferences about the class. At the conferences they would provide parents with detailed information about the class. The teachers then passed a sign-up sheet to two parents sitting near us and asked if they were interested in attending. Parents would be provided babysitting and transportation assistance if they needed them. A male parent signed up. Another parent, a woman who had two children in the class, said she could not sign up because she had to work that night. However, she would try to get the day off to attend. The lead teacher suggested, that she sign up tentatively so that they could keep in touch her. She did, making a note that she needed babysitting. Later, the lead teacher told us that it was that important to them that the parents come to the conference; that was why they arranged for transportation and baby-sitting. When we left the class after further discussions with the teachers, we felt that they really tried to show parents that they were concerned about their children's academic growth as well as the opinions of the parents.

In this and other classes we observed there were fewer Black parents than the Whites even in the classes where most of the students were Black. Furthermore, Black parents usually did not ask questions relevant to their children's academic work. Another interesting point was that Black parents were often accompanied by their children. We didn't know whether it was because the parents did not feel comfortable attending the Open House on their own or because they did not know the purpose of Open House. We did not see any White children accompanying their parents, but then, we did not observe every class.

Why Black Parents' School Involvement Was Limited

Lack of Education

One popular explanation for the low school involvement of Black parents offered by teachers and people in the community was that they were not well educated. Therefore they did not understand the school system and did not know how to get their children through it. An example given for this lack of understanding was the inappropriate responses of parents when contacted about their children. According to one teacher, whenever he called a parent to touch base and warn of a potential problem, the parent would immediately conclude that his or her child was already in trouble. The parent would then offer to discipline the child and end the phone discussion with a threatening voice warning that the child had better change. Another teacher said that parents were concerned about their children's education, but "it's just that some of them don't know what to do." Teachers believed that relatively uneducated Black parents expected the school to do everything necessary for their children to succeed. These parents did not think that they themselves had to participate in school programs or meet with teachers for their children to succeed. The problem with this explanation was that it did not account for the low involvement of well-educated middle-class parents.

Employment

Another reason offered was that Black parents worked many hours with no time left to participate in school events. It was sometimes said that working-class parents held two or three jobs. In our comparative observations of White and Black neighborhoods we often saw more White mothers with elementary school-age children during working hours than Black mothers with similar school-age children. This suggested that more White mothers were home during the day. We saw several White mothers going for walks together in the late morning. We got to know some of these moms quite well. They devoted a large part of their time to the local PTO and other school matters. They had a lot of time to investigate what was going on in the community. Some shared with us newspaper clippings on local affairs or told us about local gossip and events that they thought might be of interest to us or would be relevant to our study. On the whole, mothers in the White community were highly involved in the local PTO and school programs in their neighborhood school.

But what about Black middle-class and professional parents? From our observations, and by all accounts, Black middle-class parents were not any more involved than Black working-class parents. School personnel reported that Black middle-class parents were not sufficiently involved with the schools but did not explain their lack of involvement. The explanation offered by their children and by other Black people in the community was that they, too, did not have time because they were struggling to maintain their middle-class or professional status. Like the working-class parents, they worked long hours or held more than one job. They went to school mainly when there was a crisis. One female student described her professional parents' involvement as crisis oriented:

> OK. For instance, my parents are married. They live together. You know, we're upper middle class, but they started early ... They didn't come up to the school; I mean, they were like not involved unless there is some problem. If there is some altercations [i.e., crisis], then they would come up and, you know, they talked to teachers and whatever.

Alienation From the System

Some school personnel and community informants believed that Black parents were not actively involved in school because they were alienated from the White-controlled school system. The first-grade teacher who had earlier described how she was unable to get Black parents to come to meetings about her program believed that alienation was at the root of the problem. As she put it, "Some African-American parents have told me that maybe school wasn't a positive experience for the parents. So they already have a negative attitude and feel fearful about approaching teachers." One parent described herself as one of a few Black professionals active in the local PTO. Her PTO had eliminated dues to attract more Black parents, but that did not work. Some parents perceived the PTO as made up of as made up of "a bunch of do-gooders and stay-home White moms." Blacks did not interpret the PTO as White parents did; neither did they feel at home as members.

Mistrust of the System

In addition to alienation, Black parents mistrusted the school system as a White institution. At a discussion with a group of school personnel someone from the community spoke at length of the history of mistreatment of Blacks by White institutions. He said that the mistreatment forced Blacks to become highly mistrustful not only of the economic system but also of White schools. Black people distrusted the schools because of generations of discrimination and the collective struggle Blacks had had to wage for equal educational opportunity. He implied that the mistrust of the school system permeated all segments of the Black community; it was not limited to poor and working class Blacks. That was why middle-class Black parents were not involved.

Cultural Model of Teaching and Learning

Still another reason for the low parent involvement was their understanding or notion of who should educate their children, that is, their cultural model of school teaching and learning. Observations and interviews in Shaker Heights and elsewhere suggested that Black Americans have what may be called "a beer mug" model school teaching and learning. In this model, students learn and perform well if the teacher pours knowledge well into students. The teacher is accountable for students' learning and performance because it is his or her duty to pour the knowledge well.

Students are more or less passive receivers or drinkers of the knowledge. We saw in chapter 2 that some students in Shaker Heights blamed teachers for not motivating them to learn. As for parents they did not perceive themselves as active agents in the education process. They did not think they needed to be involved in the teaching process for their children to learn. The role of parents is apparently limited to putting pressure on teachers to do their job of teaching well; that is, limited to pushing teachers and other school personnel to educate their children. Parents' involvement also occurred, perhaps more actively, during crises when they went to push the school system to push teachers or to push some other school personnel to "do right" by their children. We now consider how this model of teaching and learning affected what parents did, especially at home, about their children's schoolwork in Shaker Heights.

Some Shaker Heights teachers appeared to recognize this model intuitively. In the words of one teacher, "Many Black parents just expect that the school will do everything necessary to make sure that their children will get an education." The model was clearly evident in our discussion with some members of the community. An example occurred on one occasion when we were discussing a significant improvement in the proficiency test of a cohort of students in one elementary school. Our informant emphatically let it be known that the increase in the children's test scores was entirely due to what the teachers and the school did. "And," our informant concluded with emphasis, "the parents and the students did not do anything. That's right. They did not do anything."

Inadequate Knowledge of Differences Between Class Levels

One other explanation was that parents did not know enough about the significance of the difference between AP and honors courses, on the one hand, and skills and college preparatory courses, on the other hand. Many Black parents missed the opportunity to learn about the differences, because they did not attend school meetings, participate in school programs, go to parent-teacher conferences, or do volunteer work at school. They did not emphasize enough to their children the importance of taking the honors and AP courses. Neither did they know when or how to intervene to ensure that their children took these courses. One teacher believed that the reason few Black students went into honors and AP classes was that their parents did not fully understand the meaning and implications of these classes. He tried to organize a program to help parents better understand the classes. If parents learned about what was taught and how it was taught in the classes then they would be in a better position to help their children get into the classes. It was not only the honors and AP classes that parents did not know enough about; they were similarly lacking in understanding of the skills and college prep classes. It was partly for this reason that teachers organized the math conference described earlier in this chapter.

This lack of understanding of what and how their children were taught might be one reason why the parents did not prepare their children more effectively to meet the requirement for participation in academic enrichment classes at the upper elementary school. It might also, as already noted, be a reason for not intervening when their children were placed in inappropriate classes. Older students reported that more Black students would be participating in the academic enrichment program at the upper elementary school and in the honors classes at the middle school if their parents intervened. A female student described the difference her mother's intervention had made in her case.

> I think a lot happens between Woodbury and the middle school, because that's when different classes start. At that point they'll have like enrich classes, advanced classes, and regular classes. I know, like my mom had to talk to the administration about putting me in the enrich classes because it was just like, you know, my test scores were high enough to be in there. Everything was, you know. I'm doing well in math or whatever, *but* (emphasizes word) for whatever reasons they didn't want to put me in those classes. And people ... in the honors and advanced placement classes in the seventh and eighth grades [middle school] have had the background, the experience, and the knowledge from the enrichment classes to get into those classes. Then once they got to the high school, the transitions into the honors and AP classes [they] were much easier. It was easier to maintain and stay in those honors and AP classes.

Parents' Involvement With Their Children's Education at Home

If parents were not actively involved with their children's education at school, to what extent they were involved at home? The involvement of parent in their children's education ideally should begin with preparing them for initial entry into school. As their children get older, parents should explain to them it is important for them to go to school; let them know of the parents' expectations; check on their children's schoolwork and homework; and, if they can, assist with their homework. When children are having difficulty in a subject, parents would try to find out the reasons; they could then go to the teacher to find out more about the problem and what can be done about it.

In Shaker Heights, students, parents and other members of the Black community discussed patterns of parents' involvement with their children's schoolwork at home. We describe some of these patterns in this section.

Preschool and Early Grades

Some, but not all, parents prepared their children for entry into kindergarten. One active member of a local PTO reported that a former kindergarten teacher once told her that professional families of four or five children did not prepare them adequately for her kindergarten class. The informant dismissed the teacher's assessment as unfair and as an excuse not to teach Black children effectively to close the academic gap between them and White children.

Other informants believed that Black parents did not pay enough attention to their children's schoolwork in the early grades, especially in reading and math. Furthermore, Black parents did not check their children's schoolwork and homework regularly. At formal and informal discussions, students stated that one reason more Black students did not get into the academic enrichment classes at the upper elementary school was that their parents did not push them enough in the earlier grades. In comparing their parents with White parents they believed that White parents pushed their children more. Their parents did not supervise their schoolwork in the early grades as much as White parents supervised the schoolwork of their own children. The contrast between their parents and White parents was made by several high school students during a discussion with the anthropologist:

> Oh, um, I think it also starts at home, too. Um, I think that um part of the reason that maybe Blacks just don't do as well, is because maybe Black parents don't push them as hard to do well as maybe White parents. I'm not saying that all Black parents don't try and want their kids to do well, but it somehow told us, that's not um a major criteria in their household, and they're not so concerned about if their kids do well in school.

Another student cautioned against generalization, saying that there were differences among Black parents just as there were differences among White parents. He concluded, "It all depends on where you're coming from ... like, you can't say [it's every] Black family. 'Cause it could be two Black families [that] could be extremely different, and two White families [that] could be extremely different."

Homework Supervision

We became aware of parents' supervision of homework, or lack of it, during a visit to Woodbury Upper Elementary School in the early part of our fieldwork. A teacher approached us as we were about to leave to let us know that parental supervision of homework was an important factor in students' school success. She suggested that we look into that. She said that as a teacher she was responsible for what happened in the classroom but that it was the responsibility of the parents to ensure that their children completed their homework and that many children would not do their homework without their parents' supervision. She went on to report the case of a parent whom she described as "a complainer." Yet her child would never complete homework assignments. Whenever she asked the child why he did not complete his homework, he would say "I was tired and I fell asleep" or give other excuses. The teacher concluded by saying that she believed one of the reasons African American students were not doing well was that they came from low-income and working-class families where parents did not supervise their homework.

Teachers, students, and others more or less agreed that many students did not take their homework seriously and that their parents did not adequately supervise it. A comparison was often made between White parents and Black parents. White parents expected more homework and made sure that their children completed and returned it to the teacher. This was less true of Black parents. Teachers were aware of this difference, and it influenced their homework policies and practices. The difference was evident in the way they talked about homework during the Open House at the middle school and high school. For example, in one AP class at the high school the teacher told parents that homework was very important. She showed them their children's folders with corrected assignments. She reminded them that homework could be a difficult assignment or overwhelming. She provided students with planners to help them organize their homework assignments. She asked the parents to monitor their children's academic progress by checking the planners. She usually signed the planners to show that she had recorded all completed assignments. The parents were requested to include a note in the planner returned by the student if they had questions or suggestions.

In contrast, teachers of skills and college prep classes tended to de-emphasize the importance of homework. During the Open House one teacher of a skills class told the parents that "there was not a lot of homework in the class." He did not explain why there was not a lot of homework. He did not show the parents their children's folders with completed homework assignments. Neither did he talk of providing students with planners to be signed to show that their homework was completed and recorded.

We learned more of parents' supervision of homework, or lack of it, from their children's descriptions of their own experiences. The importance of parents' supervision of homework was not lost on the students. For example, MAC scholars reported that parents' supervision of their schoolwork and homework was an important reason for their academic success. The parents of the scholars not only expected them to do well in school but also saw to it that they did their homework. In the words of one scholar, "My parents make sure I have done my homework before I can watch TV."

In general, however, in group discussions or at interviews students reported that many Black parents, including their own, did not supervise or check their children's homework closely or often. Recall that in chapter 2, in which we discussed students' effort or lack of effort, one student reported that he usually did only a part, not all, of his homework. His parents apparently did not check on his homework. Another student described what happened where there was no adequate supervision:

> If it's a nice, sunny day outside, you'd rather go outside and play with your friends than do your homework. And if you don't have parents who are telling you or making you do your homework, or who … will go down to school a few times and check out and make sure you're doing okay, then you can just slack off and go [and do other things]. I know. But for you to do your homework, your parents need to help you and keep you on the right tack.

Monitoring Children's Use of Time: Television

Students reported that they were distracted from schoolwork and homework by inappropriate role models on television. They complained that their parents did not sufficiently monitor the kinds of television programs they watched or how much time they spent watching television. As a result, they not only spent too much time watching television but they also watched programs that exposed them to role models that were detrimental to their school interest and striving.

Controlling Peer Pressures

Neither did parents scrutinize enough their children's friends. As we discussed in chapter 10, there were many negative peer pressures on students in regard to schoolwork. Just as parents did not monitor adequately television watching, they did not monitor their children's friendships. Hence, many children were distracted from their schoolwork by their friends and inappropriate role models. One high school student put the matter this way:

> If you have good parents, and a good home ... you may see on television someone smoking weed or somethin' like that, and your peers may smoke. Those two factors can, you know, make a dramatic change in your success. So, ... I really think that ... what the community can do is to monitor television programs so that we do not watch movies in which some bad things happen to you. And I think that parents ... should, if they're not already involved in the community, I think they should take a larger part in the involvement in the community and at home to monitor what we are exposed to.

Motivating Children: Reward and Punishment

Parents used rewards and punishment to implement their academic expectations. Students experienced this twin practice beginning at the elementary school. All but one elementary school student interviewed were rewarded for good grades or punished for bad grades. Three students had always done well in school and had never been punished. Rewards for good grades included money and a treat. One student who usually got both money and a treat, described her experience "And ... every time I get good grades on my report card, my Mom takes me out to Wendy's. 'Cause you get a free happy meal." Punishment for poor grades included loss of some privileges; a student might not be allowed to go to parties. In addition, he or she might be forced to stay home and study.

Older students were also rewarded for good grades and punished for poor grades. Some felt that the rewards constituted a powerful incentive to do better, as in the case of this student:

Student: My parents would give me, um, we'd call them report card treats, literally. And, um, for every good report card or almost every good report card or anything like that, it's sort of things that I needed anyway [that his parents would give him]. But I'd get a new pair of shoes, so I'd associate good grades with new things.

Anthrop: Rewards.

Student: Right, reward, constant reward versus punishment. And uh, I
never really thought about it much, but that's really, I guess,
that was the basis. Yeah, even from kindergarten, just a pack of
football cards, if I brought home a good grade or something
like that. And I never, I never really thought about it like that,
but my mom was a psychology major.

Students who were not rewarded for getting good grades felt that they
should. They felt that their parents were not doing enough to encourage
them to do well in school. Parents punished older children for poor
grades. However, as students got older punishments usually lost their effectiveness. Here is an example of an older student for whom punishment
for bad grades had lost its power to motivate him to improve his school
performance.

Student: And like if I get a D or a F, my father just won't accept it, 'cause
he knows I'm a smart kid; and he know I could do the work. He
said like if I got a D or somethin', he said, he'd be mad because
he know I could do the work. He said it'd be different if I could-
n't do the work, you know, he'll understand. But I can do the
work so he wants me to get to my ability.

Anthrop: So what happens when you do bring home a D? What does he
do?

Student: He usually puts me on punishment for a while. I usually can't
talk on the phone or watch TV; I have to like come straight
home from school. I can't play any sports.

Anthrop: Does that work for you?

Student: Huh?

Anthrop: Does that work to make you change and start getting better
grades?

Student: Sometimes. I mean, it doesn't as much now because before [in
the earlier grades], [when I was] on punishment ... I get a
whuppin'. So ... instead of gettin' a whuppin', I rather do my
work. But now, [when] I'm on punishment and he's not-he's
not like ever in my room to tell me what to do. And I have a TV
in my room, I could turn it down low. I got a PlayStation. I be
playin' PlayStation and stuff ... so he doesn't really come in my
room nowadays and stress it as much. But I used to get a
whoopin' and he'd take all that away ...

There were parents who did not punish their children for getting poor grades; instead, they discussed the grades with them to find out why they did not do well. They then encouraged them to do better next time. This was the experience of the next student.

Anthrop: OK. And what happens when your report card comes? What do you guys do?

Student: (laughs). OK, like for instance this time, I kind of strayed from what I was supposed to get. I got a couple of C's and my parents at first were kind of disappointed. They were, they told me. They gave me the support and, first of all, they asked how did my grades come down, to get to this level, like a B– or a C+ or anything like that. And I told them. And they said that um, that I know that I could raise my grade up because ... its just that ... the first grading period is kinda shaky for me. 'Cause if I have to get into certain subjects [honors or AP class], and actually be involved in it, I have to get really good grades and study right.

The extent to which Black parents rewarded or punished their children for good and bad grades was impressive. Their behaviors suggested that they very much wanted their children to do well in school. They were happy and rewarded them when they did well; they were unhappy and sometimes punished them when they did not. However, the effectiveness of these behaviors should be seen in its proper context. According to the children and some adults, many parents discussed their children's work with them, and rewarded or punished them, only when report cards arrived.

REASONS FOR INADEQUATE INVOLVEMENT AT HOME

Communication Barriers: Limited Parental Education

Some of the reasons for the parents' limited guidance and supervision were the same as or their limited involvement with the school system. Not being well educated was the reason most often given by school authorities. Students had a different interpretation of the effect of their parents' limited education: They believed that their poorly educated parents had difficulty convincing them, their children, that education was important or convincing them to study hard and make good grades. In other words, the students did not usually listen to their parents, whom they did not think were educated enough to advise them about such matters. One female high school student described the problem like this:

> I think [there is] something else that kinda goes along with [what has been said]. Maybe [even] a stronger reason. Like if [parents] like didn't get as good of an education—the parents I'm talking about—um, if they didn't have that good education … it's harder for them to tell their children that, "You have do this stuff that I never did," you know. Like if you have a parent that was like really successful and got like this really good education, it's easy to be like convince you by tellin' you, "I did it. You do it now." But like if they didn't do it, it's a lot harder for them to like—convince their kids that like "You have to be better than I was," you know. That's hard for a parent to say to a kid. But I don't even put the blame on the parents or anyone or the teachers, because it's really up to the student. Because I know a lot of people who are not financially as stable as a lot of people here in Shaker, you know. And they go to school in Cleveland. But their parents are always saying, "Because we don't want you to live this life that we had to live, we want you to do better, so please try hard. Try hard." And a lot of parents are saying that to their children, you know. It's no parents that—well, there are some—but most parents, they want their child to do well in school. But when you talk about when you talk about … Black students who aren't doing well, I think their parents want them to do good just like any others, any other parent wants her child to do good. It's just the student. And it's like, when you come to school, it doesn't matter what your parents have, uh, told you, it's up to you.

She went on to say that students were responsible for choosing between their education or schoolwork and their peer groups:

> You're [i.e., the student] the one who have, … you know, to make the decisions; and you're the one who has to decide, "Well, my mother wants me to do good, but am I gonna do that?" The reason is that when a lot of students come to school, school isn't school to them. School is just a place where they meet and … hang with their friends. It doesn't even matter what … their parents told them. It could go completely, you know, into one ear and out the other. It's just the whole mind set of the student.

Communication Barriers Between Generations

The generation gap was another reason students did not listen to their parents. Some students were unwilling to follow their parents' advice about education because they considered their parents' views to be old-fashioned. A student illustrated the problem with a description of her relationship with her parents. She said that her parents did not understand her teenage problems and how to relate to her about these problems. So, she turned to her teenage cousins who had gone through similar problems.

Competing Inappropriate Societal Role Models

Another reason students did not listen to their parents was that society and the media presented them with role models whose paths to fame or status did not depend on school success.

> And it's the image thing too, like, Lana was saying. The image of role models that the society has set for the uh Black male or the Black female is, you know, that of rappers, or gang bangers, or dope dealers, and a lot of other kinds of people. [students] feel that that's what is the in-thing to do, and they feel that getting good grades and being successful, that's not the in-thing. And I think it has to do with role models and everything. And people can't separate the fact that entertainment—you know, gangster, rap music—they can't accept the fact that that's just entertainment. They see that that's the way of life, and that's the cool way to be. They can't separate that in their heads that this is music. You know, and it's just music. These people are out to make money, but I want to do good in school, you know. I want to, I want to do something with my life. They want to be like the rappers and everybody else they hear about, so that's what I think.

Employment Constraints on Parents' Time

Although some working-class parents who found time to talk to their children about the need to do well in school supervised or checked their homework, most did not do so because they had no time because of their jobs. Students believed that their parents' work affected their ability to motivate them and to supervise or help with their homework. The following student described her own experience of the work constraints on her parents' time. She also provided a general picture of the situation among the working-class:

Student: My neighbor found time to talk to his children. But my parents are like [the] opposite. They're the opposite 'cause like a lot of parents, you know, they don't have the time to, you know, motivate you by telling you things like that. So you know, you're kinda just on your own and put aside 'til they got time, and yet by the time they have time, they, it's like it's too late.

Anthrop: So your parents don't have time?

Male Student:	A lot of people's parents don't have time.
Anthrop:	Do your parents have time?
Male Student:	No. Never.

It was not only working-class parents who did not have time to help their children at home and monitor their homework; some children from middle-class and professional families also reported that they received little or no assistance from their parents because of their employment schedule. They described their parents' working life as "struggling." Thus, it appears that both working-class and middle-class parents had no time because they were struggling, although for different reasons. Working-class parents struggled by working two or three jobs to earn enough money to pay the bills; middle-class parents, on the other hand, struggled by working at more than one job or long hours to earn enough money to maintain their middle-class status.

Allocation of Educational Responsibility

Another reason for the low involvement of working-class parents was that some parents felt their role in their children's education was paying the high tax rate and meeting the high cost of living in Shaker Heights so that their children would graduate from the Shaker Heights school system. They wanted their children to graduate from Shaker Heights because of the prestige of school credentials from the school district. They moved to Shaker Heights for this reason, knowing that it would mean working at more than one job to pay the bills. That is, they believed that by moving to Shaker Heights and working hard and long hours to meet the financial cost of living and sending their children to Shaker schools, they had fulfilled their own responsibility of educating their children. It was up to the school to teach and make sure that their children learned and it was up to their children to study and do well in school. One student from a working-class background described this allocation of educational responsibility and his own experience this way:

Male Student:	I just wanted to make one point. That is, that a lot of times Shaker is looked at as like a goal. It's to, it's like to my mom, I know that she grew up in a project and her dad started going to

[jail].... I mean, if you could picture in your mind the projects, [it's] like the worst projects you can think of. That's where my mom [grew up]. I mean, she had no money at all. And my daddy gone to school, when she met him [and they decided] just to [move] to Shaker. And I think [there is] a lot of um people's parents [who] don't have quite that much money. They want their children to have better lives, and they say about their child, "Well, if I can just get him into Shaker, if I can get him into Shaker schools, he'll be all right." So we get here, and we're in Shaker schools and everything. [But] if you are here in Shaker and you don't go to class, [and] you don't get the A's and B's then, I mean, what's the point? Your parents are just paying a lot of taxes that ain't doing nothing.

Anthrop: You know, you sound to me like Chinese students who said that their parents suffered to come to the U.S. so that they can get "American education." Your parents suffered to come to Shaker, right? so you can go to school ... Chinese students take that as a challenge to do well [in school] in order to make their parents feel that at least they are getting something for their effort and sacrifices. Am I hearing the same thing from my fellow brothers and sisters whose parents are working so hard so they can live in Shaker and give them a chance for "better education?"

Male   Well, anyway, you know, [they will say] once I got here, I'm
Student: gonna [get good education]. But by the time [students] get to Shaker, and their parents are *inspired* (emphasizes the word) to come, [parents] still got to work. They still got to pay the bills.

Lack of Awareness of Children's Academic Problems

Finally, some parents did not help their children with their schoolwork because they were not aware that their children had academic problems. They thought that their children were doing well when they were not. An example of this was the case of a mother who attended the math conference described earlier. In a discussion with the teachers after the conference we told them that when we talked with the mother in the community she thought that her son was doing an amazing job in the class. The teachers said that this was definitely not so. The boy received a B for the first marking period. Compared to other students, in the class he didn't do well; he barely met the minimum expectation. They explained that they did not give failing grades because they didn't want to discourage the students in the math lab class. The work for which they gave passing grades in the lab class would receive failing grades in regular math classes. They said that the woman's son was easily distracted and was not doing so well. Their overall description of him suggested that he was really one of the problem children in the class, yet his mother didn't have a clue of his academic performance or behavior problems.

ASPIRATION AND EXPECTATION
VERSUS BEHAVIOR

As has already been pointed out, Black parents had very high academic expectations for their children, and their children knew this. But the children felt that high expectations were not sufficient to help them do well in school. Several students pointed out what was missing: Their parents did not show them how to succeed in school. They did not, for example, supervise their schoolwork closely. Thus, there was a discrepancy between parents' expectations, such as telling them that they should make good grades, and actually showing them how they should make good grades. The male student who reported earlier that his parents never had time to supervise his homework also spoke to this:

Anthrop:	So they haven't really communicated to you something to motivate you to work hard in school, right?
Male student:	Well, they say, "Go to school and do good," but really that's not enough. Anybody can tell you that. "Go to school and do good." I mean, that's not all parents expect will make you do well in school. But, I mean, they're never there.
Anthrop:	Are your parents middle class? Upper class?
Male student:	None.

Some students living with both parents in working-class families did not necessarily see any of the parents when they got home from school, because both parents were working, perhaps, on two jobs. The student extended his description to this situation:

The students don't see [their parents]. They don't come home until ten o'clock and [the students], you know. They might not even get dinner. They might have to make dinner for themself (sic). They ... don't ever see their parents. And by the time they get up to go to school, their mother's at work already. They, they don't even see [their parents] for a week. I see my mother on like, maybe, Monday, and I might see her (again on) Friday, Friday night. You know what I'm sayin'? So, there's not even thinkin' of my schoolwork, 'cause I don't even see my mom for, I mean, a week.

School authorities and some people in the Black community usually assumed that the problem of inadequate guidance and supervision was limited to working-class, poor families and single-parent families. However, we learned from students and some adult informants that it also existed among middle-class and professional families. Students from professional or middle-class families described their own experiences that were similar to those of students from working-class families. Some of the former described themselves as *latchkey kids*. The advantage of middle-class latchkey kids was that they might have received more or better preparation for their academic careers in early school years. This enabled them to handle their schoolwork more effectively in the absence of later parental guidance and supervision. The following self-portrait of an upper middle-class student is representative of the middle-class latchkey kids:

OK. My parents are married. They live together, you know. We're upper middle class. But they married early. They told us what we needed to know. We're latchkey kids, and they left. We raised ourselves. So, I think my situation is a little bit different from those of working-class families. My parents gave us a lot of good things before they left, but then, they're … basically gone. They didn't come up to the school; I mean, they were like not involved unless there is some problem. Then they would come up and, you know, they talked to teachers and whatever. But basically everything I have done in my education have been by my decisions to be in whatever classes. I usually do some research before the classes to know well enough about them before taking them.

12

Community Forces
and Academic Disengagement:
A Summary of Findings

We started this book by stating the three objectives of our study. One was to discover the factors that contributed to the low school performance of Black students in the Shaker Heights school district. The second was to examine one of these factors, their academic disengagement. Finally, we hoped to bring community forces into the present discourse, policy, and practice in Black education. Our framework for the study was the cultural–ecological theory of schooling, which posits that minorities' school engagement and performance would be influenced by two sets of actors: (a) societal and school factors, and (b) community factors. The societal and school factors (the system) are the treatments of Blacks by Whites in society and in education, and the community factors are people interpretations of and responses to schooling (community forces) because of the way they interpret and respond to the societal and school treatments as well as their mode of incorporation into minority status. We did not downplay the role of societal and school mistreatment of Blacks in Shaker Heights, but we focused on the role of community forces; that is, we concentrated on the educational beliefs or interpretations and behaviors of Blacks, especially those of the students. Specifically, we examined how the following features of the community forces affected the academic engagement and school performance of the students: frame of school or educational comparison; beliefs about the instrumental value of school credentials; relationship with White people and the schools they controlled; symbolic beliefs about or interpretations of cultural, language, and intellectual differences; and educational strategies or how Blacks strived to acquire formal education.

We took into account three other contextual factors, namely, (a) that the United States is a settler society, (b) that the formal education system in the United States is a delegate agency, and (c) that Black Americans are *an involuntary minority* (see chap. 3).

The preceding chapters were not organized around our findings on the community forces, because these factors were interlocking so that a given factor permeated the topics described in several chapters. In this chapter we draw from various chapters to summarize our findings on specific community forces. The primary focus of this chapter is on community forces, for two reasons. First, as we indicated in the Preface, one of the objects of this book is to introduce the community forces as a part of the discourse, policy, and practice in minority education. The second reason is that our findings on community forces are the basis of our recommendations in the next chapter.

FRAMES OF REFERENCE

Throughout the study, Blacks compared themselves with Whites in Shaker Heights and in the whole United States. In the comparison, they always concluded that they were worse off than the Whites in jobs, income, housing, political power, and education for no other reason than their minority status. This inequality had been a part of their experience since they were emancipated from slavery. As evidence, they cited several historical landmark court decisions, such as Plessy v. Furguson. As for unequal educational opportunity, they noted that it took the U.S. Supreme Court decision in the case of Brown v. Board of Education to end de jure school segregation and inferior education in the South. But that did not necessarily end de facto segregated and inferior education in the South and in the North. From their point of view, at the time of our study in 1997, Blacks in Shaker Heights High, like those in Little Rock High in Arkansas, were still segregated and disadvantaged in education in the absence of legal barriers.

Adults and children compared the two races politically. From the middle school the students were aware of the unequal power relations between the two races both locally and nationally. For example, one middle school student noted that no Black American had ever been elected President of the United States (chap. 4). The students believed that Black people were judged by the color of their skin rather than ability in many areas of life. They wished that society would stop stereotyping them and would judge them on the basis of their ability.

Another negative frame of comparison was about the criterion for evaluation of performance. They believed that Black Americans were compelled to work twice as hard as their White peers for the same societal reward. High school students complained most that Black employees were expected by White employers to work twice as hard as White employees with the same qualification or education to prove themselves. Black workers usually knew that their White employers had lower expectations of them, and for that reason they felt that they had to prove themselves.

The students also believed that for a Black person to compete successfully with a White person for the same job, wage, or job promotion he or she had to be twice as good as the White competitor. We did not directly inquire into the effects of these beliefs on the students' academic engagement, but it is not far-fetched to think that they might in some way contribute to the academic disengagement.

OPPORTUNITY STRUCTURE AND INSTRUMENTAL LINKAGE TO EDUCATION (FOLK THEORY OF "MAKING IT")

In Shaker Heights, Blacks verbally emphasized the importance of education for adult futures. They also said that they were determined to get a good education themselves or for their children to get a good education in order to get good jobs. At the same time, however, they verbalized other beliefs and described experiences that appeared to undermine their educational beliefs and commitments. As involuntary minorities with a long history of discrimination in the opportunity structure, it appeared that our informants were not really sure that education was the key to upward social mobility or to the achievement of the American Dream. This apparent ambivalence was evident in our subsequent analysis of three issues in education and opportunity structure.

Education and The American Dream

Before the civil rights movement and legislation of the 1960s, Black Americans were prevented by a job ceiling from receiving equal benefits of school credentials with Whites (chap. 8). The job ceiling was lowered by the civil rights legislation and extra government policies, such as affirmative action. Civil rights legislation and affirmative action attempted to enable Blacks and other minorities get the jobs and other benefits of education that their

White peers with similar educational qualification got without special legislation and government programs. The job ceiling was not lowered, because Blacks had become more educated. Thus, for Black Americans the link between school credentials, on the one hand, and upward social mobility, on the other hand, remained relatively weak in the context of the civil rights legislation and affirmative action: From the 1960s, Blacks needed the special legislation and affirmative action program to get the jobs open to Whites without these extra helps.

Shaker Heights Blacks believed that they had benefitted from civil rights legislation and affirmative action. They did not face the same degree of discrimination in the opportunity structure experienced by their forebears. Many, like their White peers, could now get the same jobs, wages, and job promotions on the basis of education and ability. However, informants were skeptical. It is significant to note that even some elementary school students discussed the racial barriers in opportunity structure. Some middle school students felt that affirmative action and other special government programs were still needed, not to enable Blacks to close the gaps caused by past discrimination but because of residual of racial barriers. From the students' point of view, White people were criticizing affirmative action because they were not aware of the extent of the barriers endured by Blacks in the past. Furthermore, White critics know how deeply those barriers affected the current occupational status and education of Blacks. High school students repeatedly explained that affirmative action program was developed to remedy the damage resulting from the long history of discrimination and that the affirmative action should continue to enable Blacks to catch up with White people.

Perceptions of Unequal Opportunity and Academic Engagement

The belief that unequal opportunity still persisted had two opposite effects on students' academic engagement. On the one hand, it made some students skeptical as to the real value of school credentials and discouraged some students from striving to maximize their academic performance. On the other hand, it motivated some students to work hard in school in order to compete more successfully with their White peers in the job market. Thus, during one Minority Achievement Committee meeting one scholar admonished the potential scholars that as Black men they should work as hard or even harder than their White peers in order to compete successfully with the Whites in the job market.

There were other effects of discrimination in opportunity structure on the academic engagement of which Black students and the community were not necessarily aware. We call these effects missing connections, and we describe three of them here briefly.

1. *Schooling is not perceived as a preparation for the job market.* Black students in Shaker Heights did not generally discuss their present schooling as a preparation for their adult futures in the job market. They rarely made a connection between what or how they were doing in school and what they would become or do when they grew up. We reported earlier that in a class discussion in high school the students repeatedly said that they would think of careers when they grew up. The teacher told them that they were already grown up. He informed them that in some other societies people of their age already had families and other responsibilities. The point to stress is that the students at all levels did not make adequate connection between their academic performance and their adult futures in the labor market. Their schooling was not goal oriented and lacked motivating direction.

2. *Inadequate knowledge of educational requirements of future jobs.* Many students, even at the high school, did not seem to have a good understanding the educational qualification required by the jobs they would like to do when they finished school. They did not seem to know that some jobs or professions required certain skills and knowledge that students might begin to acquire during their education. For example, a student desiring to become an engineer would start taking certain math courses at a precollege level of schooling.

3. *How courses at school levels are related is not understood.* The students did not seem to understand that the sequence of their courses or that their present course enrollment would determine their future course enrollment. For example, Black students at the elementary school were apparently not thinking or concerned about how their performance would affect their course enrollment at the middle school. Likewise, those at the middle school did not seriously consider how their performance would affect their enrollment in various course levels at the high school.

We speculate that these missing connections arose from the barriers between education and opportunity structure that Black Americans experienced historically and that were manifested among the students in lack of pragmatic goals and directions in their school careers.

Alternative and Survival Strategies

Black Americans turned to sports, athletics, entertainment, and drug dealing, according to students, because racial barriers and the job ceiling made it difficult for them to achieve the American Dream or gain upward social mobility by acquiring school credentials. They turned to alternative strategies that did not require school credentials. These strategies were discussed during class lessons, in interviews with individual students, and at group meetings. Black Americans who turned to the alternative strategies were "smart." Such intelligent Blacks diverted their "smartness" from academic pursuit into pursuits because of racial barriers. On a number of occasions the students reminded the researchers that Black drug dealers were very intelligent people. It was widely believed that nowadays sports provide Blacks the best opportunity for getting ahead. Students and some school personnel were aware of the adverse effects of these alternative strategies on academic engagement. Some teachers discussed the risks of students neglecting the academic route to professional careers and putting their hopes in professional sports. Yet for some students it appeared that all that mattered was sports. Students engulfed in sports and entertainment cultures showed little interest in doing schoolwork and making good grades.

Role Models

Black students chose well-educated and successful professional Blacks in Shaker Heights and elsewhere in the nation as role models. However, the role models were admired because of their leadership in the "collective struggle" against White oppression or in the civil rights movement rather than because of their academic and professional success or other attributes that made them successful in the corporate economy or wider societal institutions.

The people most admired were Black athletes, sports heroes, and famous entertainers. The students explained that these categories were admired more because the media made them, their wealth, and their fame more visible than Blacks who achieved success through school credentials, such as doctors, engineers, lawyers, and university professors. The students' dominant role models were, therefore, characters lacking in attributes conducive to academic success.

RACE RELATIONS AND SCHOOLING

Race relations in many ways adversely affected the schooling of Black Americans in the Shaker Heights school district as they did elsewhere in the nation. This was not only because of the way White people have treated Black people in school and society but also because of the way Black people have interpreted and responded to their schooling because of their involuntary minority status and the White mistreatment. White enslavement and mistreatment of Blacks after emancipation are well documented in the literature (Bullock, 1970; & Williams, 1989; Ladenburg & McFeely, 1969; Litwack, 1991; Myrdal, 1944; Ogbu, 1978). What have not been adequately studied and understood are the educational consequences of what Blacks believe about their relationship with Whites and White institutions and Blacks' responses to them. In the present study we examined three aspects of the latter, namely, social distance and fear, conflict and mistrust, and an affective rather than pragmatic relationship with the system.

Social Distance and Fear

In the Preface we reported a public image of racial harmony in the Shaker Heights community and schools. What we found was a significant social distance between the two racial groups, at least from the point of view of Blacks. They did not believe that race relations in Shaker Heights were as harmonious or good as Whites claimed them to be. Blacks believed that the public image of racial harmony was maintained by a code of silence imposed by the Whites and that, in reality, White people disparaged, misrepresented, and feared them. These treatments created social distance and mutual ignorance between the two races that affected any discourse about Black education. For example, White fear of Blacks prevented some White candidates for a school board election from attending a candidates' forum in a predominantly Black segment of the city.

Conflict and Mistrust

The nearest thing to open conflict that we noticed was the dispute over the publication of the article on the academic achievement gap between Black and White students in *The Shakerite*. The students commented on the absence of open conflict by contrasting their suburb with Parma, a neighboring suburb.

But beneath the seeming racial harmony was deep mistrust. Immediately after we arrived to conduct our research we discovered that the Black community did not trust the White community, whose members constituted the school authorities. As we noted in the Preface, the mistrust was a matter of concern to us, because Blacks feared that White school authorities would provide us with data that would bias our research against them. The mistrust showed up on several occasions when Black education in the district was discussed. For example, the Black community and school officials agreed that Black students were achieving academically below White students, but the two sides had different explanations for the academic performance gap. White school officials said that the gap was due to differences in social class. The Black community attributed it to racism. Blacks and Whites accepted the facts about the academic achievement gap published in *The Shakerite*. Blacks suspected that White people had published the article to humiliate them. Even some Black school personnel shared this community interpretation, as could be seen in the dialogue between a Black school counselor and a Black community representative during our meeting with one group of school authorities. White school officials denied that the article was published to humiliate Blacks.

Affective Interpretation of Schooling

When Blacks evaluated their teachers and schools, they emphasized the importance of "caring" for students and the inclusion of their experience and perspectives in the curriculum or pedagogy. Their emphasis is not so much on teachers' expertise in the subject matter. Gay (2000, p. 47) explained that by *caring* Blacks mean that they want their teachers and schools to be nourishing, supportive, protective, and encouraging. Furthermore, Blacks hold teachers accountable for students' performance. Gay (2000) added that if teachers and schools manifest this type of caring, they would create a consistently caring climate that would make Black students more willing to participate in learning tasks and demonstrate higher achievement [italics added].

A frequent complaint of Black students in the Shaker school district was that their teachers, counselors, and administrators didn't "care." Our impression was that the students emphasized their need for more caring more than their need for teachers and schools as experts from whom they could learn useful knowledge and skills. They were apparently not engaged in their schoolwork partly because they were not getting enough "caring" and partly because they did not evaluate their teachers and schools more in terms of expertise in useful knowledge and skills.

EXPRESSIVE RESPONSES: IDENTITY, CULTURE, LANGUAGE, AND ABILITY

The expressive mistreatment of Black Americans included denigration of their identity, culture, language, and intelligence. We examined Black people's responses in terms of their collective identity, cultural and language frames of reference, and beliefs about their own intellectual capacity. We must emphasize that the intellectual, cultural, and language beliefs and behaviors of Blacks in Shaker Heights were not just the products of their mistreatment by White people in Shaker Heights. Rather, these beliefs and behaviors originated from historical and wider societal mistreatment. At the same time, we do not deny that contemporary race relations in Shaker Heights contributed to the beliefs and behaviors. The important thing to bear in mind is that these beliefs and behaviors, as well as their effects on schooling, are historical and national.

Collective Identity and Cultural and Language Frames of Reference

Blacks in Shaker Heights were aware of their collective identity or a sense of who they were as Black Americans and that this identity was different and perhaps to their perceived White collective identity. Similarly, their cultural and language frames of reference were different, and in some domains oppositional, to those of their fellow White citizens. Although they behaved and talked like White people in some domains, there were cultural rules as to when these incidents happened at school and in the community.

Collective identity and cultural and language frames of reference entered into the schooling of Black students in Shaker Heights. Of particular note is how these factors affected the way that Black students perceived the school curriculum, language, and classroom pedagogy. As we reported in chapter 10, some defined these phenomena—and therefore, consciously or unconsciously, the attitudes and behaviors associated with them—as White. This led to some academic disengagement, as the students avoided the attitudes and behaviors conducive to school success. Students who defined the curriculum, standard English, and classroom pedagogy as White accused other Black students who spoke standard English, enrolled in honors or advanced placement classes, or had many White friends and made good grades, of abandoning their racial identity.

The accusers did not necessarily reject making good grades because it was acting White. What they seemed to object to were adopting certain White attitudes and behaviors adopted by the students who made good grades. As we reported, the students accused of acting White did not necessarily reject their racial identity, culture, or dialect. Nevertheless, the fear of the accusation, and the actual accusation discouraged some students from engaging in their schoolwork.

Peer Pressures

Negative peer pressures resulting from oppositional identity, and cultural and language frames of reference reduced academic engagement and achievement, but not all peer pressures against academic engagement came from these phenomena. As we showed in chapter 10, there were other sources of peer pressures that were detrimental to academic success.

Internalized White Beliefs and Self-Doubt

The debate about Black American intellectual ability continues today in the popular media and in scientific publications. Even as we are writing this book, we have an invitation to a forum at the New York Academy of Sciences to discuss the issue of Black intellectual status! Black Americans over the course of their history have to some extent internalized White Americans' beliefs that they are not as intelligent as White people (chap. 5). The internalization has decreased over historical period, particularly since the civil rights movement of the 1960s and the Black power movement of the 1960s and 1970s (, 1992). However, our research in Shaker Heights and elsewhere shows some residue of the internalization.

What Blacks came to believe about their own intellectual ability vis-à-vis White intellectual ability resulted in some self-doubt and lowered academic expectations and effort among Blacks. We reproduced a vivid account by one high school student of how the internalization came about and the continuing effects on both teachers and students. It is significant that Black students in Shaker Heights made a connection between the internalized White beliefs and their own academic beliefs and behaviors in the classroom. They described how some of their fellow students consciously or unconsciously acted as if they were, indeed, not as intelligent as their White classmates. Some believed that making good grades was the prerogative of White students by virtue of their superior intelligence. The students' academic effort and performance also suffered because of this self-doubt. Finally, teachers were not immune to the belief that Blacks were not as intelligent as Whites, and this affected their treatment of Black students. Thus, teachers, including Black teachers, regarded Black students who got good grades as exceptional.

EDUCATIONAL STRATEGIES

In our conceptual framework we defined educational strategies as cultural practices or customary behaviors of a given group in the domain of schooling. They are customary ways of going to school to get the school credentials that people need or desire. The cultural practices are manifested in the attitudes and behaviors of students, families, and community of a given group. We described the educational strategies of Blacks in Shaker Heights in chapters 2, 10, and 11.

Students

Black students had very high educational aspirations and made strong verbal endorsement of academic success. They were proud of the high academic standards of their school district. They said that it required a lot more effort to make good grades in their schools than elsewhere. By effort the students meant that one had to study a lot, do and a lot of homework, and pay attention in class. However, as we documented in chapter 2, they were lacking in this effort from elementary through high school. They did not work hard, admitted that they did not work hard, and believed that they could have made better grades if they worked as hard as they could and should . From our observation of more than 100 classroom lessons, and observations in the community, we had plenty of data to support their self-report, namely, that they did not work hard. We reported in chapter 2 and elsewhere several reasons for their lack of adequate academic effort. Also, earlier in this chapter we suggested how various domains of community forces might contribute to their academic disengagement. One more factor to be added here is discipline problems (see chap. 7). Many informants, including the students themselves, commented on the disruptive attitudes and be-haviors of students in general education and college prep classes, where most of the students were Black. These students knew that their attitudes and behaviors were disruptive and not conducive to school success. In fact, they contrasted the climate of pedagogy in their classes with that in the hon-ors and advanced placement classes, where most of the students were White and performed better.

The Family

Black parents admired the standards of education in Shaker Heights so much so, that some of them moved there, in spite of the financial burden, to give their children the opportunity to obtain Shaker school credentials. They expected their children to work hard, make good grades, and gradu-ate from Shaker to fulfill their goal. Overall, however, their strategies for a realizing the goal of a successful academic career in the Shaker Heights school system were inadequate. Teachers and other school personnel, Black students, and some members of Black community recognized the inadequacy of the parents' strategies. We also observed this inadequacy.

We discussed parents' strategies within the school institution and at home with their children. At school, parents' participation or involvement was dismal, even when the main objective of the expected participation was to enhance their children's academic success. We wish to emphasize that it was not just working-class parents who did not participate enough in the education of their children at school. Middle-class and professional parents likewise did not. Our description of the parents' attendance at the Open House at the middle school and high school should serve as a good example of their low institutional participation.

Parents' involvement with their children's education at home was equally dismal. They did not supervise their children's homework closely; neither did they teach their children appropriate use of their time. Many did not shield their children enough from negative peer pressures, and their methods of motivating their children to engage in their schoolwork were not usually effective.

Parents' allocation of educational responsibility also adversely affected their ability to help their children succeed in school. Their lack of involve-ment with their children's education at school was partly due to their cul-tural model of pedagogy. They thought or believed that it was the responsibility of teachers and the schools to make their children learn and perform successfully; that is, they held the teachers, rather than them-selves, accountable for their children's academic success or failure. Their role was more or less limited to sending their children to school and putting pressures on teachers and the schools to "make them" succeed. This point was noted in the report of Project ACHIEVE (1997).

There was another allocation of educational responsibility at home between parents and their children. The allocation was most evident in working-class families. Some of these families had moved to Shaker Heights in spite of the financial hardship to enable their children graduate from Shaker Heights. They interpreted their move to Shaker Heights and its economic burden as their share of the responsibility for the education of their children; their children's share was to study and do well in school. It did not work.

LEVELING OR TRACKING

We summarize some of our findings on leveling here because some of the school and community forces already discussed contributed to it. Shaker Heights had no overarching leveling or tracking program; that is, students were not assigned to general education, vocational education, or college preparatory education "tacks" that stayed with them more or less throughout their school career. Instead, they were assigned to different levels of the same course and in different subjects in a given school session. Nevertheless, this more or less resulted in de facto tracking along racial lines, because most Black students were enrolled in lower level classes, and most Whites were enrolled in higher level classes.

The tracking or leveling began in the upper elementary school, where the curriculum was differentiated into three categories: (a) skills or remedial, (b) regular, and (c) academic enrichment classes. Pronounced racial differences in enrollment between the remedial programs (mostly Blacks) and the academic enrichment programs (mostly Whites) began here. The middle school and high school had four curriculum levels: (a) skills or general education, (b) college prep, (c) honors, and (d) advanced placement classes. Most students in the skills and college prep classes in each subject were Black, and most students in the honors and advanced placement classes were White.

The potential for differential racial distributions of students at different curriculum levels, starting at Woodbury Upper Elementary School, seemed to exist as early as the first grade. Recall the report of a first-grade teacher in the school district for 17 years who made several unsuccessful attempts to get Black parents to participate in a program for first-grade students with learning difficulties, most of whom were Black. Children who received help during this early period in their school career might avoid being assigned to remedial programs or learning-disability curriculum at the upper elementary school. We may assume that the failure of Black parents to get the help described by the first-grade teacher for their children during the early years contributed to the disproportionate assignment of Black students to the remedial programs and their under-representation in the academic enrichment programs at Woodbury. This was likely to happen whether student assignments were based on teacher recommendations, test scores, or both.

During interviews and group discussions, students pointed out that their academic tracks were often determined by the program to which they had been assigned at the upper elementary school. When they arrived at the middle school, counselors assigned them to various course levels in each subject on the basis of their performance at Woodbury and on teachers recommendations. In subsequent years and at the high school students were assigned to their course levels on the basis of their record of performance and teachers' recommendations. Students often said that their previous performance did not necessarily reflect their ability. However, counselors worked with the record before them: grades, test scores, and recommendations. In our discussion with counselors they seemed overburdened with scheduling students for grade or school transfers and with students' behavior problems with teachers. They had little time for explaining to students the importance of enrolling in honors or advanced placement classes. Blacks interpreted this to mean that counselors did not "care" and did not encourage them to enroll in the higher level classes. Some students believed that they were actually discouraged from enrolling in the higher level classes until their parents intervened.

Black parents contributed to the uneven racial distribution at the middle school and high school partly because they did not seem to understand the leveling system. They did not know enough about how honors and advanced placement classes differed from skills and college prep classes. Perhaps for this reason they did not emphasize to their children how important it was for them to take the honors and advanced placement classes, did not prepare them to take those classes successfully and did not intervene to enroll their children who had the potential in the honors and advanced placement classes.

Finally, self-elimination played a role in Black under-representation in the honors and advanced placement classes. Self-elimination took three forms. One was avoidance of the honors and advanced placement classes because most other students in the classes were White. Another was lack of effort; that is, the students did not work hard enough to make good grades to qualify for those courses. The third mechanism was the personal decision not to enroll in an honors or advanced placement class by a student who qualified to be in the class by virtue of his or her academic record. In this case, after consulting with the counselor the student might decide not to enroll in spite of the counselor's recommendation because he or she did not think that he or she could handle the work. The counselor was not always the gatekeeper.

Students, teachers, and some other school personnel were aware that leveling affected instruction. We also observed differences in the instructional patterns at different course levels from upper elementary school through high school. Students who participated in the academic enrichment program at Woodbury Upper Elementary School believed that they were taught better and learned more than those who were assigned to remedial programs. Students in the honors and advanced placement classes at the middle school and high school praised the curriculum materials and teaching styles, while those in skills, regular, and college prep classes criticized the curriculum materials and teaching styles. We found in our classroom observations that the latter paid less attention during lessons, were less willing to do classwork, less likely to return their homework, and were generally more disruptive than the former. Teachers acknowledged that they taught the same subject differently at different levels even when using the same curriculum materials. For example, one teacher who taught the same literature with the same textbooks in an advanced placement class and a college preparatory class usually assigned more reading materials to the advanced placement class. The students in this class read the assignments and critically and enthusiastically discussed them. In contrast, students in the college prep class usually did not read the assigned passages; the teacher read for the class. The students discussed not the reading assignment but rather their personal or group experiences. The ideas for the discussion of the personal or group experiences might, however, have come from the reading.

13

Policy Implications

SOME CURRENT APPROACHES TO THE ACADEMIC ACHIEVEMENT

In Shaker Heights and elsewhere in the nation the Black community, school authorities, education policymakers, and researchers are searching for ways to improve the academic achievement of Black students. We have identified four approaches pertinent to our research, namely: (a) choice (e.g., voucher plan), (b) performance contract, (c) cooperative learning (e.g., accelerated learning, Advancement Via Individual Determination (AVID), Comer, etc.), and (d) culturally responsive pedagogy. Common to these approaches is an assumption that conventional public school policies and practices are the reasons why Black students are not academically successful.

Choice

Advocates of school choice want to empower parents to choose where to educate their children through open enrollment, magnet schools, school vouchers. The idea of using market strategy to improve academic success in the public schools has been around since the 1950s when it was suggested by economist Milton Friedman (1955). He argued that all parents should have more freedom to choose where to educate their children because parents know more about their children's abilities and needs than anyone else.

School Vouchers

The use of school voucher as the market strategy to improve the academic performance of Black students is now accepted and being tried in some school districts (Good & Braden, 2000, p. 96; see also Fuller & , 1992). It is also popular with politicians in some states, even where it is opposed by the educational establishment, as in Wisconsin (Ruenzel, 1995). However, the voucher approach has yet to be proved as an effective remedy for the poor academic achievement of Black students (Good & Braden, 2000, pp. 99, 110).

Charter Schools

Charter schools are another avenue to improve the school performance of minority and poor children. Charter schools are public schools operating under a contract within a school district with a charter granted by a state charter agency. They are funded by the state like other schools in the school district and are accountable for students' academic performance. Although charter schools are popular, they have yet to prove that they can effectively improve students' academic achievement (Contreras, 1995; Good & Braden, 2000, pp. 137, 173–174; Wells, 1998).

Performance Contracts

Some school districts have entered into contractual agreements with for-profit private companies to operate some of their schools for payment. The school districts hope that the companies will raise the academic achievement of the students, as measured by test scores. The companies hope to raise the students' test scores and make profit. Edison contracts with the school systems of New York City and San Francisco are examples of this approach (Bradley, 1994). Educational performance contracting is not new. It dates back to the 1970–1971 school year, when the Office of Economic Opportunity contracted with private firms to teach some 20,000 "unresponsive" school children in 20 public school districts for $6 million. When the "experiment" was evaluated it was found that the "results did not materially affect student achievement" (Gramlich & Koshel, 1975).

Merit Pay

Merit pay, or pay-for-performance, is another market approach. It is based on the assumption that schools should operate like businesses and that teachers are to be paid according to their productivity, which is to be measured by students' test scores. Proponents believe that teachers are not sufficiently motivated under the current pay structure. The latter should, therefore, be replaced with a market-oriented structure under which teachers who are more productive or who teach better should receive higher pay.

Opponents argue that it is divisive, that the nature of teachers' work is different from that of the workers in business, and that merit pay has been tried in the past and did not work (Cuban & Tyack, 2000; S. M. Johnson, 1984; Murnane & Cohen, 1986; Pederson, 2000).

One common assumption of the choice or market strategies is that the conventional structure and process of the public schools, or the system, must be changed or modified in order to increase the academic performance of Blacks, similar minorities, and in general poor students. The modification can be achieved by giving parents education vouchers to enable them to choose the school to which they send their children, authorizing charter schools within the public school system, contracting with private corporations to run public schools for profit, or paying teachers according to merit or productivity as measured by children's academic performance.

To date there is no convincing evidence that these strategies are more effective than conventional public school practices in increasing the academic achievement of Black students. More important, we are not convinced that they will close the academic performance gap between Black and White students in Shaker Heights, because they do not address the influence of community forces such as those described in preceding chapters. This is evident in Table 13.1.

TABLE 13.1

Lack of Acknowledgment of the Role of Community Forces in Strategies to Increase Black Academic Achievement Under the Current School Reform Movement

Community Forces	Voucher	Charter	Performance Contract	Merit Pay
Frame of reference	No	No	No	No
Opportunity structure & beliefs in school credentials	No	No	No	No
Relaxation with whites and schools	No	No	No	No
Collective identity	No	No	No	No
Cultural frame of reference	No	No	No	No
Language frame of reference	No	No	No	No
Beliefs about intellectual differences	No	No	No	No
Black educational strategies	No	No	No	No

Cooperative Learning Approach

The cooperative learning strategy consists of programs that emphasize cooperation and collaboration among the school or teachers, the minority community, and students. The cooperative learning approach is based on the assumption that Black and similar minority cultures in the United States value cooperation and use collaboration to solve problems. It is also assumed that an important feature of the learning styles in minority cultures is cooperation. Examples of programs using this approach include Comer's School Development Program, Levin's Accelerated Elementary School Education for Disadvantaged Students, and Mehan's AVID. These programs have been adopted by many school districts, including Shaker Heights. For example, as a part of its school reform effort, Merce Elementary School in Shaker Heights adopted the Accelerated Schools Model program to promote "the academic acceleration of all students. The goal would be achieved by the integrating instructional/curricular practices, and active community involvement (Project ACHIEVE 1997, p. 14)." There were no detailed reports of the results of this program at the time of our study. The programs are generally reported to be successful by their proponents, but where they have been independently evaluated the results are equivocal (T. D. Cook, Habib, et al., 1998; T. D. Cook, Hunt, & Murphy, 1998). Our overall impression is that although the programs in the cooperative learning approach help to improve the school performance of some Black students, they will not lead to an overall increase in the academic achievement of Black students because they do not take into account the community forces we have described in this book (see Table 13.2).

We should mention two intervention programs that have benefitted from our earlier studies, although this has not always been acknowledged in print. One is Treisman's who developed his program while he was a graduate student at Berkeley partly from reading my study of Black and Mexican-American students in Stockton, California. (Although Treisman, 1985, made no reference to my work—or to any other work, for that matter—in his doctoral dissertation, this information about the use of my research findings in Stockton was provided by Singham, 1997; see Ogbu, 1974.) Among these minorities, the academically successful students in high school were loners, and few were successful through this strategy. In contrast, Chinese or Asian high school students worked together and shared knowledge. More of them were successful. So, Treisman designed a program to teach Blacks and Mexican Americans to "act Chinese" or "Asian."

The other is Hugh Mehan's AVID program. Mehan thought that he was going to disprove Ogbu's theory (Ogbu, 1987, 1991) by showing that invol-

TABLE 13.2

Cooperative Learning and Community Forces

Community Forces	Comer's Program	Accelerated Education	Avid
Frames of reference	No	No	No
Opportunity structuring & beliefs in school credentials	No	No	No
Relation with Whites and schools	No	No	No
Collective identity	No	No	Yes
Cultural frame of reference	No	No	?
Language frame of reference	No	No	?
Beliefs about intellectual differences	No	No	?
Black educational strategies	No	No	No

Note. Avid = Advancement Via Individual Determination.

untary minorities can succeed through "untracking." In his program, now called AVID (Advancement Via Individual Determination), he formed Latino and African American students into academically oriented peer groups, developed strategies for managing an academic identity, adopted strategies for maintaining a community identity among friends, and reaffirmed their ethnic identity. These students were taught the accommodation ideology usually associated with voluntary minorities. They were taught how to take notes and how to study as well as an achievement strategy (Baca, 1994; Mehan, Hubbard, & Villanueva, 1994; Mehan, Hubbard, Villanueva, & Lintz, 1996; U.S. Department of Education, 2001). The author's claim to the contrary, the AVID program actually confirms Ogbu's theory. One problem overlooked in the evaluation of AVID is selection bias. By focusing on "linguistic minorities" it is likely that Latino immigrant and nonimmigrant students wee lumped together in the program (Baca, 1994, p. 25).

Culturally Responsive Education

We use the term culturally responsive education for the third major approach to improve minority or Black academic achievement. Culturally responsive education includes African-centered pedagogy, Afrocentric education, African immersion academies, cultural diversity, culturally responsive pedagogy, and multicultural education (Asante, 1991; Dei, 1994; Gay, 2000; C. Lee, 1995; Ogbu, 1992). We focus our comments on culturally responsive pedagogy because it incorporates many features of other specific approaches in culturally responsive education. Furthermore, it emphasizes raising academic achievement as a major goal.

Proponents of culturally responsive pedagogy argue that Black students and other students of color are failing in public schools because the conventional classroom processes are based on European-American (or Eurocentric) cultural practices, while teaching and learning styles vary from culture to culture. Because minority children, such as Blacks, have been socialized into different styles before entering the public school, they encounter discontinuities between their own styles and the school practices. Proponents contend that the academic achievement of minority students will increase "if schools and teachers are changed so that they reflect and draw on (the) cultural and language strengths of the minorities" (Banks, 2000, p. ix). This is similar to anthropological mismatch theory reviewed in chapter 3. The difference is that contemporary proponents of culturally responsive pedagogy are primarily minority scholars (Boykin, 1986; DelPit, 1995; Gay, 2000; Irvine, 1991).

One example of the cultural difference in classroom teaching and learning styles is that during classroom lessons in Eurocentric cultures teachers expect "protocols of attentiveness (with) emphasis placed on them" (Gay, 2000, p. 22). Apparently in Black culture students are not expected to pay attention during lessons! Gay went on to describe the problem in their public school classroom lesson process as follows:

> During classroom lessons in the Eurocentric cultural practice, students are expected to pay close attention to teachers for a prolonged, largely uninterrupted length of time. Specific signs and signals have evolved that are associated with appropriate attentive behaviors. These include nonverbal communicative cues, such as gaze, eye contact and body posture. When they are not exhibited by learners at times, at intervals and for intervals designated by the teachers, the students are judged to be uninvolved, distracted, having short attention spans, and/or engaged in off-task behaviors. All these are "read" as obstructive to effective teaching and learning. (Gay, 2000, p. 22)

Gay (2000) then described two experiments by Allen and Boykin (1991, 1992) that show that Black students learn more in the Black cultural style than in the conventional public school style. In one experiment in which the performance tasks were accompanied with music and movement rather than sitting and paying attention, Black students performed better than White students. In the second experiment, in which the tasks were not accompanied with music and movement, students were required to concentrate on the tasks at hand. White students did better than Black students. Furthermore, during the task with no music or movement, Black students showed "signs of restlessness and boredom; their eyes frequently wandered from the task, and they attended to their hands and feet more so than to the learning materials and tasks" (Allen & Boykin, 1992; Gay, 2000, p. 171).

It follows from the perspective of culturally responsive pedagogy that asking Black students to pay attention during lessons is an imposition of a Eurocentric cultural hegemony or style that contributes to their low academic achievement. To increase the academic performance of Black students, teachers and schools should stop imposing the Eurocentric cultural style on the students, endorse Black cultural practices, and learn and use them to educate Black students. According to Gay, (2000, p. 25) "It is incumbent upon teachers, administrators and evaluators to deliberately create cultural continuity in educating ethnically different students."

In our comparative research we have found that other non-White or non-European minorities, including immigrants from Africa, have their own indigenous teaching and learning styles. We have also found that when immigrant minorities enter the public school they change by adapting to the conventional pedagogy of the public school, which includes paying attention during lessons, following rules and doing what the teachers say, and focusing on and doing classwork and homework. They do not consider these behaviors an imposition of Eurocentric hegemony; rather, they think that they are adopting behaviors that are conducive to making good grades, and they usually achieve academic success. In contrast, other minorities, including Black Americans, Native Americans, and Native Hawaiians, who are targets of culturally responsive pedagogy, seem to resist adopting the conventional classroom attitudes and behaviors. Apparently, they expect teachers to endorse and use their indigenous styles. Under this circumstance these minorities fail to do well in school. The theoretical and policy-related question is: Why do some minorities adopt the conventional public school style, while Black students do not?

Our research findings in Shaker Heights suggest that culturally responsive pedagogy is not an adequate solution to the academic disengagement and low achievement of Black students. In fact, culturally responsive pedagogy is problematic as a theory and in practice. As a theory, culturally responsive pedagogy implies that in order to educate minority students successfully, the public school must teach the students from each minority group according to their own indigenous pedagogic style. But it cannot explain why immigrant minority students from Africa and Asia in Shaker Heights were doing better than Black Americans under the same conventional public school pedagogy.

As a practice, teaching every group according to its cultural pedagogic style it is not feasible in contemporary American public school classrooms. Now, consider how this will work in a school system such as that in Oakland, California, where most of the classrooms have students from 5 more minority groups. The school district as a whole is educating students from more than 60 ethnic or cultural groups, each of which, presumably, has its own indigenous pedagogic style.

From a comparative perspective, in contemporary societies every educational system has its own conventional classroom practices. The classroom practices are based on the culture and language of the dominant group, which in turn are the medium of polity and commerce in society. Members of the society, majority as well as minority, are expected to master the attitudes and skills imparted through the conventional pedagogy for competence in adult life. In other words, the schools are functioning as a delegate agency. Immigrant minority students do better in school than the nonimmigrants do because they seem to understand and accept the role of the schools as a delegate agency. For this reason, they adopt and conform to the conventional pedagogy of the public schools.

Some Black students may benefit from culturally responsive pedagogy, Afro-centric education, African-centered pedagogy, and the like, but these approaches are limited as a solution to academic disengagement and performance, because they do not address two crucial issues in Black children's education in the United States: First, why are some minorities more academically successful in the public school than Black students, even though they are culturally different, with different pedagogic traditions? Why do African American students need a pedagogic style unique to their own culture in order to do well in school? The second is a policy issue: Given that most school systems attended by Black children have many other minorities, how feasible is it to provide Black students with culturally relevant pedagogy in the same classrooms with students from five or more other cultural groups? Our conclusion is that the culturally responsive strategy is a limited solution because, after all, most Black children will continue to be educated in the public school with White and other minorities rather than in African- immersion academies and other such institutions.

RECOMMENDATIONS

One remarkable feature of all three of the approaches to bridging the academic gap just reviewed is that they are not based on knowledge derived from actual study of Black Americans as a functioning component of U.S. society. Rather, they are based on what the proponents know about the public schools and their treatment of Black students. Proponents of these approaches seem to be prescribing solutions for the low Black academic achievement almost as if they assume that Black Americans are passive victims who play no part in their poor school performance. Furthermore, they assume that Black Americans share their definitions of the problem and its solution. Another remarkable thing, already discussed, is that these three approaches lack a comparative perspective. They do not ask why some other minorities are academically successful under conventional public school pedagogy.

The cultural–ecological theory is not a theory of pedagogy; it is not a theory of how teachers can teach Black students to be more academically successful. The pedagogical value of the theory is that the research findings described in previous chapters will help education authorities, including policymakers, teachers, and the Black community, to better understand why Black students are disengaged from their academic work. With such an understanding they should find ways to help the students become more engaged with their academic work. In the remainder of this chapter we suggest things that might be done to increase the academic engagement and performance of Black students in Shaker Heights based on our research findings. The focus of our recommendation is the academic re-engagement of Black students in the public school systems, because that is where most of them are going to be educated, with White students and other minority students.

According to the cultural–ecological theory underlying our study, there are two parts to the problem. Our findings suggest that increasing the academic engagement of Black students, thereby closing the academic achievement gap, requires changes in the system as well as changes in the community forces.

Our recommendations are not prescriptions; they are suggestions for study and dialogue before action. They are not put forward as solutions that have been tested and found successful. We put them forward because they make sense to us on the basis of our research experience and findings.

The first step in developing our recommendations was our inquiry into what Blacks and school authorities in Shaker Heights knew about or considered to be the causes of Black students' academic disengagement and the academic achievement gap between Black and White students. We also inquired about what could be done about the two problems. We presented this knowledge along with our own observations and interpretations in the foregoing chapters. Although the focus of our fieldwork was on community forces, our knowledge of the system came from various documents that the school district made available to us, our discussions with school authorities, and the perceptions and interpretations of Black students and members of the Black community.

In chapter 12 we briefly summarized the effects of the community forces on the academic engagement of Black students in Shaker Heights. Our major finding was that the Black community and the school system were both responsibility for the academic disengagement of Black students. Our recommendations are based on this joint responsibility and our belief that the community and the school system also share the responsibility for solving the collective problem.

We recommend that both community and school authorities should read and critically discuss our research findings. This should be followed by a three-way dialogue: between (a) the community and the anthropologists, (b) school authorities and the researchers, and (c) among the three parties: the community, school authorities, and the anthropologists. The extent to which each stakeholder—the community and the school—accepts the researchers' analysis of the problems will determine the likelihood of acceptance and implementation or our recommendations. Also, the feedback from the community and the school will enable the researchers to improve more their recommendations.

RECOMMENDATIONS
FOR THE BLACK COMMUNITY

The Black community and Black families must assume a proactive role to increase the academic orientation, effort, and performance of their children. Although, good teaching and some changes in the educational process are important, the academic achievement gap is not likely to be closed by restructuring the educational system or by what the schools, Shaker community, and U.S. society at large can do for Black students. Equally important are what the Black community can do or the changes that must take place within the community and community forces. To emphasize the important role of the community, we start with recommendations for the Black community.

Framework for Community Action

Throughout its history, and all over the United States, the Black community has fought against de jure and de facto racial barriers in society at large and in the education system in order to enable their children to have educational opportunities equal to those of their White peers. Black children at Shaker and elsewhere are aware of this collective struggle. The collective struggle has, understandably, emphasized collective effort at the collective or intergroup level rather than individual effort at individual level. Although collective struggle remains an important educational strategy, it must now be combined with other strategies that enhance academic orientation and effort at community, family, and individual levels. We believe that in Shaker Heights and elsewhere the academic re-engagement of Black students requires a new framework for reconstructing the positive functions of the community forces in the Black community.

Throughout our study we were impressed by the interest of the community in the education of the children. Attendance at each of our two public presentations at the beginning of the study was impressive. In the second presentation, in a large church, the audience was almost entirely Black. The people listened attentively, and after the presentation they discussed several educational issues critically. However, we learned during the course of our research that this was a pattern of response in times of educational crisis. The publication of the article in high school paper, *The Shakerite*, on the academic performance gap between Black and White students represented such a crisis. We have also observed a similar response by Black communities during a study conducted in other cities (Luster, 1992; Ogbu 1974, 1999). What seemed to be missing in Shaker Heights and elsewhere, and what we want to address in our recommendations, are the actual educational efforts of the Black community as a cultural practice.

To explain what seemed to be missing in Shaker Heights' Black community, namely, educational efforts as a cultural practice, we use the findings in one East Asian community reported by the Task Force of The College Board. In a study commissioned by the Task Force, it was found in one community there were "about 300 non-profit and for-profit after-school and weekend supplementary education programs ... from pre-school through high school" (College Board, 1999, p. 18). The report goes on to say that "The researcher concluded that the community had essentially organized a parallel educational system to the schools—and parents were paying for most of these services" (College Board, 1999, p. 18).

In our own comparative studies we have found similar, although not as extensive, programs in some minority communities. Minority students from communities with such programs were academically successful (Fong, 1992, 2001; Ogbu, 1974, 1998). Like the College Board's Task Force study, we have also found that parents in communities with the parallel educational programs seem to teach their children to believe that academic success is based on effort and personal responsibility. In one study in which we specifically asked parents what they did to ensure that their children are academically successful, they were almost unanimous in their high expectations of their children, in holding their children and themselves, rather than teachers and school, responsible for academic performance (Ogbu, 1998). Parents were unequivocal in support of their children to learn English and the school curriculum, because they saw this as a necessary requirement for making good grades, and for later success in the job market. When asked about the kinds of attitudes, skills, and behaviors that helped children adjust well in school and make good grades these parents almost unanimously said that they taught their children to pay attention in class and take notes during lesson whether or not they liked the teacher, to learn to be self-motivated to do their work or to be willing to learn, and to finish their homework every day. They checked their children's homework every day. The children who were asked in separate interviews about their parents supported their parents' account of their role in their children's education at home.

Our comparative work suggests that it is not only East Asian immigrant communities that have parallel educational programs or teach their children attitudes, skills, and behaviors that are conducive to academic success, monitor their school progress, and when they can assist with homework. These educational practices have also been found to some extent among other non-White immigrants (Ogbu, 1998). The point we wish to stress here is that the educational orientations and practices that are conducive to making good grades are limited among Blacks in Shaker Heights because of their community forces. For this reason we make the following specific recommendations.

The Black Community Should Enhance Academic Orientation With Supplementary Educational Programs

The Black community should establish a variety of supplementary afterschool and weekend educational programs, both for profit and not-for-profit, to increase its academic orientations and performance.

The Community Should Develop a Cultural Context to Increase the Value of Academic Success and the Visibility of Academically Successful Blacks as Role Models

At present, the most visible and appealing role models for Black youth in Shaker Heights and elsewhere in the nation are stars in the sports and entertainment fields. These categories appeal not only to the youth but also to Black adults. Although not necessarily in Shaker Heights, we have come across many a Black parent who proudly told us that his or her child would be attending such and such a college on an athletic scholarship; rarely have we heard of academic scholarships. We recommend that the Black community develop a Black heritage month similar to the Chinese New Year and use the occasion to promote the value of academic success and role models of academic achievers. For example, organized events can be used as occasions to present Blacks who have achieved professional success in several fields by virtue of their academic success and/or hard work. This would provide an excellent opportunity for the youth to adopt them as role models and learn how success and rewards are achieved through education and hard work. The Black community nationwide has established halls of fame for athletes and entertainers. These are well known to Black children. But Black children do not know of halls of fame for successful Black doctors, college professors, and engineers. We believe that through public recognition of Blacks who excel in mathematics, science, and other academic fields the community will be sending a powerful message to the Black youth about the importance of academic success.

Establish a Local ACT-So

In 1977, the National Association for the Advancement of Colored People began an important program to recognize accomplishments of Black high school students. It is called the Afro-Academic Cultural and Scientific Olympics (ACT-So). Students are given medal awards for accomplishments in architecture, biology, computer science, chemistry, dance, chemistry, music, painting, physics, poetry, sculpture, and so on (see National Association for the Advancement of Colored People, 2001, p. 75). We believe that duplicating this program at the local level, such as in Shaker Black community, would enhance the academic engagement and performance of the students. Although we did not make a systematic study of it, we know from our research in other Black communities there are usually a number of scholarship programs in the community, such as those organized by churches, The Links, and other organizations. The award ceremony should be held in the community and be open to everyone in the community. This would act as a powerful incentive for younger students to strive for higher academic achievement so that they, too, can receive the awards when they reach the appropriate age and achievement.

Distinguish the Affective From the Pragmatic Value of Education

We found in Shaker Heights and in a literature review some lack of clarity regarding the purpose of the conventional public school curriculum or education. Some advocates of multicultural education or cultural diversity criticize the conventional public school curriculum for being "too White" or reflecting mainly the experience and perspectives of White Americans and excluding those of Black Americans. They contend that because of this Black children come to believe that academic skills and knowledge are the properties and prerogatives of White Americans. It is for this reason that some Black students interpret making good grades or school success as "acting White" (College Board, 1999). Multicultural education, or curriculum infusion (inclusion of minority experiences and perspectives), is required to prevent Black students from equating school success with acting White and to enhance their self-esteem, increase self-awareness, and interracial understanding; make learning more relevant to their lives, and increase their academic performance (Prince George's County Public Schools, 1990). We also found both in the literature and in our fieldwork that teachers and the public schools are evaluated according to their degree of "caring" rather than their expertise in knowledge, skills, language, and other attributes required under contemporary corporate economy (Gay, 2000; Singham, 1997).

This affective evaluation of conventional public school curricula in terms of representation and teachers as "caring" or "not caring," as well as the interpretation of attitudes and behaviors conducive to making good grades as White are characteristic of involuntary minorities almost everywhere. The affective component of schooling is also important for immigrant minority students but, regardless of race, the immigrants emphasize pragmatic criteria more in evaluating the school curriculum and teachers as well as in interpreting attitudes and behaviors conducive to making good grades. Because their primary concern is school success to enhance their success in the labor market, they treat school curriculum contents—mathematics, language, science, social science, and so on—as subjects to be learned; evaluate their teachers in terms of their expertise in the subject matters of the curriculum, and interpret the conventional classroom instructional requirements of paying attention, doing classwork and homework, studying, and working hard desirable and necessary for making good grades. The result is that they make good grades.

We recommend that members of the Black community teach their children to separate the affective meaning of the school curriculum and instructional processes and student learning behaviors from their pragmatic or instrumental meaning. Black students should learn the curriculum contents as subjects with pragmatic values while the community continues to press for curriculum infusion to reflect their experiences and perspectives. As we suggested in presenting the cultural–ecological theory, the public school is, after all, a delegate agency and not necessarily an agency to displace Black cultural and language identity. Black students should recognize and judge their teachers as "experts" in useful knowledge, skills, and language as well as interpret the pedagogic process pragmatically.

Develop and Institutionalize Appropriate and Effective Parental Educational Strategies

Our research findings indicate that Black parents' educational strategies are not adequate and not effective in helping their children succeed in Shaker Heights schools. This inadequacy shows up, for example, in (a) parents' allocation of educational responsibility among them, school authorities, and their children; (b) lack of participation in their children's education at school; and (c) lack of close supervision of their children's work at home. To increase parents' involvement, the school district was using or planning to use the following techniques: a parent liaison, parent resource centers, parenting workshops, distribution of handbooks on achievement, and school/community outreach programs. These approaches are designed to deal with the lack of parental involvement as an individual problem rather than in the context of the community forces. Current inadequate and ineffective strategies of Black parents are embedded in cultural and race-relation contexts.

The community should also reconsider its allocation of educational responsibility at home. Good teaching is always very important, but students do not succeed in school merely because of it. Neither do children always do their schoolwork and homework without parent supervision and assistance. Black parents need to get inside the school and participate in appropriate school programs to become knowledgeable about what their children are learning and how they are doing. In this way they find out when and where their children need help and what help they can give or get for them. Some claim that Black parents are not involved in school even when the latter is integrated because they are marginalized (Shujaa, 1996). From our discussion with some involved Black parents, Black teachers, some highly concerned White teachers, and Black students, as well as our own observations of several situations, we are unable to attribute their lack of involvement to marginalization by the school district.

If Black parents are not involved in school, then they should be involved in their children's education at home. We are, therefore, recommending parent education on how to promote their children's school success at home. The community, not the school district, should take the initiative in providing this education for parents. The community should develop both for-profit and not-for-profit programs to teach parents how to help their children with academic and nonacademic school problems. By developing and institutionalizing effective parents' educational strategies the children will perceive this as a powerful indigenous message and will be motivated to engage more seriously with their schoolwork.

Teach Children How to Work Hard and Persevere to Make Good Grades

In Shaker Heights, Black American students verbally emphasized the importance of effort in achieving school success. But they do not work hard. This contributes to their school failure. In chapter 2 we considered several factors that mitigate against maximizing their academic effort. We suspect that for several reasons Black Americans did not historically develop effort optimism or the norm of maximum individual effort in schoolwork as a part of their culture, even though they value education. We know that there are other minorities, usually immigrants, with no tradition of effort optimism in education in their indigenous cultures. But when they arrive in the United States they develop or adopt educational effort optimism and thereby do well in the public school. They adopt the norm of maximum effort because of the belief that success in adult life, in the job market, or in achieving the American dream depends on school success, and school success depends in part on effort. We believe that as the opportunity structures or chances for upward social mobility through education continue to improve, Black students will increasingly see a strong connection between school success and self-betterment. With this perception they will apply themselves to, or engage more with, their academic work. The community should, therefore, establish programs to help children learn how to be self-motivated, work hard, and persevere in their schoolwork.

RECOMMENDATIONS FOR THE SCHOOL SYSTEM

Initiatives by the School District

Shaker Heights, like many school districts, has initiated a number of programs to help all students improve their academic achievement. They include staff development, tutoring centers, all-day kindergarten, school reforms, accelerated schools, Comer's program, the Minority Achievement Committee Program (MAC), special education services, programs for low-and underachieving students, an English as a second language program, Learning-To-Learn project, mathematics labs, Proficiency Review of Basic Essentials, and so on. From our observations, discussions with school authorities, and review of the evaluations of these programs we were impressed by the efforts of the school district to find solutions for the low academic achievement of its students, especially the low performance of Black students. We note in particular two initiatives that are successful because of their relevance to our finding: (a) reform at Lomond Elementary School, and (b) MAC.

Lomond School Reform

The reform at Lomond Elementary School took the form of changing teaching skills and concepts in mathematics and science. About 54% of the students were Black. The major changes included a shift from individual, independent work to community learning. Furthermore, there was a change from traditional skill-based work, to mathematical ideas and processes. Instead of uniform grade teaching, the assessment changed to individual student performance and growth. According to the evaluation, the reform was very successful.

The Lomond reform certainly offers some insights into major school change, but it does not specifically address the issue of differences in academic performance between Black and White students. It works better than the traditional mathematics and science pedagogy among the students, but it does not address the issues of community forces as described in the foregoing chapters of this book.

MAC

We described this effective program briefly in chapter 2. Instead of repeating the description, we want to (a) indicate how it has already incorporated some of our findings on community forces, and (b) suggest how to use it even more effectively to further increase the academic achievement of the scholars, potential scholars, and others.

We believe that one of the reasons MAC is effective is because it incorporates three positive features of the community forces we identified in the study. One of these is collective identity. The MAC program integrates Black collective identity with academic identity. This can be seen in the MAC pledge:

> I am an African American and I pledge to uphold the name and image of the African American man. I will do so by striving for academic excellence, conducting myself with dignity and respecting others as if they were my brothers and sisters.

The MAC pledge is an initiation to a community of scholars with a collective identity, marked with symbols of handshake, dress, and other forms of behaviors. MAC scholars are known and respected as a category by other students and, as role models, attract potential scholars to their status. The second positive feature is positive peer pressures: Among MAC scholars, emerging scholars, and potential scholars peer pressures are directed toward making good grades. One of the precepts of the MAC scholars is to show pride in their own school success. We heard that these students were able to resist pressures toward academic disengagement. In addition, they call upon former scholars, including those in college or into their own professional careers as role models. The latter were invited to address current scholars and potential scholars. The third positive feature was educational strategies: Some of the strategies for school success we observed at several MAC meetings we attended were discussions of study habits, taking notes during lessons, preparing for examinations, time budgeting, and the like. MAC thus provides an opportunity for an effective socialization for academic achievement or acquisition of the norm for maximum academic effort.

We now discuss some recommendations.

Expand the Use of the MAC Program for Academic Engagement. By every account, the MAC program was both effective in raising Black students' academic achievement and popular among the students. One of the most important contributions of MAC to the academic engagement of Black students was the creation of a community of students/scholars where academic identity was valued, supported and sought after. We believe that its effectiveness and popularity can be further increased by formally incorporating some of our research findings into its routine activities. We recommend that the periodic MAC meetings should focus on different specific themes designed to reconnect students with learning and performance. The following are examples of such specific themes:

1. *Future-oriented or pragmatic education.* Students should discuss and learn about the connection between their schooling or their present academic effort and their adult futures (chap. 6).

2. *Academic responsibility and effective school strategies.* Effective school strategies include effort, study habits, budgeting use of time, and setting priorities. This is already done but should continue to be emphasized (chap. 2).

3. *Role models and their academic influence.* In a session, the group might consider the following: what role models are; types of role models; the importance of role models who have become successful in life through education and hard work; the attributes that enabled such role models to succeed in school and, later, professionally. Students need to distinguish two types of valuable attributes of well-educated and professional Blacks role models: (a) their leadership quality in the "collective struggle," and (b) the attributes that made them successful in school and in their professions (chap. 6).

4. *Internalization of beliefs about Black intelligence and its educational consequences.* Students should discuss how to deal with the self-doubt that arises from internalized White beliefs. Students should discuss the beliefs of Black people about their own intelligence and the educational implications of their beliefs. In previous research, students reported what people in their families and community "knew" about what White people believed about the

intellectual ability of Black people, what people in their families and community believed about their own intellectual ability, and what the students believed about the beliefs of the school authorities about their intellectual ability vis-à-vis their White schoolmates. Explicit discussion of these issues will reduce or eliminate the adverse effects of the internalized beliefs (chap. 5).

5. *Teacher expectations and factors that shape them.* Among the things to consider here are the following: What are lower teacher expectations? What brings about lower teacher expectations? How do students contribute to lower or higher teacher expectations? How do teacher expectations affect students' academic performance? How can teacher expectations of Black students be raised? (see chap. 7).

6. *Leveling or tracking.* Students should learn about differences between course levels beyond the level of difficulty and workload. Why are course level differences important? How do students get into higher or lower course levels? (see chap. 6).

7. *Identity, culture, language, and the curriculum.* We strongly recommend helping Black students to distinguish the affective meaning of the school curriculum (e.g., representation of Black experience and perspectives) from the instrumental or pragmatic meaning of the curriculum (e.g., learning math, science, standard English, and so on as acquiring useful knowledge, language, or tools for future job and upward social mobility). Both are important. Both are very important. However, it seems to us that in current ideology surrounding minority education the affective interpretation seems to take precedent. There is something more here. Black students and the Black community in Shaker Heights do not relate to teachers as experts in knowledge, skills, and language who have something useful to offer. Instead, they seem to be overly concerned with whether teachers and the school system "cared" for them. It is important for teachers and schools to care for their students; but caring is not enough (chap. 8).

8. *Peer pressures.* The group should discuss peer pressures, types of peer pressures, influence of peer pressures, and how to handle peer pressures (chap. 10).

9. *Discipline and its effects on academic work.* We think that formal discussions of the issues suggested earlier during MAC meet-

ings will further increase the effectiveness of the program. The topic and discussion at each meeting should be carefully planned, with explicit objectives of what would be communicated to students (chap. 7).

Publicize the MAC Program in the Community.   We were surprised that the MAC program was not well known in the Black community. There were, for example, some Black parents employed by the school district at the middle school and high school who had not heard of the program. We recommend that the MAC program be more widely publicized in the Black community (chap. 11).

Programs for Non-MAC Members.   Students who are not yet MAC scholars or potential scholars are even more in need of the "education" we have suggested for the scholars. We recommend the introduction of a new elective social studies course for this purpose both at the middle school and the high school. The course should be open to all students, but Black students should be particularly encouraged to take it. We will comment briefly on a few of the topics to be covered in such a course.

1. *Educational strategies or how to succeed in school.* As we reported when we discussed academic disengagement, Black students were not making good grades partly because they did not work hard and lacked good study habits. We also discussed a number of factors that interfered with their academic effort. Although students verbalized attitudes, skills, and behaviors that are conducive to making good grades, they did not practice them. We think that some of these students either did not possess those attitudes and skills or did not know how to practice them. We therefore recommend that the school district develop a course or courses to teach the students how to express their abstract verbalization in concrete behaviors. Some school districts recognize this need but tend to respond to it rather late in the students' school career by instituting "study hall" at the middle school (Ogbu 1974). Study hall should start at the elementary school.

2. *Teach students to distinguish the affective from the pragmatic value of schooling.* Earlier we recommended that members of the Black community teach their children to distinguish the affective

meaning of schooling from the instrumental or pragmatic meaning. We cannot overemphasize the importance of this distinction because of the political nature of the discourse on multicultural education and cultural diversity that has now permeated the research literature, especially among minority scholars. We also recommend that the school district help the students learn to make the distinction between the affective and pragmatic values of the school curriculum. (See Community Recommendation No. 4.)

Teacher Expectations. Teacher expectations have been shown to be an important cause of academic disengagement and low performance. As we noted in chapter 2, Shaker Heights school authorities were aware of this, and it was an important theme in a speech given by a national figure at the teachers' conference during our study. We recommend a periodic workshop on teacher expectations. A workshop of 1 to 2 days should be devoted to the study of the problem by teachers. There should be a full discussion of why and how race; socioeconomic status, and other distinctions, such as gender and handicap, shape teacher expectations. Our findings in Shaker Heights indicate that the influence of race is both historical and societywide. Even the students we studied recognized that it is not just a matter of racism and prejudice on the part of individual teachers. As a result, students reported that some Black teachers in the school district also had low expectations of Black students.

Another source of low teacher expectations not usually discussed in the literature are the attitudes and behaviors of Black students. After reviewing more than 100 classroom lesson observations and discussions with student groups in the school district it is not difficult to see why some teachers may have lower expectations of students in skills and college prep classes, where most of the students were Black, than in honors and advanced placement classes, where most of the students were White. The workshop should also discuss the various forms of manifestations of teacher expectations (see Fairfax County Public Schools, 1984; Leacock, 1985; Persell, 1977; Rist, 1970; Steele, 1997).

We are not in educational practice and therefore do not know many specific programs out there that should serve as models for the type of workshop we have in mind. We will, however, mention two possible resources. One is a program that came out of our participation in a 2-year study of teacher expectations (1986–1988). This program is called "Expectations And Student Performance" and was developed by Ronald D. Reed of the Graduate School of Education at the University of California, Berkeley. The program has clear objectives and intervention strategies for changing teacher expectations of Black and other minority students. Professor Reed has retired and is probably somewhere in the San Francisco Bay Area in California (see Reed, 1988).

Another resource is GESA Facilitator (Grayson & Martin, 1990). This is a handbook for teacher workshops on teacher expectations and students' academic performance.

Parent Involvement. We described the dismal participation in of Black parents within the school system. The report of Project ACHIEVE (1997) listed newer initiatives to inform and involve parents in their children's education. We did not study these promising strategies; however, as we noted in our recommendations for the community, the new programs will have some positive effects but will not necessarily solve the problem of parent participation because they hardly address the role of community forces. We are, therefore, recommending a different approach based on what we learned about the relationship between the Black community (or Black parents) and the White community and Shaker schools as a White-controlled institution.

In the Preface and elsewhere this book we discussed the deep mistrust of the White community and the school system by the Black community. Organizations and programs set up by the school district or White parents were viewed with suspicion and regarded as foreign. We suggest an alternative approach, namely, that some school programs intended to involve Black parents should be cosponsored by organizations in the Black community, especially Black churches. We base this recommendation partly on our own research and work with communities, dating back more than 30 years. For example, between 1969 and 1973 we took part in programs that effectively reached parents by working with churches in the Black community (Ogbu, 1974; see also Litherland, 1978).

We recommend three specific programs through which the school district should make every effort to involve parents, and we recommend that the school district work with churches and other organizations in the Black community.

1. *Parent workshop on leveling or tracking.* The school district provides parents with a handbook on leveling or the academic pro-

grams starting at the upper elementary school. We strongly suspect that many Black parents were not adequately informed by simply receiving the handbook. Some probably did not treat the handbook as containing ideas that would help their children because it came from White people or the system. We recommend a conference or workshop each year for parents of children at the early elementary school about the school careers of their children entering upper elementary school. Parents need to know at the early elementary school level what they need to do so that their children will qualify for the academic enrichment program at Woodbury.

2. *Parent workshop on class level differences.* One teacher suspected that many Black parents did not know what honors and advanced placement classes were about. That was probably why they did not prepare their children for these classes. He had unsuccessfully tried to organize a program to provide Black parents with more knowledge about these courses. We had the same impression as this teacher that some Black parents in Shaker Heights did not understand the differences between the course levels and the significance of those differences.

3. *Working with teachers and monitoring children's work.* Several parents did not know how to monitor their children's work at school. They did not know how well or poorly their children were doing at school. Thus, some parents thought that their children were doing well when they were not; other parents responded inappropriately when teachers contacted them about their children's work. At Open House, Black parents did not ask questions that revealed that they knew about their children's schoolwork or academic status. We recommend a program or programs in which parents can obtain appropriate information about the process of their children's education for more effective participation in it.

Building and Maintaining Trust. There is a great need to build trust between the Black community and the school district. Lack of trust between the community and the school district appears to be reflected in a lack of trust between Black students and the school authorities. Both situations affected students' academic engagement and performance. We recommend that every effort should be made to build trust between the community and schools. One way to increase mutual trust between the school district and the community is to work with community organizations, as suggested earlier. We also suggest a community–school conference during which the two sides present and discuss their understanding of the factors contributing to the academic disengagement and what could be done about it. Shared understandings of the problems and possibilities will result in increased mutual trust and acceptance of and cooperation in implementing intervention programs at school or in the community. It should be pointed out that the mistrust of the Shaker Heights' school system by Blacks is not just a function of local and contemporary situation; it is rooted in the history of the relationship between Black Americans and the public schools nationwide. The historical and national context should be analyzed, and suggested solutions should be evaluated in that context.

THE SHAKER HEIGHTS COMMUNITY
AND U.S. SOCIETY AT LARGE

From elementary through high school, Black students talked about residual racial discrimination that prevented their forbears from getting full and equal rewards for educational achievement in comparison to the rewards given to their White peers. The belief that the residue of past discrimination persisted no doubt contributed to the students' academic disengagement. Societal denigration of Black intellectual ability and the invisibility of Blacks who have achieved success through education as role models also contributed to the academic disengagement. Therefore, we recommend that the wider society and Shaker Heights community, in particular, take every step to eliminate the vestiges of discrimination in the opportunity structure and, as the students demanded, judge everyone by his or her ability rather than skin color. Societal change is necessary if the efforts of the Black community, families, and individuals as well as the school district, are to be effective. The media can contribute to this positive change and increase in the students' academic engagement and performance by highlighting the accomplishments of educated Black professionals and the attributes that made them appropriate role models for Black youth.

References

Alexandria County Public Schools. (1993). *1992–93 CTBS/TAP Achievement Test Results, July 1993.* Alexandria, VA: Alexandria County Public Schools, Monitoring and Evaluation Office.

Allen, B. A., & Boykin, A. W. (1991). The influence of contextual factors on African-American and Euro-American children's performance: Effects of movement opportunity and music. *International Journal of Psychology, 26*(3), 373–386.

Allen, B. A., & Boykin, W. A. (1992). African-American children and the educational process: Alleviating cultural discontinuity through prescriptive pedagogy. *School Psychology Review, 21*(4), 586–598.

Ainsworth-Darnell, J. W., & Downey, D. B. (1998). Assessing the oppositional culture explanation for racial/ethnic differences in school performance. *American Sociological Review, 63*, 536–553.

Anton, K. (1980). *Eligibility and enrollment in California public higher education.* Unpublished doctoral dissertation, University of California, Berkeley.

Anyon, J. (1981). Social class and school knowledge. *Curriculum Inquiry, 11*, 2–44.

Anyon, J. (1997). *Ghetto schooling: A political economy of urban educational reform.* Albany: State University of New York Press.

Arlington County Public Schools. (1991). *Report on the achievement and participation of Black students in the Arlington public schools, 1986–1990.* Arlington, VA: Arlington County Public Schools, Division of Instruction, Office of Minority Achievement.

Artiles, A. J., & Zamora-Duran, G. (1997). Disproportionate representation: A contentious and unresolved predicament. In A. J. Artiles & G. Zamora-Duran (Eds.), *Reducing disproportionate representation of culturally diverse students in special and gifted education. Reston, VA: Council for Exceptional Children.*

Asante, M. (1991–1992). Afrocentric curriculum. *Educational Leadership, 49*(4), 28–31.

Baca, R. R. (1994). *Persistence and secession: Toward an understanding of first generation Mexican binational migrant students in high school.* Unpublished doctoral dissertation, University of California, Berkeley.

Banks, J. A. (2000). Series foreword. In G. Gay, *Culturally responsive teaching: Theory, research and practice. New York: Teachers College Press.*

Baratz, J. C. (1970). Teaching reading in an urban Negro school system. In F. Williams (Ed.), *Language And poverty: Perspectives on a theme* (pp. 11–24). Chicago: Markham.

Belluck, P. (1999, July 4). Sensitive issue debated: Experts grow more troubled by showing of students in the middle class. *New York Times.*

Berkeley Unified School District. (1985). *An equal education for all: The challenge ahead.* A report to the Berkeley Board of Education by the Task Force on School Achievement). Berkeley, CA: Berkeley Unified School District, Department of Research and Evaluation.

Bond, G. C. (1981). Social economic status and educational achievement: A review article. *Anthropology and Education Quarterly, 12*(4), 227–257.

Boykin, A. W. (1986). The triple quandary and the schooling of Afro-American children. In U. Neisser (Ed.), *The school achievement of minority children: New perspectives* (pp. 57–92). Hillsdale, NJ: Lawrence Erlbaum Associates.

Braddock, J. H., II. (1990). *Tracking: Implications for student race–ethnic subgroups.* Baltimore: Johns Hopkins University, Center for Research on Effective Schooling for Disadvantaged Students.

Brown, P. R., & Haycock, K. (1984). *Excellence for whom?* A report from the Planning Committee for the Achievement Council. Oakland, CA: Achievement Council.

Bullock, H. A. (1970). *A history of Negro education in the South: From 1619 to the present.* New York: Praeger.

Campbell, F. (1982, December). Black executive and corporate stress. *The New York Times Magazine,* 1–42.

Caplan, N., Whimore, J. K., & Choy, M. H. (1991). *The children of the Boat People: A study of educational success.* Ann Arbor: University of Michigan Press.

Carpenter, M. E. (1941). *The treatment of the Negro in American history school textbooks.* Menasha, WI: Banta.

Carter, P. (1999). *Balancing acts: Issues of identify and cultural resistance in the social and educational behaviors of minority youth.* Unpublished doctoral dissertation, Department of Sociology, Columbia University, New York.

Clark, E. M. (1971). *A syllabus for an interdisciplinary curriculum in African-American studies.* Oakland, CA: Merritt College & Berkeley Unified School District, Mimeo.

Clark, R. M. (1983). *Family life and school achievement: Why poor Black children succeed or fail.* Chicago: University of Chicago Press.

The College Board. (1993). *College bound seniors profile of SAT and Achievement Test-Takers: California Report.* New York: Author.

The College Board. (1997). *College bound seniors profile of SAT and achievement test-takers: California report.* New York: Author.

The College Board. (1999). *Reaching the top: A report of the National Task Force on Minority High Achievement.* New York: Author.

Contreras, A. R. (1995). Charter school movement in California and elsewhere. *Education and Urban Society, 27*(2), 213–228.

Cook, P. J., & Ludwig, J. (1998). The burden of acting White: Do Black adolescents disparage academic achievement? In C. Jencks & M. Phillips (Eds.), *The Black–White academic gap* (pp. 375–400). Washington, DC: Brookings Institute.

Cook, T. D., Habib, F.-N., Phillips, M., Setterston, R. A., Shagle, S. C., & Degirmencioglu, S. M. (1998). *Comer's School Development Program in Prince George's County, Maryland: A theory-based evaluation.* Evanston, IL: Northwestern University, Institute for Policy Research.

Cook, T. D., Hunt, H. D., & Murphy, R. F. (1998). *Comer's School Development Program in Chicago: A theory-based evaluation.* Evanston, IL: Northwestern University, Institute for Policy Research.

Council of Great City Schools. (1999). *Closing the achievement gaps in urban schools: A survey of academic progress and promising practices in the great city schools.* Washington, DC: Author.

Cuban, L., & Tyack, D. B. (2000). Lessons from history. *Rethinking Schools, 14*(3), 11.

Curtis, J. (1988). Parents, schools and racism: Bilingual education in a northern Californian town. In T. Skutnabb-Kangas & J. Cummins (Eds.), *Minority education: From shame to struggle.* Philadelphia: Multilingual Matters.

Darlington, R. B. (1986). Long-term effects of pre-school Programs. In U. Neisser (Ed.), *The school achievement of minority children: New perspectives* (pp. 159–167). Hillsdale, NJ: Lawrence Erlbaum Associates.

Dei, G. J. S. (1994). Afrocentricity: A cornerstone of pedagogy. *Anthropology and Education Quarterly, 25*(1), 3–25.

DelPit, L. D. (1995). *Other people's children: White teachers, students of color, and other cultural conflicts in the classroom.* New York: New Press.

DeVos, G. A. (1973). Japan's outcast: The problem of the Burakumin. In B. Whittaker (Ed.), *The fourth world: Victims of group oppression.* New York: Schocken.

DeVos, G. A. (1984, April). *Ethnic persistence and role degradation: An illustration from Japan.* Prepared for the American–Soviet Symposium on Contemporary Ethnic Processes in the USA and the USSR. New Orleans, LA.

Diaz-Soto, L. (1997). *Language, culture and power.* Albany: State University of New York Press.

Elson, R. M. (1964). *Guardians of tradition: American schoolbooks of the nineteenth century.* Lincoln: University of Nebraska Press.

Engelmann, J. (1970). How to construct effective language programs for the poverty child. In F. Williams (Ed.), *Language and poverty: Perspectives on a theme* (pp. 102–121). Chicago: Markham.

Epstein, J. (1995, May). School/family/community partnership: Caring for the children we share. *Phi Delta Kappan,* 701–712.

Fairfax County Public Schools. (1984). *Report of the Advisory Committee on the Academic Performance of Minority Students in Fairfax County Public Schools.* Fairfax, VA: Fairfax County Public Schools, Office of Research and Evaluation.

Fairfax County Public Schools. (1988). *Annual report on the achievement and aspirations of minority students in the Fairfax County Public Schools, 1986–1987.* Unpublished manuscript, Fairfax County. Public Schools, Office of Research, Fairfax, VA.

Fell, J. C. (1990). *The painting of America: Evolution of the portrayal of minorities in American history textbooks.* Unpublished manuscript, University of California, Berkeley.

Ferguson, C. A. (1959). Diglossia. *Word, 15,* 325–340.

Ferguson, R. F. (1998). Can schools narrow the Black–White test score gap? In C. Jencks & M. Phillips (Eds.), *The Black–White Test Score Gap* (pp. 318–374). Washington, DC: The Brookings Institute.

Fine, M. (1991). *Framing dropouts: Notes on the politics of an urban public high school.* Albany: State University of New York Press.

Fishman, J. A. (1967). Bilingualism and diglossia. *Journal of Social Issues, 23*(2), 29–57

Fong, J. C. (1992). *The educational and cultural practices of the Chinese family and community in Oakland.* Unpublished manuscript, University of California, Berkeley.

Fong, J. C. (2001).*Complementary education and cultural models: The Chinese students' strategy of schooling in the San Gabriel Valley.* Unpublished doctoral dissertation, University of California, Berkeley.

Ford, D. Y. (1993). Black students' orientation as a function of perceived family achievement orientation and demographic variables. *Journal of Negro Education,* (62), 47–66.

Fordham, S. (1996). *Black out.* Chicago: University of Chicago Press.

Fordham, S., & Ogbu, J. U. (1986). Black students' school success: Coping with the Burden of acting White. *The Urban Review, 18*(3), 1–31.

Foster, H. L. (1974). *Ribbin', jivin' and playin' the dozens: The unrecognized dilemmas of inner-city schools.* Cambridge, MA: Ballinger.

Friedman, M. (1955). The role of government in education. In R. A. Solo (Ed.), *Economics and public interest* (pp. 123–144). New Brunswick, NJ: Rutgers University Press.

Fuller, B., & Elmore, R. F. (Eds.) (1992). *Who chooses? Who loses?: Culture, institutions, and the unequal effects of school choice.* New York: Teachers College Press.

Gallagher, J. J., & Remy, C. T. (Eds.). (1987).*The malleability of children.* Baltimore: Brookes.

Gay, G. (1979). Changing conceptions of multicultural education. In H. P. Baptiste & M. L. Baptiste (Eds.), *Developing multicultural process in classroom instruction: Competencies for teachers* (pp. 18–27). Washington DC: University Press of America.

Gay, G. (1990, September). Achieving educational equality through curriculum desegregation. *Phi Delta Kappan,* 56–62.

Gay, G. (1994). *At the essence of learning: Multicultural education.* West Lafayette, IN: Kappa Delta Pi.

Gay, G. (2000). *Culturally responsive teaching: Theory, research & practice.* New York: Teachers College Press.

Gelb, S. A., & Mizokawa, D. T. (1986). *Special education and social structure: The commonality of exceptionality.* Unpublished manuscript.

Gibson, M. A. (1988). *Accommodation without assimilation: Punjabi Sikhs in an American high school and community.* Ithaca, NY: Cornell University Press.

Glazer, N. (1994, Summer). A new word for an old problem: Multicultural "school wars" date to the 1840s. *Multicultural Education,* 6–9.

Good, T. L., & Braden, J. S. (2000). *The great school debate: Choice, vouchers, and charters.* Mahwah, NJ: Lawrence Erlbaum Associates.

Gordon, E. W., & Wilkerson, F. (1966). *Compensatory education for the disadvantaged: Pre-school to college.* New York: College Entrance Examination Board.

Gramlich, E. M., & Koshel, P. P. (1975). *Educational performance contracting: An evaluation of an experiment.* Washington, DC: The Brookings Institute.

Grayson, D. A., & Martin, M. D. (1990). *GESA: Gender/Ethnic Expectations and Student Achievement: The GESA Facilitator.* Earlham, IA: Gray Mill.

Grier, W. H., & Cobbs, P. M. (1968). *Black rage.* New York: Bantam.

Gumperz, J. J., & Cook-Gumperz, J. (1994). Changing views of language in education: Anthropological perspectives. *International Encyclopedia of Educational Research, 6,* 3235–3238.

Gutman, L. M., & McLoyd, V. C. (2000). Parents' management of their children's education within the home, at school, and in the community: An examination of high-risk African American families. *Urban Review, 32,* 1–24.

Hale-Benson, J. E. (1986). *Black children: Their roots, culture, and learning styles.* Baltimore: Johns Hopkins University Press.

Hanna, J. L. (1988). *Disruptive school behavior: Class, race & culture.* New York: Holmes and Meiers.

Harris, O. (1991). Athletics and academics: Contrary or complementary activities. In O. Jarvie (Ed.), *Sport, racism, and ethnicity* (pp. 124–149). London: Falmer.

Harry, B., & Anderson, M. G. (1994). The disproportionate placement of African American males in special education programs: A critique of the process. *Journal of Negro Education, 63*(4), 602–619.

Haynes, R. L. (1985). *Minority strategies for success.* Unpublished manuscript, Department of Anthropology, University of California, Berkeley.

Heller, K. A., Holtzman, W. H., & Messick, S. (Eds.). (1982) *Placing children in special education: A strategy for equality.* Washington, DC: National Academy Press.

Herrnstein, R. J., & Murray, C. (1994). *The bell curve: Intelligence and class structure in American life.* New York: Free Press.

Hilliard, A. G., Payton-Stewart, L., & Williams, L. O. (1991). *Infusion of African and African American content in the school curriculum: Proceedings of the first national conference, October 1989.* Morristown, NJ: Aaron.

Hoberman, J. (1997). *Darwin's athletes: How sport has damaged Black America and preserved the myth of race.* Boston: Houghton Mifflin.

Holland, D. C., & Eisenhart, M. A. (1990). *Educated in romance: Women, achievement and college culture.* Chicago: University of Chicago Press.

Holt, G. S. (1972). Inversion in Black communication. In T. Kochman (Ed.), *Rappin and stylin' out: Communication in urban Black America* (pp. 152–159). Chicago: University of Illinois Press.

Hoover-Dempsey, K. V., & Sandler, H. M. (1995). Parental involvement in children's education: Why does it make a difference. *Teachers College Record, 97*(2), 310–331.

How Whites think about Blacks. (1979, February 26). *Newsweek, 48.*

Howard, J., & Hammond, R. (1985, September 9). Rumors of inferiority: The hidden obstacles to Black success. *The New Republic,* pp. 17–21.

Hu, A. (1997). Education and race: The performance of minority students in affluent areas refutes the prevailing educational shiboleths. *National Review, 49*(17).

Hymes, D. (1967). Models of the interaction of language and social setting. *Journal of Social Issues, 23*(2), 8–28.

Hymes, D. (1971). On linguistic theory, communicative competence, and the education of disadvantaged children. In M. L. Wax, S. Diamond, & F. O. Gearing (Eds.), *Anthropological perspectives on education* (pp. 51–66). New York: Basic Books.

Irvine, J. J. (1991). *Black students and school failure: Policies, practices, and prescriptions.* Westport, NY: Praeger.

Ito, H. (1967). Japan's outcasts in the United States. In G. A. DeVos & H. Wagatsuma (Eds.), *Japan's invisible race.* Berkeley: University of California Press.

James, W., (2001). *Fierce hatred of injustice: Claude McKay's Jamaica and his poetry of rebellion.* London: Verso.

Jaynes, G. D., & Williams, R. M. Jr. (1989). *A common destiny: Blacks and American society.* Washington, DC: National Academy Press.

Jensen, A. R. (1969). How much can we boost IQ and scholastic achievement? *Harvard Educational Review, 39,* 1–123.

Johnson, C. (1999, November). *An assessment of African descent from their own set of normative behaviors in Miami–Dade County Public Schools.* Poster presented at the Stanford University Conference on Race: African American Research and Policy Perspectives at the Turn of the Century, CA.

Johnson, S. M. (1984). Merit pay for teachers: A prescription for reform. *Harvard Educational Review, 54,* 175–185.

Katz, I. (1967). Socialization of academic achievement in minority group children. In D. Levine (Ed.), *Nebraska Symposium on Motivation.* Lincoln: University of Nebraska Press.

Kerber, A., & Bommarito, B. (1965). Preschool education for the developing cortex. In A. Kerber & B. Bommarito (Eds.), *The schools and the urban crisis* (pp. 345–349). New York: Holt.

Kochman, T. (1983). *Black and White styles in conflict.* Chicago: University of Chicago Press.

Kunjufu, J. (1988). *To be popular or smart: The Black peer group.* Chicago: African American Images.

Labov, W. (1972). *Language in the inner city: Studies in the Black English vernacular.* Philadelphia: University of Pennsylvania Press.

Lacey, C. (1970). *Hightown grammar.* Manchester, England: University of Manchester Press.

Ladenburg, T. J., & McFeeley, W. S. (1949). *The black main in the land of equality.* New York: Hayden.

Leacock, E. (1985). The influence of teacher attitudes on children's classroom performance: Case studies. In K. Borman (Ed.), *The social life of children in a changing society* (pp. 47–64). Norwood, NJ: Ablex.

LeCompte, M. D. (1978). Learning to work: The hidden curriculum of the classroom. *Anthropology and Education Quarterly, 9,* 22–27.

Lee, C. (1992). *Signifying as a scaffold for literacy interpretation: The pedagogical implications of an African American discourse genre.* Urbana, IL: NCTE Press.

Lee, C. (1995). African-centered pedagogy: Complexities and possibilities. In M. J. Shujaa (Ed.), *Too much schooling, too little education: A paradox of Black life in White societies* (pp. 295–318). Trenton, NJ: African World.

Lehrer, J. (Producer). (1997, May 16). An apology 65 years late. *The News Hour with Jim Lehrer transcript.* (What is Tuskegee Experiment?) Retrieved 7/16/02 from http://www.pbs.org/newshour/bb/health/may97/tuskegee

Levy, G. E. (1970). *Ghetto school: Class warfare in an elementary school.* New York: Pegasus.

Lieberson, S. (1980). *A piece of the pie: Black and White immigrants since 1880.* Berkeley: University of California Press.

Lightfoot, S. L. (1978). *Worlds apart: Relationship between families and school.* New York: Basic Books.

Litherland, R. H. (1978). *The role of the church in educational change: A case history of a feasible strategy.* San Francisco: San Francisco Theological Seminary.

Litwack, L. F. (1991). *Trouble in mind: Black Southerners in the age of Jim Crow.* New York: Vintage.

Lombana, J. H. (1983). *Home-school partnerships: Guidelines and strategies for educators.* New York: Grune & Stratton.

Lucas, S. R. (1999). *Tracking inequality: stratification and mobility in American high schools.* New York: Teachers College Press.

Luster, L. (1992). *Schooling, survival, and struggles: Black women and the GED.* Unpublished doctoral dissertation, Stanford University.

Math, S. (1997). *Shaker Heights: The struggle for integration.* Unpublished documentary proposal.

Matute-Bianchi, M. E. (1986). *Ethnic identities and patterns of school success and failure among Mexican-descent and Japanese American students in a California high school: An ethnographic analysis.* Unpublished manuscript, University of California, Santa Cruz.

McCleod, J. (1987). *Ain't no makin' it: Leveled aspirations in a low-income neighborhood.* Boulder, CO: Westview.

Mehan, H., Hubbard, L., & Villanueva, L. (1994). Forming academic identities: Accommodation without assimilation among involuntary minorities. *Anthropology and Education Quarterly, 25*(2), 91–117.

Mehan, H., Hubbard, L., Villanueva, L., & Lintz, L. (1996). *Constructing school success: The consequences of untracking low-achieving students.* New York: Cambridge University Press.

Mickelson, R. A. (1990). The attitude–achievement paradox among Black adolescents. *Sociology of Education, 63,* 44–61.

Mickelson, R. A. (1998). *A report to the U.S. District Court for the Western District of North Carolina in the Case of Capacechione v. Charlotte–Mecklenburg Schools et al.* Unpublished Manuscript.

Mickelson, R. A. (2001). The effects of segregation on African American high school seniors' academic achievement. *Journal of Negro Education, 68*(4), 566–586.

Mickelson, R. A., Smith, S. S., & Oliver, M. L. (1993). Breaking through the barriers: African American job candidates and the academic hiring process. *Beyond silenced voices: Class, race, and gender in United States schools* (pp. 9–24). Albany: State University of New York Press.

Miller, H. L. (Ed.). (1967). *Education for the disadvantaged.* New York: Free Press.

Minority Achievement Committee. (1997). *Students leading students to greater school success: Resource guide.* Unpublished manuscript, Shaker Heights School District, Shaker Heights, OH.

Miller, L. S. (1995). *An American imperative: Accelerating minority educational advancement.* New Haven, CT: Yale University Press.

Miramontes, O. B., Nadeau, A., & Commins, N. L. (1997). *Restructuring schools for linguistic diversity: linking decision-making to effective programs.* New York: Teachers College Press.

Montgomery County Public Schools. (1984). *A study of children at risk: A report by the Citizen's Minority Relations Monitoring Committee, Report for 1982–83 school year.* Rockville, MD: Board of Education and Montgomery County Public Schools.

Montgomery County Public Schools. (1993). *School performance program report, 1993.* Rockville, MD: Montgomery County Public Schools, Office of Evaluation.

Murnane, R., & Cohen, D. (1986). Merit pay and the evaluation problem: Why most merit pay plans fail and a few survive. *Harvard Educational Review, 56,* 1–17.

Myrdal, G. (1944). *An American dilemma: The Negro problem and modern democracy.* New York: Harper.

Naphin, D. (Producer). (2201, May 27). Gold in them thar schools. *60 Minutes XXX111*(37), 14–20. New York: CBS Television Network.

National Association for the Advancement of Colored People. (2001, September–October). ACT-SO competition showcases future leaders. *The New Crisis,* p. 75.

Nesteby, J. R. (1982). *Black images in American films, 1896–1954: The interplay between civil rights and film culture.* New York: University Press of America.

Nobles, W. W. (1991). The infusion of African and African-American content: A question of content and intent. In A. G. Hilliard, III, W. W. Payton-Nobles, & A. Mann (Eds.), *Achieving educational and cultural excellence for African American students.* Oakland CA: Center for Applied Cultural Studies and Educational Achievement.

Oakes, J. (1985). *Keeping track : How schools structure inequality.* New Haven, CT: Yale University Press.

Oakland Unified School District. (1996). *Average 1995–96 language NCE by language category.* Oakland, CA: Oakland School District, Division of Planning, Research, Evaluation and Policy Development.

Oakland Unified School District. (1999). *Third year report.* Oakland, CA: Oakland School District, Task Force on the Education of African-American Children.

O'Connor, C. (1997). Disposition toward (collective) struggle and educational resilience in the inner city: A case analysis of six African American high school students. *American Educational Research Journal, 34*(4), 593–629.

Ogbu, J. U. (1974). *The next generation: An ethnography of education in an urban neighborhood.* New York: Academic.

Ogbu, J. U. (1977). Racial stratification and education: The case of Stockton, California. *IRCD Bulletin, 12*(1), 1–26.

Ogbu, J. U. (1978). *Minority education and caste: The American system in cross-cultural perspective.* New York: Academic.

Ogbu, J. U. (1981, July). *Economic realities and the minority school child.* Paper presented at a colloquium on Integrating the Schools, University of Wisconsin, Milwaukee.

Ogbu, J. U. (1983). Minority status and schooling in plural societies. *Comparative Education Review, 27*(2), 168–190.

Ogbu, J. U. (1992). Understanding cultural diversity and learning. *Educational Researcher, 21*(8), 4–14.

Ogbu, J. U. (1987). Variability in minority school performance: A problem in search of an explanation. In E. Jacob & C. J. Jordan (Eds.), *Minority education: Anthropological perspectives* (pp. 83–111). Norwood, NJ: Ablex.

Ogbu, J. U. (1994a). Language and learning in education. In *International Encyclopedia of Education* (Vol. 6, pp. 3213–3216). Oxford, England: Pergamon.

Ogbu, J. U. (1994b). Racial stratification and education in the U.S.: Why inequality persists. *Teachers College Record, 96*(2), 264–298.

Ogbu, J. U. (1995b). Cultural problems in minority education: Their interpretations and consequences—Part One: Theoretical background. *Urban Review, 27*(3), 189–203.

Ogbu, J. U. (1995b). Cultural problems in minority education: Their interpretations and consequences—Part Two: Case studies. *Urban Review, 27*(4), 271–297.

Ogbu, J. U. (1998). *Community forces and minority education strategies: The second part of the problem.* Unpublished manuscript, University of California, Berkeley.

Ogbu, J. U. (1999). Beyond language: Ebonics, proper English, and identity in a Black American speech community. *American Educational Research Journal, 36*(2), 147–184.

Ogbu, J. U. (2001). Cultural amplifiers of intelligence: IQ and minority status in cross-cultural perspective. In J. M. Fish (Ed.), *Race and intelligence: Separating science from myth* (pp. 241–278). Mahwah, NJ: Lawrence Erlbaum Associates.

Ogbu, J. U., & Simons, H. D. (1994). *Cultural model of school achievement: A quantitative test of Ogbu's hypothesis.* Unpublished manuscript, University of California, Berkeley.

Ogbu, J. U., & Simons, H. D. (1998). Voluntary and Involuntary minorities: A cultural–ecological theory of school performance with some implications for education. *Anthropology and Education Quarterly, 29*(2), 155–188.

Ogbu, J. U., & Stern, P. (2001). Caste and intellectual development. In R. J. Sternberg & E. L. Grigorenko (Eds.), *Environmental effects on cognitive abilities* (pp. 3–37). Mahwah, NJ: Lawrence Erlbaum Associates.

Oliver, M. L., Rodriguez, C., & Mickelson, R. A. (1985). Brown and black in white: The social adjustment and academic performance of Chicano and Black students in a predominantly White university. *Urban Review, 17*(1), 3–34.

Palmer, R. W. (1990). *In search of a better life: Perspectives on migration from the Caribbean.* New York: Praeger.

Park, C. C., & Chi, M. M.-Y. (Eds.). (1999). *Asian-American education: Prospects and challenges.* Westport, CT: Bergin & Garvey.

Patterson Research Institute. (1997) *The African American education data book: Vol. 1. Higher education.* Fairfax, VA: College Fund/United Negro College Fund.

Patton, J. M. (1998). The disproportionate representation of African Americans in special education: Looking behind the curtain for understanding and solutions. *Journal of Special Education, 32,* 25–31.

Payne, C. M. (1984). *Getting what we ask for: The ambiguity of success and failure in urban education.* Westport, CT: Greenwood.

Pederson, B. (2000). Merit: To pay or not pay? Teachers grapple with yet another marketplace reform. *Rethinking Schools, 14*(3), 1, 9–11.

Persell, C. H. (1977). *Education and inequality: The roots and results of stratification in American schools.* New York: Free Press.

Petroni, F. A. (1970). Uncle Toms: White stereotypes in the Black movement. *Human Organization, 29*(4), 260–266.

Petroni, F. A., & Hirsch, E. A. (1972). *Two, four, six, eight, when are you gonna integrate?* New York: Behavioral Publications.

Polite, V. C. (1991). *All dressed up with no place to go: A critical ethnography of African American male students in an urban high school.* Unpublished doctoral dissertation, Michigan State University, East Lansing.

Pollard, D. S., & Ajirotutu, C. S. (1997). *Five year report: Dr. Martin Luther King Jr. Elementary School.* Unpublished manuscript, University of Wisconsin, Milwaukee.

Pollard, D. S., & Ajirotutu, C. S. (Eds.). (2000). *African-centered schooling in theory and practice.* Westport, CT: Bergin & Garvey.

Prince Georges' County Public Schools. (1988). *Percentile ranks for the California Achievement Test results by race, within grades, within school 1984, 1985, 1986 and 1987.* Upper Marlboro, MD: Prince Georges' County Public Schools, Department of Evaluation and Research.

Prince George's County Public Schools. (1990). *Black Male achievement: From peril to promise.* Upper Marlboro, MD: Prince George's County Public Schools, Office of the Superintendent.

Prince Georges' County Public Schools. (1993). *1993 Maryland school performance program report*. Upper Marlboro, MD: Prince Georges' County Public Schools, Department of Evaluation and Research.

Project ACHIEVE. (1996). *Progress report*. Unpublished document, Shaker Heights School District, Shaker Heights, OH.

Project ACHIEVE. (1997). *Report*. Unpublished document, Shaker Heights School District, Shaker Heights, OH.

Reed, R. (1988). *Expectations and student performance: Vol. 1. Ethnicity, gender, school practices and the communication of expectations*. Sacramento: California State Department of Education.

Rist, R. (1970). Student social class and teacher expectations: The self-fulfilling prophecy in ghetto education. *Harvard Educational Review, 40*, 411–451.

Rockquemore, K. A., & Brunsma, D. L. (2002). *Beyond Black: Biracial identity in America*. Thousand Oaks, CA: Sage.

Ruenzel, D. (1995, September 27). A choice in the matter. *Education Week*, 23–27.

Russo, C. J., & Talbert-Johnson, C. (1997). The over-representation of African American children in special education: The re-segregation of educational programming. *Education and Urban Society, 29*(2) 136–148.

St. Lawrence, T. J. (1977). *Kids' culture in an urban school: The role of culture conflicts in the maintenance of social inequality*. Unpublished doctoral dissertation, University of Pittsburgh.

School District of Philadelphia. (1999). *Realities converge: The facts about public schools in Philadelphia*. Philadelphia: Office of Government Relations.

Scrupski, A. (1975). The social system of the school. In A. Scrupski & N. K. Shimahara (Eds.), *Social forces and schooling: An anthropological and sociological perspective* (pp. 141–186). New York: McKay.

Shack, W. A. (1970). *On Black American values in White America: Some perspectives on the cultural aspects of learning behavior and compensatory education*. Paper prepared for the Social Science Research Council: Sub-Committee on Values and Compensatory Education, 1970–1971.

Shaker heights school district best in state: America's best schools. (1994, April). *Redbook*.

Shaker Heights School District. (1996). *Annual report*. Unpublished document, Shaker Heights School District, Shaker Heights, OH.

Shaker Heights School District. (1998). *Woodbury Elementary School: Advanced programs in language arts and mathematics,1998–99, A guide for parents*. Unpublished document, Shaker Heights School District, Shaker Heights, OH.

Shaker Heights School District. (1997). *SHTA Newsletter, 11*(8). Shaker Heights Teachers Association, Shaker Heights, OH.

Shannon, S. M., & Latimer, S. L. (1996). Latino parent involvement in schools: A story of struggle and resistance. *Journal of Educational Issues of Language Minority Students, 16*, 301–319.

Sheppard, S. M., & Rose, H. (1995). The power of parents: An empowerment model for increasing parental involvement. *Education, 113*(3), 373–377.

Shimahara, N. K. (1991). Social mobility and education: Burakumin in Japan. In M. A. Gibson & J. U. Ogbu (Eds.), *Minority status and schooling: A comparative study of immigrant and involuntary minorities*. New York: Garland.

Shujaa, M. J. (Ed.). (1996). *Beyond desegregation: The politics of quality in African-American schooling*. Thousand Oaks, CA: Corwin.

Singham, M. (1997).*The canary in the mine: Closing the academic gap between Black and White students*. Unpublished manuscript.

Slade, M. (1982, October 24). Aptitude, intelligence, or what? *New York Times*, p. E22.

Smith, K. L. (1989). *An exploration of the beliefs, values, and attitudes of Black students in Fairfax County*. Unpublished doctoral dissertation, Virginia Polytechnic Institute and State University, Blacksburg.

Smitherman, G. (1977). *Talkin' and testifyin': The language of Black Americans.* Detroit, MI: Wayne State University Press.

Solomon, R. P. (1989). Dropping out of academics: Black youths and the sports culture in a cross-national perspective. In L. Weis, E. Farrar, & H. G. Petrie (Eds.), *Dropouts from school: Issues, dilemmas, and solutions* (pp. 79–93). Albany: State University of New York Press.

Solomon, R. P. (1992). *Black resistance in high school: Forging a separatist culture.* Albany: State University of New York Press.

Stewart, L. (Ed.). (1990). *Infusion of African and African American content in the school curriculum: Proceedings of the first national conference, October 1989.* Morristown, NJ: Aaron.

Spencer, L. (1999, February 6). School network targets score gap: Suburban network is led by Evanston. *Chicago Tribune,* p. 1.

Spencer, M. B., Noll, E., Stoltzfus, J., & Harpalani, V. (2001). Identity and school adjustment: Revising the "acting White" assumption. *Educational Psychologist, 36*(1), 21–30.

Stanback, A. M. (1992). *The testing of a new integrative model of cognition within the context of a continually existing educational problem.* Unpublished doctoral dissertation, Biola University, La Mirada, CA.

Stasiulis, D., & Yuval-Davis, N. (1995). *Unsettling settler societies.* Thousand Oaks, CA: Sage.

Steele, C. (1992, April). Race and the schooling of Black Americans. *Atlantic Monthly,* 68–75.

Steele, C. (1997). A threat in the air: How stereotypes shape intellectual identity and performance. *American Psychologist, 57*(6) 613–629.

Stern, S. P. (1986, December). *School imposed limits on Black family participation: A view from within and below.* Paper presented at the 85th annual meeting of the American Anthropological Association, Philadelphia.

Stupay, D. S. (1993). *The Shaker Heights City Schools: An overview.* Shaker Heights, OH: Shaker Heights School District.

Suarez-Orozco, M. M. (1989). *Central American refugees and U.S. high schools: A psychosocial study of motivation and achievement.* Stanford, CA: Stanford University Press.

Treisman, P. M. (1985). *A study of the mathematics performance of Black students at the University of California, Berkeley.* Unpublished doctoral dissertation, University of California, Berkeley.

Under survey. (1956). *Southern School News, 3*(1), 2.

U.S. Department of Education. (2001). *Paving the way to post-secondary education: K–12 intervention programs for under-represented youth.* Washington, DC: National Center for Educational Statistics.

Warner, W. L., Havighurst, R. J., & Loeb, M. B. (1944). *Who shall be educated? The challenge of unequal educational opportunities.* Westport, CT: Greenwood.

Webster's ninth new collegiate dictionary. (1990). Springfield, MA: Merriam-Webster.

Wehlage, G. G. (1989). Dropping out: Can schools be expected to prevent it? In L. Weis, E. Farrar, & H. G. Petrie (Eds.), *Dropouts from school: Issues, dilemmas, and solutions* (pp. 1–19). Albany: State University of New York Press.

Weis, L. (1985). *Between two worlds: Black students in an urban community college.* Boston: Routledge & Kegan Paul.

Wells, A. S. (1998). *Beyond the rhetoric of charter school reform: A study of ten California school districts.* Unpublished manuscript, University of California, Los Angeles.

White, B. L. (1979). *The origins of human competence.* Lexington, MA: Heath.

White, S. H., Day, M. C., Freeman, P. K., Hartman, S. A., & Messenger, K. P. (1973). *Federal programs for young children. Review and recommendations: Vol. 1. Goals and standards of public programs for children.* Washington, DC: U.S. Government Printing Office.

Whittington, D. (1996). *Analyses of under-achievement.* Unpublished document, Shaker Heights School District, Shaker Heights, OH.

Williams, F. (Ed.). (1970). *Language and poverty: Perspectives on a theme.* Chicago: Markham.

Williams, M. D. (1990). Afro-Americans in the cultural dialogue in the United States. In G. D. Spindler (Ed.), *The American cultural dialogue and its transmission.* New York: Falmer.

Williams, T. R. (1972). *Introduction to socialization: Human culture transmitted.* St. Louis, MO: Mosby.

Willis, P. (1977). *Learning to labor: How working class kids get working class jobs.* New York: Columbia University Press.

Wilson, H. C. (1972). On the evolution of education. In S. T. Kimball & J. Hill-Burnett (Eds.), *Learning and culture* (pp. 211–241). Seattle: University of Washington Press.

Author Index

Subject Index

A

Academic achievement
  choice and, 265–267
  cooperative learning approach and, 268–269
  culturally responsive education and, 269–272
  effect of role models on, 166
  teacher expectations of Black student, 124–129
  vs. academic aspiration among Black students, 122–123
Academic achievement gap, 3–11
  explanations for, 33–55
    cultural differences and conflict, 37–41
    inadequate IQ, 33–34
    language/dialect differences and conflicts, 42–44
    racial segregation, 36
    role of community forces, 44–55
    social class status, 34–36
    teacher expectations, 10, 36–37, 45
  historical and national contexts, 3–4
  in Shaker Heights (Ohio), xi, xii–xv, 4–7
  local knowledge of, 7–11
  race and interpretation of, 71–74, 257
  racism and, 73–76
Academic aspiration
  vs. academic achievement among Black students, 122–123
  vs. behavior, 248–249
Academic disengagement, of Black students from academic work, xiii, 250

acting "White" and, 258–259
Black and White academic effort compared, 15–17
Black peer groups and, 189–190, 191–192
classroom discussions on, 20–21
classroom observations of, 22–23
"cool" status and, 213–214
discipline and, 134
expanding use of MAC program to combat, 283–285
failure to connect schooling and adult future and, 123, 167–171, 254
ghetto lifestyle and, 215–216
keeping friends and, 214–215
leveling and, 110
low effort syndrome and, 17–20
MAC meetings and, 21–22
opportunity structure and, 154
part-time jobs and, 215
peer pressures and, 191–194, 197–216
perceptions of unequal opportunity and, 253–255
quest for popularity and, 214
recommendations to combat Black students, 273–274
residual racial discrimination and, 289
school level and academic effort and, 20
student explanations of, 12–15, 23–32
tutoring sessions and, 22
Academic expectations, of Black parents, 219–221
Academic problems, lack of parents' awareness of, 247–248
Academic programs, Black parents' involvement in, 222–233